GOD THROUGH THE STORMS

by
Dot Roberts
with Ricky Roberts, Ph.D.

EA Books Publishing

Copyright @ 2020 Dot Roberts and Ricky Roberts

All rights reserved. No part of this publication may be reproduced or transmitted in any form or by any electronic or mechanical means including photo copying, recording, or any information storage and retrieval system now known or to be invented, without permission in writing from the publisher or the author.

Unless otherwise noted, the Scripture quotations are from The King James Version of the Bible, public domain in the United States.

Name: Dot Roberts and Ricky Roberts

Title: God through the Storms by Dot Roberts and Ricky Roberts

Identifiers: ISBN: 978-1-952369-56-8

LCCN: 2021904038

Subjects: 1. Religion/Christian Living

2. Religion/Christian Living/Spiritual Warfare

3. Religion/Christian Living/Inspirational

Cover Designer: Krystine Kercher

Author Photo: Edgars Studio, Baxley Ga.

Cover photo: Sailboat In Stormy Seas, Lighthouse In, Photographer John Lund/Getty Images 2019

Published by EA Books Publishing, a division of Living Parables of Central Florida, Inc. a 501c3

EABooksPublishing.com

I have had many storms in this world, but now my vessel will soon be on shore in heaven
–Thomas Bilney (1531)

ACKNOWLEDGEMENTS

We acknowledge all those who have helped us in this endeavor. We also thank those who helped in the proofreading of this manuscript.

AUTHOR'S NOTE

God Through the Storms is a follow-up book to our book, *A Walk Through Tears*[1]. While much of this book is written by me, Dot Roberts, my son had an integral part in all the portions dealing with theology, Greek and Hebrew texts, and ancient writings. For ease of reading, we have left the book in my voice, but we would like the reader to be aware that Dr. Ricky Roberts contributed much of the theology contained herein.

TABLE OF CONTENTS

INTRODUCTION..1
CHAPTER 1 DID SATAN KNOW? 8
CHAPTER 2 WHY?...11
CHAPTER 3 EARLY MIRACLES...40
CHAPTER 4 LIFE GROWING UP...48
CHAPTER 5 INTRODUCTION TO PENTECOST.................................68
CHAPTER 6 MY HUSBAND'S FAMILY..73
CHAPTER 7 FIRST EXPERIENCES WITH GOD...................................84
CHAPTER 8 MINISTERS WHO HELPED US......................................113
CHAPTER 9 TEACH ME TO PRAY..145
CHAPTER 10 PRAYER AND TRIALS...176
CHAPTER 11 WARFARE AND INTERCESSION................................203
ENDNOTES...253
ABOUT THE AUTHOR..260

INTRODUCTION

Margaret Glidden, a respected principal, writer, and teacher in Jacksonville, Florida, once said, "God is not the God over troubled waters; He is the God through them."

The biblical narrative depicts many examples of this truth.

For example, in 1 Timothy 1:18–19, the apostle Paul knows of no Christian life that does not involve severe tests and struggles. Without these severe tests and struggles, a Christian's life will lean toward theoretical and practical forgery. In other words, in all ways and manners, such a life becomes a forgery of the Christian life. Such a life falls victim to both deception and sinful behavior. And it finally becomes shipwrecked.

Therefore, a Christian walk that does not cost anything or fight against evil is a perversion of the pure and absolute walk, and that perverted walk follows the walk of the Gnostics, who through their deception had, and continue to have, horrible results upon many Christians. Many perversions of Christianity go back to the Gnostics. Many denials of sin and its practices promoted by any Christian make that Christian a modern Gnostic.

Often, we see that the Bible uses times of trouble in the lives of its heroes and other characters to teach the rest of us some precious lessons about faith, God, and life itself.

Nowhere does the Bible guarantee the saints of God will be free from the storms of life. On the contrary, the Bible informs the saints that the storms will come, and they are expected to be part of the life of a Christian (See Job 14:1; Ecclesiastes 2:23; John 16:33).

Too many Christians believe that they are free from all the storms of life. However, troubles can and will touch all of us.

The idea that we are safe from all the troubles of life is not found in the ancient church either. Problems and perils were to their left, right, front, and back. Difficulties of various kinds affected the ancient saints. Many went through the troubles and only found rest when they died.

John Wesley, one of the greatest revivalists in history, saw storms in his life as standard. If they disappeared, he questioned whether he had sinned or backslidden. It is said about him,

John Wesley was riding along a road one day when it dawned on him that three whole days had passed in which he had suffered no persecution. Not a brick or an egg had been thrown at him for three days. Alarmed, he stopped his horse, and exclaimed, "Can it be that I have sinned, and am backslidden?" Slipping from his horse, Wesley went down on his knees and began interceding with God to show him where, if any, there had been a fault. A rough fellow, on the other side of the hedge, hearing the prayer, looked across and recognized the preacher. "I'll fix that Methodist preacher," he said, picking up a brick and tossing it over at him. It missed its mark and fell harmlessly beside John. Whereupon Wesley leaped to his feet joyfully exclaiming, "Thank God, it's all right. I still have His presence."[1]

In his journal, John Wesley wrote the following:

> By how gentle degrees does God prepare us for His will! Two years ago, a piece of brick grazed my shoulders. It was a year after that the stone struck me between the eyes. Last month I received one blow, and this evening two; one before we came into the town and one after we had gone out; but both were as nothing: for though one man struck me on the breast with all his might, and the other on the mouth with such force that the blood gushed out immediately, I felt no more pain from either of the blows than if they had touched me with a straw.[2]

Throughout the history of the church, it is rare to find saints without storms of life. The saints were open to these storms in whatever manner they appeared.

Many believe that a holy life will keep away all the storms of life. It is thought that holiness is all we need to live a trouble-free experience. Impossible! Others have concluded that if they can be good enough, all the problems of life will fade away or never see the light of day in their lives. But that is wrong too. No matter how right a person may be, or how holy a person may live, it does not remove the human condition—the troubles connected to this fallen life. Nor does it eliminate the problems we must go through to become developed in our character and our faith. And last, many saints have the mistaken idea that obedience to the will of God will produce laid-back, cost-free, and smooth navigation throughout life. But that is a sad view. We, as faithful saints, will actually find ourselves in storms because we have obeyed the Lord. In such cases, we must remember that the Lord brought us into the storms.

The Book of Job testifies that Job was a man of God, "perfect and upright, and one that feared God, and eschewed evil" (Job 1:1). Yet Job's experience with God reveals that a holy and obedient life does not necessarily mean a protected and thriving life. In truth, God will take the most sacred, pure, respectable children He has and place them amid the storms of life to prove that He is still God through the troubles.

A well-developed character and a well-tested faith are keys in the storms of life. Our character and faith will cause us to endure the storms of life (Proverbs 10:9).

When studying faith, it is important to know that faith must have an object. That object must be God. But faith must also be tested. It must go through the storms, the waters, and the fires. All these trials prove faith and show that the faith is not a paper tiger but a mighty fortress.

The necessary testing of faith denies the Christian immunity to the sorrows and tragedies of life. Instead, real faith gives Christians the power to triumph in the sorrows and tragedies of life if they will use it.

Too often, Christians have faith in faith rather than having faith in God. Faith must not be our object. Instead, faith must have God as its object. If we have faith in faith, it will fail. But if we place our faith in God, we will see results.

Frequently the Lord allows things in our lives that are hard for us to endure. We are loaded with circumstances and fear we may break under their weight. In such cases, the Lord is molding us into His image. A lump of clay must go through a lot of squeezing and molding to become a useful vessel. Likewise, we must undergo squeezing and molding to become kings and priests. A piece of coal can only be transformed into a diamond by high pressure. We, as saints, have a choice to remain a piece of coal or allow the Lord, through force, to change us into diamonds. There are many coals in the church, but there are few diamonds.

When the trials of life come, we must change our human viewpoint to the divine perspective. If we view the storms of life from a human perspective, we will always think according to self. On the other hand, if we think from the divine perspective, which is based upon faith, obedience, and moral conscience, we will see the divine plan woven through the storms. We will come to know that they are molding our character and faith. They are preparing us to reign as kings and priests.

This is why we must follow the perspective of God in all matters. We must come to the place where the way of God is the only way for us. We arrive at this place only through prayer, studying the Bible, God's grace, and our faith, obedience, simplicity, and purity in daily life.

The storms of life reveal that God is still in control and moving among us. It is only during the storms of life that our profession of faith in Christ is shown to be real and secure.

It is wise for the saints to look for the rainbow in the midst of the storms. The rainbow is there—if only we can see it (Genesis 9:8–17). The rainbow is a sign that the Lord God of Covenants keeps His promises, and He will be there.

In the storms of life, the Lord must remain our center with His Word. If the Lord is our center, there will be calmness and peace during the dark times.

God allows His children to go through the storms. And if they will listen to Him, they will be brought through to their end stronger and more determined to follow Jesus Christ.

All saints should study Matthew 7:24–27. In this passage, Christ speaks of two builders, one wise and the other foolish. We are to follow the instructions of Christ for building our house, which is our Christian life, and which determines our ultimate fate. Each saint must select the right site and build a solid foundation (see also 1 Timothy 6:19).

The wise builder builds upon the Rock, which is Jesus Christ (1 Corinthians 3:11; 1 Peter 2:2–5). Building upon the Rock takes time and commitment. Those who build upon the Rock are wise, prudent, and sensible (Proverbs 16:21), and they will survive the storm. The wise builder is not exempt from the storms because he builds an excellent house. The primary reason for making a strong house is to assure that he will be able to weather all storms. It rains "on the just and on the unjust" (Matthew 5:45).

Similarly, storms come upon the just as well as the unjust. No one can stop them. For all of us, the day is coming when it will be too late to build. So build now.

If a person truly builds and continues to build his life upon Christ, he never falls, no matter the severity of the storms. This reason is seen in the promises of God.

1. God receives us in Christ.
2. He adopts us as His children.
3. God promises to provide for our lives.
4. God promises that the end will work out for those who are wise builders.
5. God blesses those who follow His commandments and His Word (Luke 11:28).

Further, Matthew 14:24–33, Mark 6:47–52, and John 6:17–21 all relate the story of Jesus's walking on the water and reveal how Christians react to the storms of life. These passages prove that Jesus will guide us through our storms.

They also show that He will stop them when they have finished their purpose.

In these passages, the storm that caught the disciples by surprise and pulled them out to sea was not an average storm; it was a great and violent storm.

The disciples thought, like so many others, that there would be no storm. When they began their journey, the waters were calm and peaceful. They thought their trip would be successful with no trouble at all. The violent storm did come, and it threatened their lives.

These passages reflect the violent storms in our lives. They unexpectedly strike and cause upheaval in our lives.

The disciples had been struggling against this storm for hours and had only progressed three or four miles. They were exhausted and mentally drained, fighting for life.

The storms of life can cause horror and death if we are not careful. But deliverance came to the disciples when the God of the storms entered the storm and carried them through it. This deliverance could not have occurred had the disciples submitted to the storms.

Furthermore, the walking of Jesus on the sea showed His disciples that the storm was the means He used to come to them and show His great power.

Similarly, when we find ourselves in the storms, we can rest on several assurances. For example, the storms of life come because of the will of God and not outside the will of God. In other words, God permits them.

Next, Jesus was not ignorant of the coming storm (Matthew 14:24–33; Mark 6:47–52; John 6:17–21). He knew it was coming. He directed the disciples into the storm rather than away from it. Jesus Christ also leads us into the storms rather than driving us away from them. This is a significant fact and spiritual principle. Those who follow Christ will follow Him into the storms. He leads us into the storms and through them. On the other hand, Satan and the world's systems will lead us away from the storms until they cannot use us anymore. And then Satan and the world's systems will turn on us and try to destroy us.

Last, the voice of Christ will lead the saints not away from troubled waters but right into them. Prior to this storm, Jesus had tested the disciples in another storm (Matthew 8:23–27). In both cases, He was testing their faith.

It is better to be in the most severe storm and be within the will of God than to be at peace and outside the will of God. Circumstances can never be used to determine our faith. So we must believe and hold on, regardless of our circumstances.

As other writers have also pointed out, the Bible includes storms of correction and storms of perfection. Storms of correction are judgments used as discipline against the saints; storms of perfection are circumstances and incidents for growth and maturity.

How can Psalm 18:1–2 ever be true for the saints if there are no storms? From this passage, the care of God for us is seen as personal. He is our strength, our light, our fortress, our shelter, our deliverer, and our shield amid these storms of life. Each type of storm determines just how God is there. If we need strength, He is there as a fortress. If we are in darkness, God is the light through that oppression. If we need shelter, He is there as our shelter. If we are going through temptation, God is there as our deliverer. If we are threatened, He is our shield. In all cases, He is there to prove His grace, goodness, care, and mercy amid our human condition.

Today, the people of God are more than ever on the sea amid great storms. We need to follow Him through the storms and have faith that He will lead us through them and beyond them. And we must always remember that storms and intercession are mingled together.

In Acts 27:29, during a storm at sea, the sailors threw out four anchors. Paul admonished the men to stay in the boat, saying, "Except these abide in the ship, ye cannot be saved" (v. 31). The experience of Paul shows us that if we abide in the ship, we will be saved. Just as the sailors used four sea anchors, Paul saw four anchors that are effective in protecting the people of God.

In Acts 27:23–44, four anchors for the saints are emphasized:

1. God's presence (v. 23)
2. The promises of God (vv. 24–25
3. The protection and prosperity of God (v. 24)
4. God's awesome power (v. 44)

From Paul's experience, we see that God will get us through our storms and land us safely beyond them. The storms may seem to be prevailing and winning, but God is still in control. Sooner or later, He will speak to the waves, winds, rains, and storm clouds to settle down and cease. For example, in Mark 4:38–41, the Lord commanded the storm and the winds and said, "Peace be still." For that to happen, the Lord must be with us in the storms, and He must go with us through them. The phrase "peace be still" is not really what is meant by the Greek. The Greek is better translated as, "Shut up, put the muzzle on, and keep it on. Do not let me ever catch you with that muzzle off again." A day will come when the storms must have a muzzle put on them, and only the Lord can do that. When the Lord puts a muzzle on the storms, they must stop and do stop.

When we are in the storms, we must remember the following:

1. Jesus leads us into the storms of life.
2. He knows that the storms are coming before they come.
3. The storms are used for our development.
4. We should not be fearful of the storms.
5. We must call upon Him in the storms of life (Hebrews 4:14–16; 1 Peter 5:7).
6. In due time, Jesus will calm the storms.

Jones Lewis wrote the following hymn:

> *Upon life's boundless ocean where mighty billows roll*
> *I've fixed my hope in Jesus, the anchor of my soul*
> *When trials of life surround me as storms are gathering o'er*
> *I rest upon His mercy and trust Him more*
> *I've anchored in Jesus, the storms of life I'll brave,*
> *I've anchored in Jesus; I fear no wind or wave,*
> *I've anchored in Jesus for He hath power to save,*
> *I've anchored to the Rock of Ages.*[3]

CHAPTER 1
DID SATAN KNOW?

Sixteen years before I received one of the biggest miracles in the twentieth century, I wrestled with God so many days and nights. In these times of fighting with God, I prayed unto Him that I was not strong enough for battle. It scared me to even think about that. I was not a Jacob who wrestled with an angel (Genesis 32:24–30). But little did I know those many nights and days, not only would I fight with God, but I would also grapple with the devil and his demons. We must aggressively confront the forces of evil; there cannot be any coward here in the front line of the battle. The shame is that few are on the front line of the fight. Most are not even in the battle itself.

As I have repeatedly said, much of the church of today is miles wide but only a few inches deep. Because of that, many churches are shallow, and few are hostilely fighting against the forces of evil.

While Satan and his evil spirits are powerful and knowledgeable, they are not omniscient. They do not know all the things that God will do, all things about us, or all the things that God has in store for us. Satan and his evil spirits are significantly limited and know most about us from us; this is seen from the demons called "familiar spirits." They are familiar with our families and those who have died in our families because they watch and listen. Not only that, but they are also great at judging our emotions, feelings, actions, reactions, and even our body language. And mostly, Satan and his evil spirits would remain ignorant if we could learn to keep our mouths shut. What a joy that would be. He and his forces would question all day long about what we were doing if we could say no negative word. Indeed, if the only words that would come out of our mouths were words of praise unto the King of the Universe, Satan and his evil forces would be greatly confused. That is easily said. And hard to do. So too many of us are hung by our tongues after all.

First Corinthians 2:6–8 gives great proof that Satan and his evil spirits are not omniscient.

> "Howbeit we speak wisdom among them that are perfect: yet not the wisdom of this world, nor of the princes of this world, that come to

nought: but we speak the wisdom of God in a mystery, even the hidden wisdom, which God ordained before the world unto our glory: which none of the princes of this world knew: for had they known it, they would not have crucified the Lord of glory."

Only God knows the heart (mind and thoughts) of people (Psalms 44:21; 1 Chronicles 29:17). Satan and his evil spirits can only gain insight into our minds and thoughts through observation.

There is a clear argument that Satan is ignorant of the things of God in detail. While he does know specific facts, he does not know all things about a person's life or the plans of God for that person. And further, the ignorance of the angels about the plan of salvation is well attested. Even the chief-adversary of God was ignorant of the plan of salvation. So ignorant were Satan and all his forces about the plan of salvation that the ancient fathers of the church could not help but write about this significant fact. For example, Ignatius, an apostolic father of the ancient church, writes,

> And the virginity of Mary escaped the notice of the prince of this age, and likewise her childbearing, and the death of the Lord; three mysteries were to be loudly shouted, which were done in the silence of God.[1]

While the spurious epistle of Ignatius, known as the "Epistle to the Philippians," was not written by Ignatius, it shows the overall view of the early church about Satan and his ignorance.

> For many things are hidden from you Satan: the virginity of Mary, the wonderful birth; Who was the One that became incarnated into her body; the star which led those men who were in the east; the Magi who brought the gifts; the greeting of the archangel to the Virgin; the wonderful conception of the Virgin who was betrothed; the proclamation of the child-forerunner regarding to the Son of the Virgin, and the leaping of the child-forerunner in the womb from that which was considered foreseen; the hymns of the angels over Him that was to be born; the Good News announced unto the shepherds; the fear of Herod unto the removal of his kingdom; the command of murdering children; the migration into Egypt; the return back from there unto the same region; the infant swaddling-clothes; the human census; the nourishing with milk; the name of the father that was given unto Him, which did not beget Him; the manger because there was no place elsewhere; no human preparation for the infant; the progress of growth,

human speech, hunger, thirst, journeying, tiredness; the oblation of sacrifices, and then also circumcision, baptism; the voice of God speaking above Him who was baptized, who He was and where He came; the witness of the Spirit and the Father from above; the voice of John the prophet when it signified the passion through the title of the "Lamb;" the working of different miracles, various kinds of healings; the Master's rebuke commanding both the sea and the winds; the evil spirits were banished; you, O Satan, yourself were subjected to be inwardly tortured with pain and anxiety, and when you were tortured by His power who was seen, you had no power whatever to do anything.[2]

Such was the ignorance of Satan and all his evil forces about Christ that they willingly moved toward the undoing of themselves. Their defeat occurred by their wanting Christ's death on the cross. If they had only known that the death of Christ would be their undoing, they would have never wanted and pushed for His death. They would have tried everything possible to keep Him alive.

Undeniably, the ancient church concluded that Satan, recognizing that through the cross his destruction would be gained, attempted to put a stop to its erection, but he failed.[3]

Satan knew someone was to be the Deliverer and Messiah. He knew this from the messianic prophecy mentioned in Genesis 3:15: "And I will put enmity between thee and the woman, and between thy seed and her seed; it shall bruise thy head, and thou shalt bruise his heel." And that the ancients had a view of the coming Messiah, the Redeemer, is without dispute. They knew someone was coming; it was common knowledge that the Redeemer would come, die, and rise again; it was common knowledge so much that the ancients (those who were godly) celebrated this even before it took place. One very ancient form of Psalms 96:10 reads, "The Lord reigns from the cross."

CHAPTER 2
WHY?

My husband, George Elias Roberts, and I were raised just twenty miles apart from each other. Both our fathers were farmers during the Great Depression, and both families knew what troubles were.

Often in times of trouble, we ask the question, "Why me? What is the reason, cause, or purpose for my difficulties?"

In Genesis 32:24–30, if Jacob had a choice to ask a question, it would have been something like, "Why should God be so firm? Why should the struggle go on all night? Why should I struggle with God and with men?" The result of this struggling was that his name became Israel (Genesis 32:22–30). Notice the words of Hosea: "Yea, he had power over the angel, and prevailed: he wept, and made supplication unto him: he found him in Beth-el, and there he spake with us" (Hosea 12:4). And we should notice another passage:

> "How long wilt thou forget me, O LORD? forever? how long wilt thou hide thy face from me? How long shall I take counsel in my soul, having sorrow in my heart daily? How long shall mine enemy be exalted over me? Consider and hear me, O LORD my God: lighten mine eyes, lest I sleep the sleep of death; Lest mine enemy say, I have prevailed against him, and those that trouble me rejoice when I am moved. But I have trusted in thy mercy; my heart shall rejoice in thy salvation. I will sing unto the LORD, because he hath dealt bountifully with me" (Psalms 13:1–6).

All my life since being saved, I have asked God, "Why this? Why did my daddy become an alcoholic? Why did I have to be born between the Great Depression and World War II? Why was my father's first wife murdered? Why did my only son have to be born with brain damage and dyslexia?"

Since being in the ministry, I've seen the same with others. Too many people ask the question in various forms, but still, it is the same question: "Ms. Dot, why this? Why did God take my husband? Why do I have cancer? Why does God not heal me? Why does God not move for my family and me? Why does God not bless me? Why does God allow the wicked to be blessed while His children live paycheck to paycheck? Why do we have to wait so long for the Lord to move?"

The simple answer is "because." But that is no answer. To answer the question requires understanding where men and women were, where they are, and where they shall be. While the central theme of the Bible is Christ, another main subject of the Bible is where men and women were, where they are, and where they will be.

Why was I born? I was born to be an intercessor and a handmaiden of the Lord.

There are many *whys* in my own life. And I have not always understood them. Nor have I understood why my life had to be so hard. And a great "why" in my life is this question: "Why have I had to wait so long for my prayers to be answered?" Because of all these questions, many times in my life, I thought God hated me.

The Old Testament has been a great help in understanding all these *why* questions. So looking back to the Old Testament, we can see how God did things that caused the saints to ask the same question.

Amram and Jochebed

Exodus 2:1 reads, "And there went a man of the house of Levi and took to wife a daughter of Levi." His introduction in the biblical narrative was simple. No name was given, just a vague mention of him by the phrase "a man of the house of Levi." The writer of Exodus, Moses himself, points out that his father was not as famous in the biblical narrative as he and his mother were.

Later, we are told that his name was Amram and that he belonged to the family of the Kohathites. The Kohathites were descended from Kohath, Levi's second son (Exodus 6:16–18).

Further, Josephus wrote that the father of Moses was named Amram. Josephus continued and said that Amram was a noble of the Hebrews, though not of the highest class, and very upset because his wife was with her third child.

According to Josephus, Amram ran toward prayer as a means of help, and God was moved by such practices and supplication. No angel appeared to Amram; the Lord God, God the Word, the defender of the covenant, appeared before him in a dream. He gave Amram courage that he and his son had favor with God. The Lord informed Amram that because of his child, the Egyptians doomed the children of other Hebrews to destruction, but He, the Lord, would protect his child.[1]

Jochebed was born in Egypt and married to her nephew, who was of the same tribe of Levi. She and her husband Amram were steadfast and godly people. There was no hint that they ever compromised their faith in God.

The tribe of Jochebed, which was the tribe of Levi, was to become the tribe of the Levites, the priests, and the high priests. This tribe's duties included taking care of the tabernacle and later the temple.

In history, Jochebed is considered one of the greatest mothers. Her actions, practices, and conduct—unselfish love and self-sacrifice—made possible the Exodus of the Israelite people from Egypt. This one woman changed the course of history. God placed her in the path of a pharaoh and his will. This simple, uneducated woman was more than enough to face a highly educated pharaoh, his empire, his soldiers, and all the evil spirits associated with Egypt. Just one godly person is more than enough to change the course of history because that one pious person serves an awesome God.

Jochebed's Various Questions

Jochebed, the mother of Moses, must have asked many questions. She could have desired not to have a boy but rather a girl. In contemplating the birth of a son, surely she must have wondered: *Why is pharaoh killing all the baby boys? He has put all of us into slavery. Both men and women have been put into labor camps. Would not my boy be one more man working in these labor camps?* She would have rather seen her son alive and in slavery than be dead. Finally, she did give birth to a son after the issuing of the evil decree of pharaoh (Exodus 1:22–2:2).

She had no way of knowing that pharaoh had wise magicians to foretell future events. According to Josephus, there was one magician, also known as a priest and a prophet of Egypt, who predicted the coming of a child who would deliver the Hebrews from the Egyptians and bring destruction upon them.[2] Further, the Targum of Jonathan mentions Jannes and Jambres, two other great enemies of Moses and the Hebrews, as the heads of the Egyptian sorcerers. Both these men interpreted this dream of pharaoh. "Behold, all the land of Mizraim was placed in one scale of a balance, and a lamb, the young of a sheep, was ill the other scale; and the scale with the lamb in it overweighed."[3] These two men told the king that about this time, there would be a child who was to be born to the Israelites. If such a child were born, he would bring low the Egyptian dominion.

Such a child would cause any king to fear. If this child were born and lived, pharaoh would have to fight to keep his power over the Egyptian empire. The child would be a lamb that outweighed the whole Egyptian empire.

So why did pharaoh order the death of all male Hebrew babies? He feared the coming deliverer.

Pharaoh also wanted to stop the population of the Israelites from growing, and Satan attempted to destroy all the males of Israel so that the Messiah could not come to bruise his head (Genesis 3:15).

As a mother, I can feel Jochebed's pain as she held her baby boy close to her; she cried and prayed that the God of her fathers would move. She surely prayed with tears. Nothing touches God's heart like the tears of a mother.

Satan must have tormented Jochebed's mind and tried to bring fear before her. She must have remembered all the babies that had been thrown into the River Nile.

Other questions must have come to her mind: *I fear putting my baby into the River Nile! Did God speak to me? Will He protect my baby? Did He tell my husband that after three months, I am to put this beautiful baby in the river—the same river in which babies have been sacrificed to a false god?* She must have been praying something like, "Please God, do not let my child drown."

Birth of Moses

At birth, Moses was protected through two Hebrew midwives named Shiphrah and Puah (Exodus 1:15). During this time in Egypt, there were from five hundred to one thousand women working in the union of midwives. Jochebed knew if other Hebrew mothers found out that the midwives had protected her baby, her whole family would be killed. Perhaps she chose these two midwives because they were the heads of the union, and they feared God more than men.

Jochebed protected her baby even though she had no idea that the little ark would hold the most magnificent cargo the world had ever known. That cargo would change a nation and an empire. That cargo was a type of Christ.

Before the birth of Moses, his family consisted of only four people: Amram (old in age), his wife Jochebed, and two children, Aaron and Miriam. Miriam was born soon after the marriage, and Aaron was born some twelve years later.

Aaron was born before the pharaoh's evil decree of oppression had been announced. From his birth, Aaron was set apart from the womb through God's choice to make him a high priest and a Levite. While Aaron did not need protection, Moses did. This protection was by the God-fearing midwives refusing to kill the Hebrew sons. So the life of Moses was saved (Exodus 1:15–

19).

When Jochebed became aware of the evil decree, she was about to give birth to her third child. She knew her infant son faced a death sentence.

Both Jochebed and her husband Amram were willing to confront, defy, and disobey pharaoh's edict, while still following the will and commandments of the Lord God of Israel. Jochebed did not have to do this alone. Like Peter and the other apostles, Jochebed and her husband likely said, "We ought to obey God rather than men" (Acts 5:29).

I do not believe Jochebed's tears and prayers to pharaoh would have moved him to pity, but I am greatly assured that the mighty and great God noticed her tears and prayers. It is almost impossible to imagine Jochebed's emotional agony and pain as she carried the child. She knew if her child Moses was born, it meant death. Such thoughts must have afflicted her hour by hour every day. There is nothing birthed without affliction, and there is nothing birthed without tears and prayers if that which is birthed is under the divine will of God.

Amram and his wife Jochebed, though believing and trusting God, must have wrestled within themselves about their decision. There cannot be any great decision like this without Satan and his forces of evil spirits working to spread doubt and confusion among the servants of God. The war is enormous.

Josephus points out that it was the faith of Amram, above that of Jochebed, that saved Moses. And Josephus points out that both Amram and Jochebed were involved in setting the ark of Moses afloat in the water.[4] However, the biblical text only points out that Jochebed had a part in this. It was her faith that brought to completion her son's rescue from the threat of death and for the plan of God to be fulfilled.

Jochebed had been watching the daughter of pharaoh and knew exactly where she went to bathe. Upon the waters, God brought the child to the right place at the right moment, and the daughter of pharaoh made the fantastic discovery. The Bible states that "the babe wept. And she had compassion on him" (Exodus 2:6). God knows when to make us cry out for help. The pagan princess recognized that the child was Hebrew and took him as her own.

Rather than having been raised amid godly surroundings, Moses was raised among the court of pharaoh in the Egyptian style. As a child, he would have walked around the Egyptian court without any clothes, and all his hair would have been shaved off, except for one small lock. He would have been kept completely clean. And almost every desire of his would have been quickly fulfilled as he was waited on by many attendants.

Despite the luxuries, as Moses grew to adulthood, a day came when he could not stand by and watch his people be oppressed. It is important to note that the life of Moses was changed in just one day. This is true for so many people. It only takes a day, a minute, a second, or even a moment to change a life from good unto evil, or evil unto good.

Moses Never a Pagan

It cannot be denied that Moses was familiar with the repulsive rites and practices of Egyptian paganism. Residing at the Egyptian court, he would have seen the pagan priests offer up prayers and sacrifices unto the pagan gods. There can be no doubt about this.

Moses was not entirely under the pagan influence. He received godly supervision and teachings from his Hebrew family during the early period of his residence as a child in Egypt. What kept Moses from falling into paganism was certainly his relationship with his family. They were anchors to his life and led him into the religious beliefs of the Israelites and his sympathy for his Jewish countrymen. If he had grown up entirely as an Egyptian, and become an idolater, he would not have concerned himself with the sufferings of his people. But the opposite is true (Exodus 2:12), for he continued to feel their sorrow and hoped in time to better their future.

The principles of the Hebrew religion were taught to Moses as a child, and that teaching safeguarded him from becoming a pagan. By this, he grew up with an unmovable faith in Jewish monotheism, believed in the covenant and promises given to Abraham, Isaac, and Jacob, and hated all forms of idolatry. It was impossible for Moses to believe in the God of Abraham, Isaac, and Jacob, and at the same time practice paganism.

Therefore, the idea of Moses being a worshiper of idols, the gods of Egypt, is groundless. And the idea that Moses was a priest of the gods is unfounded. There is nothing in the Bible, or in any historical record, to even remotely suggest this. Moses's foundation of religious beliefs and training, handed down to him from his Hebrew family, tailored him to become the deliverer and leader of his nation. Such godly beliefs and practice grounded his confidence in God and enabled him to stay the course throughout his life. Even amid idolatries and idolaters, the influence of paganism had little hold on him. What a difference between Moses and so many Christians. We who have the greater covenant seem as if we cannot withstand anything.

Moses rejected all the pleasures, vices, and perversions that a pagan society could well offer a young man in his position. He was following a destiny and a vision, and nothing Satan could provide would be accepted. Even in his early life, his eyes looked beyond the physical and into the spiritual world, where the King of the Universe resides.

According to Josephus, Moses never concealed his identity as a Hebrew; he never denied his God, his religion, nor his nationality. Josephus mentions a tradition about Moses that when he was at Heliopolis, he performed prayers unto the Lord God outside the wall of the city's temple and followed the rites of the Jewish fathers. Therefore, Moses never concealed or abandoned, under difficult circumstances, his faith, his nationality, or his religion.[5] But the Israelites would not hold to their faith and practice as firmly as Moses did, especially in the times of the wilderness, the Judges, and the Kings. Though Moses held on to his faith, his nationality, and his religion, the Hebrews in Egypt still considered him an outsider. He had not made up his mind to throw in his future with his people. He knew their sufferings, but not as personally as he would in the Exodus and wilderness.

Courage, Faith, and Compensation of Jochebed

From Scripture, we find aspects of Jochebed that stand as reminders to all of us. In the narrative of Exodus, there is enough written about Jochebed that we can conceive an overall view of what made her tick.

First, Scripture speaks of the qualifications of Jochebed. Sometimes we think that God selects us without noticing our skills, but that is far from the truth. One of the reasons God chooses us is because we are qualified to be called and arranged for divine tasks. Of course, God has been working on our whole lives, both building up and tearing down so that we can be qualified for His divine plan. Some have been, are, or will be worked on by God for a few years or a few months.

Jochebed is a picture of everything a mother must be. Every mother must have a relationship with the Lord. And every boy and girl deserves a saved, sold-out, and dedicated mother.

The courage of Jochebed is remarkable. She did not give in to a pagan ruler and defy the Lord God. And she refused to surrender to a pagan and godless system. If she had submitted to this evil system, it would have cost her the life of her son.

In thought and principle, she agreed with the words of Joshua, which were to be spoken when Israel was in the Promised Land:

"And if it seem evil unto you to serve the LORD, choose you this day whom ye will serve; whether the gods which your fathers served that were on the other side of the flood, or the gods of the Amorites, in whose land ye dwell: but as for me and my house, we will serve the LORD" (Joshua 24:15)

The faith of Jochebed was steadfast. She was a woman driven and inspired by an unmovable faith in the will of the Lord God. Her faith was so remarkable that Jochebed was named, with her husband, among the heroes of faith in Hebrews 11. Hebrews 11:23 reads, "By faith Moses, when he was born, was hid three months of his parents, because they saw he was a proper child; and they were not afraid of the king's commandment."

A person with unmovable faith can be assured that the tasks and duties ahead will be great and challenging. In truth, the greater a person's faith, the greater their difficulties. Nothing, regardless of how seemingly insurmountable or difficult, should destroy our faith. If we put our faith in God, our faith increases in power, strength, and determination step by step as we are confronted with greater and greater tasks and duties.

Unmovable faith may be passive and inactive most of the time. Others may not realize the great faith of a person. Yet when the storms rage, that unmovable faith is activated and ready for the fight.

It is during the battle that the might of a real soldier is revealed. Great difficulties require great faith. Sadly, that is the reason so many do not make it through the storms of life. They face problems with weak faith. The wise soldier builds up his or her faith before the storms rage. He or she does not wait until the storms rage to increase his or her faith.

Jochebed needed this unmovable faith to accomplish what she did for the Lord and her son. Not only did she resist the world, but she also opposed all the evil spirits in Egypt.

The world and all the evil spirits in Egypt were crying out for the death of her son Moses. Regardless, she stood firm in the face of the attack. In spite of the world, pharaoh, and all the evil spirits, she stood. She placed her son above the problems. She threw down a gauntlet before all of them and proved her faith by action. She released her son unto the Lord and put him in the river. When she put her son into the river, the meaning is so clear. She took her hands off the life of her son and left him in the will of God.

It took unmovable faith to place her son into the same terrifying river that pharaoh used to destroy the infant sons of Israel. Yet through faith, Jochebed used the river as a means of deliverance (Exodus 1:22).

Jochebed and Miriam were only able to set the next part of their plan into motion after the daughter of pharaoh found Moses.

Unmovable faith was also present in this circumstance. The mother of Moses became the nurse of Moses. She raised a child for someone else while she was still the biological mother of that child. Imagine how difficult that was. Early Jewish commentaries indicate that she could never tell the child who she was. She had to guard her mouth and her emotions for quite a time.

However, Jochebed was given several significant opportunities for raising her child for the daughter of pharaoh. The most considerable occasion was that Jochebed, for a time, was able to teach her son about the Lord God, true worship, and godly living.

Besides unmovable faith, she surrendered herself to the duty and tasks of raising her son. She did not understand or realize all the ramifications that followed her actions for the sake of her son. But she gave her son to the Lord so that a nation could be saved.

Jochebed's life reveals that when we surrender ourselves to the Lord, there will be compensation. Understanding compensation is important. When we work and live for the Lord, we will receive back. Either it is automatic, or we must ask for compensation. Regardless, Jochebed's life points to the fact that God repays us for our dedication, surrender, faith, and service unto Him. God is not heartless. He has not set it up so that He alone receives, and we alone give. Instead, He receives and gives. We are required to give and receive as well. Too many saints only receive from the Lord. They do not like giving.

Jochebed's compensation was in the form of her son's becoming the deliverer of the people of Israel, and the one who would be known as the great lawgiver of God's people.

The Life of Moses

As Moses grew, he observed the afflictions and burdens of the Hebrews, his countrymen. One day he saw an Egyptian hitting a Hebrew. In anger, Moses killed the Egyptian and buried his body in the sand (Exodus 2:12). Why would God let Moses kill the Egyptian? The Egyptian was evil, demon possessed, a reprobate, and one who practiced the vilest forms of evil. Therefore, Moses sought to defend and protect the innocent and oppressed against evil.

The practices of pagan idolatry brought demonization. Every slip into idolatry and other forms of paganism meant a slip into demon possession.

Every witch, sorcerer, and other variety of occultists mentioned in the Old Testament were demon possessed.[6]

People cannot practice idolatry and sexual immorality without falling into the state of demon possession. For example, during the kingdom of Israel, the Israelites were involved in the sacrilege and unbridled insanity of the Canaanites. They added promiscuity to promiscuity beyond the bounds of restraint and modesty. They added practices of insanity to their list of vices. In so doing, their state became that of demon possession. Simply put, demon possession, sexual sin, and idolatry always go together.

Origen, a father of the early church in the third century, discussed the condition of the world before the coming of Joshua and the Israelites.

> You see how many swarms of hostile hosts and the vilest demons may be stirred up against Joshua and the Israelite army. Before the advent of our Lord and Savior, all those demons, who were at peace and secure, possessed the human spirits and ruled in their minds and bodies. But so grace appeared in the world, and the mercy of God our Savior instructs us thoroughly so that we may live righteously and morally in this world and be separated from every contagion of sin that each spirit of a human may take back its freedom and the image of God also in which it was created from the beginning.[7]

Moses's killing of the Egyptian was the first blow of deliverance for his people. Moses did not know the full significance of his deed. He did it alone, in secret, by his strength, not at the request of the Lord, and he failed. It was not his decision to begin the deliverance of his people from the Egyptians. The decision rested with God alone. And the wrath of God was to reveal itself shortly by various means. Moses forgot what Paul knew: "Dearly beloved, avenge not yourselves, but rather give place unto wrath: for it is written, Vengeance is mine; I will repay, saith the Lord" (Romans 12:19). The phrase "unto wrath" does not refer to human wrath but to the wrath of God. Moses forgot to leave room for the wrath of God. Also, the deed of Moses was a display of his faith, though displaced, anticipating the coming divine providence. Stephen, recounting the history of Moses, says, "And seeing one of them suffer wrong, he defended him, and avenged him that was oppressed, and smote the Egyptian: For he supposed his brethren would have understood how that God by his hand would deliver them: but they understood not" (Acts 7:24–25). Stephen realized the act of Moses as a promise of the coming deliverance of the Israelites from the Egyptians, which God meant to accomplish through Moses.

Further, the killing of the Egyptian was not a case of murder nor self-defense. Moses, as a prince of Egypt, had the authority of the sword and could kill a slave driver within his legal rights under Egyptian law. The simple phrase "he slew" in Exodus 2:12 does not mean murder, but the best translation is "he was made to kill." The causative idea within Hebrew is expressed quite well here. By the actions of the Egyptian, Moses had no choice but to act as he did, regardless of its consequences. The Egyptian stepped out of the Egyptian norms of conduct; the killing was a deed of an Egyptian prince against a slave driver for the sake of innocence.

Leaving Egypt and following the Lord, Moses gave up all the things of the world and was to become a type of Christ as a deliverer. "By faith Moses, when he was come to years, refused to be called the son of Pharaoh's daughter; Choosing rather to suffer affliction with the people of God, than to enjoy the pleasures of sin for a season; Esteeming the reproach of Christ greater riches than the treasures in Egypt: for he had respect unto the recompence of the reward. By faith he forsook Egypt, not fearing the wrath of the king: for he endured, as seeing him who is invisible" (Hebrews 11:24–27).

In the next forty years, God had a plan for Moses. As a shepherd in Midian, Moses had plenty of time to die to his flesh. To do what he was called to do, he had to conquer his emotions. He had to become an empty vessel that God would fill.

Moses lived forty years being something, another forty years being nothing, and another forty years of being something again.

The Hebrews also had a strong rebellious nature, and they needed to learn how to die to the flesh and submit to God, lest death come upon them. Further, they needed to learn unconditional obedience. They also had to learn the ways and the means of the coming of the Messiah, who would die on a cross and be resurrected. Indeed, the Israelites were to learn how to march in the form of a cross. Why had God instructed them to advance that way? It was for our benefit. There are signs and symbols of the cross everywhere in the Old Testament to foretell the coming of the Messiah. These signs signaled the moving from the Dispensation of the Law into the Dispensation of Grace.

Have you ever considered how many miracles God worked through eighty-year-old Moses? The first miracle was that the rod of Moses turned into a real snake. Then the magicians of pharaoh used demonic powers to turn their rods into real snakes. The snake of Moses swallowed up the snakes of pharaoh's magicians. Moses went on to do other miracles by the power of God. All of them, especially the plagues of God against the Egyptians, show an ancient principle at work: what you sow you will reap (Galatians 6:7–8). Evil practices will produce evil consequences. Therefore, such corrupt practices will come back to haunt people.

The Coming Plagues

At the time of the Exodus, Israel's destiny seemed to hang breathlessly in the balance. After all, the Lord God had not responded to their prayers for approximately four hundred years; during this time, heaven had become like brass. In those years, many Jewish mothers cried out to the Lord God. And there are no prayers like a mother groaning and travailing, crying her heart out. Finally, God heard Israel's groaning and remembered His covenant with Abraham, Isaac, and Jacob. God saw the people of Israel and had mercy on them.

From the acts of one pharaoh and the laws of another pharaoh, consequences were finally released in the tenth plague. This plague was to repay the Egyptians for all their evil practices done against the Israelites. So no matter how hard pharaoh made their lives bitter with hard bondage, the Israelites were to survive and prosper.

Notice that pharaoh went through ten plagues before he let the Israelites go. And rather than humbling himself, he hardened himself eleven times during this time. He refused above all to submit to the rule of God; he would instead become an enemy of God, and that brought his ruin.

From the beginning to the end, the ten plagues took several weeks to be carried out. Twenty-six days are mentioned in the biblical narrative, and there must have been some time for the plagues to begin and then do what they had to do against the Egyptians. Therefore, at least fifty days span the time of the first plague to the ending of the last plague.

1. The plague of the blood lasted one week (Exodus 7:15–25).
2. The plague of the frogs took a few days to accomplish its purpose. For example, it took days for the frogs to pass through the whole land of Egypt (Exodus 8:1–8). And it took at least one day for the frogs to die out (Exodus 8:10–15).
3. The plague of lice took a few days to accomplish its purpose (Exodus 8:16–19).
4. The plague of flies took a few days to accomplish its purpose, and it

took some time to remove the flies (Exodus 8:23–29).

5. It took a set time to announce and to destroy the animals of the Egyptians (Exodus 9:1–7).
6. A specific time was given for the continual hardening of pharaoh's heart (Exodus 9:1–7).
7. The plague of boils and blains took a few days to accomplish its purpose (Exodus 9:8–12).
8. At least three days are meant next. One day was given to declare the plague of hail and fire; another day was given for the plague to accomplish its purpose, and it took at least one day to send for Moses and Aaron and have them presented before pharaoh (Exodus 9:13–27).
9. Next, at least six days are meant. The plague of locusts took two days to spread over the whole land of Egypt. The next calling of Moses and Aaron by pharaoh took another day. It took at least one day for the plague of the locusts to accomplish its purpose. And it took at least two days for the locusts to be removed (Exodus 10:4–19).
10. The plague of darkness was three days of darkness, and it took a day for Moses and Aaron to be called before the presence of pharaoh (Exodus 10:24–29).
11. It took at least a day to kill the firstborn during the Passover, accept the request of the pharaoh, and then leave the land of Egypt (Exodus 11:1–10, 12:29–36).

The ten plagues were especially designed against the demon–gods of the Egyptians. Why? God was showing the Egyptians that their gods were no match for Him; He had overcome them.

1. The first plague—the Nile River turning into blood—was designed as a direct attack against the demon–god worshiped as the Nile River itself. The god focused upon was Nilus or Hopi, the god of the Nile River and water.
2. The second plague of frogs was against Ptha, the frog-headed god, and Hekt, the goddess of reproduction.
3. The third plague of insects was against Seb, the god of the earth who blessed the earth by making it productive and protecting it, especially the land of Egypt, from natural disasters.
4. The fourth plague of flies was against Baal, the Baalim, or Beelzebub, the god of the flies. These gods were worshiped, particularly

Beelzebub, so that infected flies would go away.
5. The fifth plague of murrain (pestilence) was against Hathor and Apis, the sacred cattle gods at Memphis (Exodus 9:5–7). They were gods of reproduction and fertility; they were gods who were believed to protect from plagues, diseases, and accidents.
6. The sixth plague of boils and blains was against the Typhon, the evil-eye god who was worshiped in the hope of averting diseases.
7. The seventh plague, which was of hail and fire, was against Isis and Osiris — the gods of light, health, fertility, arts, and agriculture — and Shu, the god of the atmosphere. They were worshiped so that the Egyptians could be protected against storms and natural disasters.
8. The eighth plague, which was of the locusts, was against the Serapis, the insect god. This god was believed to protect the land from locusts.
9. The ninth plague, which was that of darkness, was against Ra, the sun god, who was to protect from any curse of the sun and provide light, warmth, and fruitfulness. Further, he was worshiped to safeguard against any natural disaster from the sun itself.
10. The tenth plague, which was the death of the Egyptian firstborn, was against Ptah, the god of life.

Hidden, but Not Forgotten

Under the most destructive plague, the tenth plague, Moses did what God said. He hid away from the angel of destruction under the protection of the blood. Moses did not dare go out of his home and enter the streets. Still, as the third child of a Hebrew family, he was only protected by following the commands and directions of the Lord. If he had gone out of his house after God spoke to him about the coming pestilence, he would have committed an act of disobedience. That deed may have cost him his life, but Moses followed all that God said. He placed the blood on the doorposts of his home, hid from the coming pestilence, and celebrated the Passover. The Lord God wrought the pestilence through the angel of destruction (Exodus 12:7–13). Of course, any firstborn male of Israel, not obeying the commandments and directions of the Lord, would have been killed, and the punishment may have extended to any person of a Hebrew household.

God protected His people and proved His power above the power of the Egyptian gods.

Many Questions

The Bible, and life in general, cause us to ask questions—especially *why* questions. First, why does God take our loved ones? Why do we suffer so much? After all, Job was only tested a few months (Job 7:3). Why has so much had to happen to my family? Why does Satan exist? Why did men and women fall? Why do we live in sin? The following analysis from the Bible and writings from the ancient church fathers answers many of these questions.

When Adam and Eve rebelled against God, Satan won a great victory. He took and gained what God had given Adam and humanity (Psalms 8:1–9). Not only did Adam rebel against God, but he also committed high treason. At the point that Adam sinned, evil, sin, death, and the power of Satan came altogether into the world. By the high treason of Adam, Satan kidnapped the human race and even wanted the land of Eden. But God drove Adam and Eve out of the garden to protect the Garden of Eden from humanity and Satan himself. He placed angels at the gate.

Genesis 3:22–24 reads,

And the LORD God said, Behold, the man is become as one of us, to know good and evil: and now, lest he put forth his hand, and take also of the tree of life, and eat, and live for ever: Therefore the LORD God sent him forth from the garden of Eden, to till the ground from whence he was taken. So he drove out the man; and he placed at the east of the garden of Eden Cherubims, and a flaming sword which turned every way, to keep the way of the tree of life.

Soon after the fall of Adam, there was given the first messianic prophecy of a coming Messiah. Genesis 3:15 reads, "And I will put enmity between thee and the woman, and between thy seed and her seed; it shall bruise thy head, and thou shalt bruise his heel."

One of the purposes for the coming Messiah was to redeem humanity from their fall into evil and depravity and save them by the blood of Jesus Christ. The blood of Christ, the death of Christ, and the cross separate men and women who are saved from the powers of evil and darkness and make them completely clean from sin and evil. They become the property of God, rather than remaining the property of Satan any longer (Romans 6:1–23).

From Genesis 3, we learn several things:
1. By an existent evil force, humanity was in rebellion against the direct rule of God.

2. Satan outwitted, fooled, and robbed the sinless but inexperienced woman of her blessings and position.
3. Adam, who was not fooled, willingly accepted the consequences of his rebellion against God.
4. As Adam was the head of humanity, if he had not rebelled, Eve's sin would have been of no effect.

Of the many consequences that took place, some were as follows:

1. The Fall defiled and contaminated the creation of God. All of creation was injured by the fall of humanity (Genesis 3:17–19).
2. The cosmic rebellion has become a cosmic-earthly rebellion.
3. Humanity now not only participates in the conflict but also has become a central figure in the warfare (Luke 4:54–6; John 12:31, 14:30, 16:11; Acts 26:18; Ephesians 2:1–3; Colossians 1:13).
4. Every race of humanity is affected by the Fall (Romans 5:12–15).
5. Death entered the world of Adam (Romans 5:12–15).
6. Due to the fall of humanity, all unsaved are in bondage to Satan, and are open to demon possession at will (1 Corinthians 10:20–21; 2 Corinthians 4:3–4; Ephesians 2:1–3; Colossians 1:13–14, 2:8–20; 2 Thessalonians 2; Hebrews 2:14–15).
7. The unsaved are all children of Satan (Matthew 13:37–39; John 8:44; 1 John 3:3–10).
8. The unsaved are in the kingdom of Satan and the property of Satan (Matthew 12:22–29; Colossians 1:12–14).
9. The unsaved are all bound by Satan (Acts 26:18).
10. The unsaved are all blinded by Satan so that they cannot in themselves receive the gospel, except for the sake of prevenient grace working in them (2 Corinthians 4:3–4).
11. The unsaved are all under the power of Satan (1 John 5:19).
12. The unsaved are all enslaved to a world-system controlled by Satan (Ephesians 4:4; 1 John 5:19).
13. The unsaved are in the flesh (Romans 7:5), under the Law (Romans 6:14, 7:6), and slaves to sin (Romans 6:6, 17–20).
14. These things indicate that humans are in a condemned state, and are lost sinners under the condemnation of death, are children of the devil, and helpless in the power of the great enemy of one's soul (Romans 1–3).

What Caused the Human Condition?

We Are the Property of Satan as Pertaining to Physical Birth

1. We were born in sin.
2. We only become the real property of God at the new birth.
3. Since we were the property of Satan, and Satan rules the world, we will suffer.
4. Satan will test us.
5. Many terrible things have happened to saints, but God is there, regardless.
6. Our strength is our faith, and we must understand that our ways are not God's ways.
7. All suffering goes back to the fall of Adam.
8. This life is a life of testing; indeed, it is a life of probation.
9. We must serve God, regardless.
10. People have free wills. I could go off tonight and get in a wreck if common sense or God's warning was not heeded.

Why Do We Suffer?

1. Suffering silences Satan, as witnessed in the life of Job (Job 1:1–22, 2:1–8, 42:10–13).
2. Suffering enables one to glorify God (John 11:4–5).
3. Suffering makes one like Christ (Philippians 3:10; Hebrews 2:10, 2:18; 1 Peter 1:7, 2:21, 3:14).
4. Suffering makes one appreciative (Romans 8:28).
5. Suffering teaches one to depend upon God (Isaiah 30:15).
6. Suffering causes one to exercise great faith (Job 23:10; 1 Peter 4:12–13).
7. Suffering will cause one to be glad when Christ appears (1 Peter 1:7, 4:12–13).
8. Suffering teaches one patience (Romans 5:3–5).
9. Suffering makes one sympathetic (2 Corinthians 1:3–6).
10. Suffering makes one what he or she ought to be (Romans 8:28–29).
11. Suffering keeps one humble (2 Corinthians 12:7–10).
12. Suffering persuades one to pray (Judges 16:28; Daniel 1–12).
13. Suffering in the present time will bring forth a right to reign with

Christ in His kingdom and will bring forth other rewards in the afterlife (Romans 8:17–18; 2 Timothy 2:12; 1 Peter 4:12–13).
14. Suffering in the present time helps one keep from sinning (Hebrews 2:10, 11:25).
15. Suffering found in the present time is seen only as a fleeting thing when one compares it to the glory, which one will see and be revealed in him or her (Romans 8:17–18).
16. Suffering brings comfort from the touch of Christ upon one's life (2 Corinthians 1:4).
17. The more suffering one has, the more grace and comfort one has (2 Corinthians 1:5).
18. Suffering causes one not to hinder the gospel of Christ (1 Corinthians 9:12).
19. One suffers for the sake of Christ (Philippians 1:29).
20. Suffering shows that one is godly in Christ (2 Timothy 3:12).
21. It is a better thing to suffer for good or for obedience than to suffer for evil or disobedience (1 Peter 3:17).
22. One glorifies God in one's suffering (1 Peter 4:16).
23. Without suffering, one will truly be deceived (Romans 8:28–29; Philippians 3:10; Hebrews 2:10, 2:18; 19 Peter 1:7, 2:21, 3:14).
24. A saint triumphs in suffering (Matthew 26:26; Romans 8:35–39; 1 Corinthians 4:9; 2 Corinthians 4:8, 6:3; Philippians 1:12–30; Hebrews 11:33–40).
25. Suffering proves that one is a saint and a minister of the highest God (2 Corinthians 6:4).

Why Does Satan Continue?

1. So that humanity may be tried (Job 1:11, 20–21).
2. So that the love and courage of a saint might be tried (James 1:12; 1 Peter 1:7–10, 5:8–9).
3. So that humility will be found to exist in the saints of God (2 Corinthians 12:7).
4. So that the saints will be provided a means of conflict that they may be rewarded through overcoming (Mark 16:17–20; 1 Corinthians 4:9; 2 Corinthians 2:5–11; Revelation 2:7–28).
5. So that the character and faith of a believer will be developed and well rounded (James 1:12; 1 Peter 1:7–13; 2 Peter 1:4–9; Jude 20–24).

6. So that the very power of God will be demonstrated over the power of Satan (Mark 16:17–20; 1 Corinthians 4:9; Ephesians 2:7, 3:10).
7. So that, as an instrument of chastisement, people will repent and come to God (Job 33:14–30; 1 Corinthians 5:1–6; 2 Corinthians 2:5–11).
8. So that the very possibility of falling will be purged from the saints in the eternal future (Daniel 9:24–27; Revelation 21).

I don't remember a season that my husband and I were not tested through the fire, nor do I remember a time when my husband and I were not in the front line of the battle.

"Now What Do We Do?"

"Now what do we do?" were the words that my son prayed and asked after we buried his father. That night, my son had such questions about our ministry. My son had no one to help him in his anguish, except God and myself. As long as my son saw his father, he knew things would be all right. The two had been inseparable.

Out of all Scriptures, Isaiah 55:9–11 helped us greatly through difficult times, both before the death of my husband and afterward.

> For as the heavens are higher than the earth, so are my ways higher than your ways, and my thoughts than your thoughts. For as the rain cometh down, and the snow from heaven, and returneth not thither, but watereth the earth, and maketh it bring forth and bud, that it may give seed to the sower, and bread to the eater: So shall my word be that goeth forth out of my mouth: it shall not return unto me void, but it shall accomplish that which I please, and it shall prosper in the thing whereto I sent it.

I often wish my family had been Christian. If they had, they could have warned me about the persecution that follows being a Christian. To my surprise, I found out that every Christian life will have persecution: "Yea, and all that will live godly in Christ Jesus shall suffer persecution" (2 Timothy 3:12). Why? Because we live in a world that hates God. And the devil is the god of this world.

Being in the ministry, I have seen people experience Jesus as their Savior and become red hot for Jesus Christ. And then, when persecution arose, they backed off.

Such people like this reminded me of myself when I was first saved. If I spent considerable time with God on my knees, trials accompanied it. I found if I stopped praying and fasting, backed away from God, and became lukewarm, the persecution ended. But I lost the ground that I had won. I heard a preacher preach that when I got saved, God would do my fighting. But that was wrong. If you don't fight Satan, he will beat you to death.

Another passage of Scripture that greatly helped us was Isaiah 43:2.

> When thou passest through the waters, I will be with thee; and through the rivers, they shall not overflow thee: when thou walkest through the fire, thou shalt not be burned; neither shall the flame kindle upon thee.

We should notice the direct and honest way in which our afflictions are mentioned in Isaiah 43:2: "the waters," "the rivers," "the fire," and "the flame." It takes for granted that we will meet with some or all these afflictions before we have finished our course of life. And Isaiah 43:2 does not mention these trials lightly. Waters may be profound. Rivers may carry us away. Fire and flame indicate that the tests of life are hard, high, various, and sure.

The phrases "when thou passest," and "when thou walkest" clearly indicate that the people of Israel are wandering and moving from one point to another. We may be quite sure that the "waters," "rivers," "fire," and "flame" have reference to all the things that met real people then as now.

In Isaiah 43:2, God has promised to be ever at our side. Through such trials are the people of God fashioned and formed. It is through many trials that the people of God enter the kingdom of God.

From Isaiah 43:2, we learn that spiritual experience and practice are definitely the same throughout all the ages. In every personal life, especially the personal lives of the saints, there are a few short-lived flashes of influential and powerful trials; that after these kinds of tests, life can never be the same; that the last trial usually is death; that human relationships in this life profit hardly anything, and that God is found with the saints in all such crisis moments and events.

Therefore, we, as the people of God, are promised to have the divine presence, divine protection, and divine deliverance.

Example of an English Reformer

In 1531, Thomas Bilney, an English Reformer, was permitted to have friends visit him in his jail cell a day before his execution. His friends found him in excellent health and eating dinner. Indeed, they had seen him with such a cheerful heart and a quiet mind.

> Then, sitting with his said friends in godly talk to their edification, some put him in mind that though the fire, which he should suffer the next day, should be of great heat unto his body, yet the comfort of God's Spirit should cool it to his everlasting refreshing. At that word, Thomas Bilney, remembering Isaiah 43:2, putting his hand toward the flame of the candle before them (as also he did divers times beside) and feeling the heat hereof, said, "O," (said he) "I feel by experience and have known it long by philosophy that fire, by God's ordinance, is naturally hot: but yet I am persuaded by God's holy word, and by the experience of some, spoken of in the same, that in the flame they felt no heat, and in the fire they felt no consumption: and I constantly believe that howsoever the stubble of this my body shall be wasted by it, yet my soul and spirit shall be purged thereby; a pain for the time, whereon notwithstanding followeth joy unspeakable."[8]

The method of death proved the truth of Thomas Bilney's inner conviction. To die well displayed faith in Christ and fidelity to Him and His Word. The night before his dreadful experience, he held his index finger in the flame for so long that he burned the flesh and bone of the first joint.

The Story of Deborah

When fighting for my life and the life of my father, I referred many times to the story of Deborah in Judges 4:4–5: "And Deborah, a prophetess, the wife of Lapidoth, she judged Israel at that time. And she dwelt under the palm tree of Deborah between Ramah and Bethel in mount Ephraim: and the children of Israel came up to her for judgment." Deborah was not only a prophetess but also a judge. The nation of Israel was going through one of its darkest times.

God spoke through Deborah:

> And she sent and called Barak the son of Abinoam out of Kedesh-Naphtali, and said unto him, Hath not the LORD God of Israel commanded, saying, Go and draw toward mount Tabor, and take with thee ten thousand men of the children of Naphtali and of the children of Zebulun? And I will draw unto thee to the river Kishon Sisera, the captain of Jabin's army, with his chariots and his multitude; and I will

deliver him into thine hand. (Judges 4:6–7)

Barak asked Deborah to go with him. She agreed, and the battle was recorded as a great victory. It always is when God is with you. Why did God use Deborah? To show that He will use anyone who is willing.

Why Did God Choose Elizabeth?

The Gospel of Luke reads as follows:

There was in the days of Herod, the king of Judaea, a certain priest named Zacharias, of the course of Abia: and his wife was of the daughters of Aaron, and her name was Elisabeth. And they were both righteous before God, walking in all the commandments and ordinances of the Lord blameless. And they had no child, because that Elisabeth was barren, and they both were now well stricken in years. (Luke 1:5–7)

The barrenness of Elizabeth was a curse in Israel. People of the time would not have imagined that God would choose a barren woman for anything. Both Elizabeth and her husband were aged and beyond the ability to have children. But God chose two people who were holy before Him; they were righteous in the sight of God and kept the moral commandments. As seen here, God seeks people who are obedient unto Him, blameless before Him, and submissive to His will.

Remember that Elizabeth was a relative of Mary, the mother of Jesus. And remember that Gabriel had appeared to her husband Zacharias and told Zacharias that his wife was going to have a child and they should call his name "John." Her child was to be the forerunner of the Messiah.

Did God Himself tell Elizabeth that John, her beloved son, was to be beheaded for the sake of the Lord? No. If so, she may not have wanted to have a son who would die as a martyr, like so many other prophets of Israel and Judah. After all, John the Baptist was the last Old Testament prophet.

Why Did the Angel Rebuke Zacharias?

Here is the question: "Whereby shall I know this? for I am an old man, and my wife well stricken in years" (Luke 1:18). Just one question asked in unbelief was enough, far enough, to bring judgment upon the person who questioned the plans and sovereignty of God. The angel answered:

I am Gabriel, that stand in the presence of God; and am sent to speak unto thee, and to shew thee these glad tidings. And, behold, thou shalt be dumb, and not able to speak, until the day that these things shall be performed, because thou believest not my words, which shall be fulfilled in their season. (Luke 1:19–20)

Why Did God Choose Mary?

The Gospel of Matthew reads as follows:

Now the birth of Jesus Christ was on this wise: When as his mother Mary was espoused to Joseph, before they came together, she was found with child of the Holy Ghost. Then Joseph her husband, being a just man, and not willing to make her a publick example, was minded to put her away privily. But while he thought on these things, behold, the angel of the Lord appeared unto him in a dream, saying, Joseph, thou son of David, fear not to take unto thee Mary thy wife: for that which is conceived in her is of the Holy Ghost. And she shall bring forth a son, and thou shalt call his name JESUS: for he shall save his people from their sins. Now all this was done, that it might be fulfilled which was spoken of the Lord by the prophet, saying, Behold, a virgin shall be with child, and shall bring forth a son, and they shall call his name Emmanuel, which being interpreted is, God with us. Then Joseph being raised from sleep did as the angel of the Lord had bidden him and took unto him his wife: And knew her not till she had brought forth her firstborn son: and he called his name JESUS. (Matthew 1:18–25)

Her purity, simplicity, virginity, obedience, and above all, her faith unto the Lord turned God's attention toward her.

Isaiah 7:14 does not speak of just any virgin, but one virgin that was to be chosen to carry and deliver the Messiah.

Mary was unmarried when she became pregnant. Culturally, this was a disgrace. Yet the Holy Spirit had overshadowed her, and she became pregnant with the Messiah who was very God and very man. What saved Mary from public disgrace? An angel appeared to Joseph and said,

Joseph, thou son of David, fear not to take unto thee Mary thy wife: for that which is conceived in her is of the Holy Ghost. And she shall bring forth a son, and thou shalt call his name JESUS: for he shall save his people from their sins. Now all this was done, that it might be fulfilled which was spoken of the Lord by the prophet, saying, Behold, a virgin shall be with child, and shall bring forth a son, and they shall call his name Emmanuel, which being interpreted is, God with us. (Matthew 1:20–23)

In my early life, it was a disgrace to have a baby before marriage. It disgraced the whole family. The Mosaic Law taught if a woman had a child out of wedlock, it was not only a public shame, but she also was to be killed. Yet Mary knew no man. What happened to her was a miracle.

Why Did Joseph and Mary Have to Wait?

In the divine plan of God, divine timing is everything.

Too many men and women have gotten into trouble because they have followed their own timing rather than the timing of God. And this is especially true when people work in the ministry.

Further, the importance of fulfilling the messianic prophecies over everything about the Messiah, including the timing and place of His birth, was paramount here, and in other places.

Like all pious and devout Jewish men and women, both Joseph and Mary knew about the messianic prophecies. One messianic prophecy was Micah 5:2: "But thou, Beth-lehem Ephratah, though thou be little among the thousands of Judah, yet out of thee shall he come forth unto me that is to be ruler in Israel; whose goings forth have been from of old, from everlasting." They knew that the Messiah was to be born in Bethlehem, no other place. And they followed and believed the message of the angel about the Holy Spirit overshadowing Mary and her conceiving a babe in her womb without knowing any man (Luke 1:26–35).

Too many Christians today want to know just why they must wait for the moving of the Lord on their behalf. Again, it is timing. And many allow timing to destroy them. It is easy to believe a prophetic word that immediately comes to pass within a few days or months. But what about years? Few have the determination and the faith to continue to hold on to that prophetic word and see it come to pass. Indeed, few believe or even know that we must pray that a prophetic word comes to pass (Exodus 2:22–24; Nehemiah 1:1–11; Daniel 9:2; Romans 4:20).

Why Did Joseph and Mary Not Stay with Others?

There were very few explanations that could be used to describe the condition of Mary. If Joseph and Mary stayed with others, whether friends or relatives, they would have had to explain the fact that Mary was pregnant, ready to give birth. She had only recently married. What a scandal. Gossip would be present all over the town. And as gossip goes, so it increases with lies.

So, staying with others, whether friends or relatives, was out of the question. And staying in an inn or other public lodging would not work either. In the times of Joseph and Mary, the inns were no place for a family, especially a woman who was about to give birth. The inns were filled with some of the worst of society and were recognized as filthy and infamous places.

While staying with inns was out of the question, stables were filthy and humiliating. For Joseph to choose a stable, he must have been desperate. The condition of Mary made everything desperate. That alone may have prompted Joseph to choose a stable.

However, the purpose of Mary giving birth to the Messiah in a stable has a deeper meaning. The place of his birth shows the humiliation of the Messiah and the fact that He came into the world in utter poverty and destitution.

Jesus Christ was not born in comfortable surroundings but a smelly stable. He was neglected and turned away from the very beginning; there was no room for him in an inn. If people had cared, they could have made room.

Also, Jesus was born in obscurity and loneliness. Jesus was born in humiliation in a sinful world full of selfishness, greed, unkindness, and every type of evil.

Why Did the Angels Appear Before Shepherds?

The shepherds were a low class in Israel. God showed that the Messiah was not only for the weak but also for the low classes. The shepherds raised lambs and later sold them for the sacrificial service of the temple. They understood that the Shepherd/Messiah was to die for the lambs, rather than the lambs for the Shepherd. The presence of the shepherds at the birth of the Messiah symbolically foretold His coming death. He, as a shepherd, was to die for the lambs.

Why Did God Use the Angels in the First Place?

Luke 2:1–15 speaks of angels' presence at the birth of the Messiah. They "shouted for joy" (Job 38:7).

Their appearance at the birth of the Messiah publicized God's approval of

Joseph and Mary and the birth of the child in the manger.

Further, in Luke 1:26–27, the angel Gabriel declares the Word of God to Mary as it related to Mary's being the mother of the Messiah. Many passages show that angels can declare God's words (Genesis 16:7–13, 32:24–30; Daniel 9:21–23; Luke 1:13). Angels are bearers of God's words, whether they are orders, commands, interpretations, judgments, instructions, comfort, encouragement, answers to prayer, rebukes, revelations, warnings, tidings, or strong requests.

Why Did Christ Have to Be God-Man?

While this question is more theological in scope than the others, it is continually on the minds of those who research Christianity and the person of Jesus Christ. The lack of apologetics taught in Christian churches, Christian schools, Christian colleges, and Christian homes has doomed many into a Christ-less and deathless form of Christianity. At least, all Christians should know this *why* question.

Few know the motive for Christ's having to be both God and man. Here are the reasons, which were entrenched into the teachings of the ancient church and reaffirmed in the teachings of the reformers and revivalists:

Why Christ Had to be Man

1. As a sinless man, Christ was able to suffer death in our stead, take upon Himself the obligations of high human treason, and pay the penalty of humanity (Matthew 8:17; Romans 3:21–25, 8:14–16; 1 Timothy 1:15; Hebrews 2:14–17, 9:26–28; 1 Peter 2:24; 2 Peter 1:4; 1 John 3:5; Revelation 1:5).
2. As a sinless man, Christ was able to satisfy the rights and claims of divine justice so that the human race could become free from the authority and power of Satan and could be given the right to receive adoption from God and partake of His nature (Matthew 8:17; Romans 3:21–25, 8:14–16; 1 Timothy 1:15; Hebrews 2:14–17, 9:26–28; 1 Peter 2:24; 2 Peter 1:4; 1 John 3:5; Revelation 1:5).
3. Because man had committed high treason, sinned, and been kidnapped by Satan, man had to suffer for sin. One innocent and sinless man had to take the place of humanity and be offered as a sacrifice to redeem mankind (Hebrews 9:22).

4. Since guilty humanity had offended God, the only means to satisfy divine justice was that one from the human race would die instead of all men and women (Luke 1:74; Romans 6:15; 2 Timothy 1:7; Hebrews 2:14–17, 4:15, 5:1–2).
5. When Satan put to death the innocent and sinless Christ, God legally canceled all Satan's claims and rights over his human victims (Luke 1:74; John 12:31; Romans 6:15; 2 Timothy 1:7; Hebrews 2:14–17, 4:15, 5:1–2).
6. All the claims and rights of Satan, which were stolen from Adam, gave Satan a pseudo-sovereignty over humanity (Mark 16:17–18; John 12:31, 14:12–15, 15:16).
7. Now Satan has a false authority over the human race (Mark 16:17–18; John 14:12–15, 15:16; 2 Corinthians 4:4; Ephesians 6:11–12; Colossians 1:13).
8. Anyone who proclaims their rights of redemption, based upon the legality of the blood of Christ, and rejects Satan, can be free from sin, the guilt of sin, spiritual death, the impending eternal death, and Satan's powers. A part of these rights of redemption includes the conditional state of healing (Mark 16:17–18; John 14:12–15, 15:16; James 5:13–16; 1 Peter 2:24).
9. All who receive Christ benefit from the death of Christ and cease being the property of Satan (1 Corinthians 6:9–11; Colossians 1:13).

Why Christ Had to be God

1. The blood of mere man could not satisfy the divine justice of God and redeem us (Psalms 49:7–8; Matthews 16:26; Acts 20:28; Romans 7:18; Colossians 1:20–22; Titus 2:13–14; Hebrews 9:12–28, 10:4–23, 13:12, 20; Revelation 1:5).
2. Only God can deliver us from evil, be everywhere to help us, give us the title to heaven, bring us to heaven, and allow us to enter (Isaiah 43:25, 44:22, 48:9, 53:6; Jeremiah 50:20; Daniel 9:17–19; Acts 3:19).
3. Only God can save to the utmost and satisfy His wrath (Isaiah 43:25, 44:22, 48:9, 53:6; Jeremiah 50:20; Daniel 9:17–19; Acts 3:19).

Why Christ's Sacrifice is Accepted and is Required for Us to Be Accepted

1. None of us are innocent and sinless.
2. Only Christ's sacrifice could be accepted because He was both innocent and sinless.
3. The sacrifice of a guilty, sinful man could not be accepted or satisfy anything.
4. An innocent and sinless man's sacrifice is the only adequate substitution for the sins of the human race.
5. The sacrifice of an innocent and sinless man is the only way to satisfy divine justice and divine law.
6. For this to take place, the sacrifice could not just be an innocent and sinless man, but the person had to be both God and man. Only by this could the penalty be paid entirely.
7. When God became a man, He became free from all charges of injustice from Satan and the world.
8. God chose to be the sacrifice and became a man.
9. When God became a man, redemption became both Godward and manward. His divine law, divine justice, and form of government became magnified before His creation forever (John 1:12, 3:16, 5:36–44; Romans 5:10, 10:17, 12:3; 1 Corinthians 12:4; 2 Corinthians 5:19; Ephesians 2:16; Hebrews 12:2).
10. The Godward aspect of redemption has God as both its subject and object. God is the Reconciler, while He is also the reconciled. God reconciles the world, but through Christ who is God Himself. God Himself demands and provides atonement for sins simultaneously.

Why Study the Old Testament?

Too many Christians continually ask this question. Their view is that we should only study the New Testament. Interesting. The ancient saints studied both the Old and New Testaments. Without examining the Old Testament, Christians cannot genuinely develop a firm foundation for their faith. The Old Testament contains many shadows and symbols of the New Testament. Therefore, understanding the Old Testament aids our understanding of the New Testament. Every Christian should know the answers to this *why* question:

1. The real revelations of God's will within the Old Testament have not

passed away.
2. The real revelations of God's holiness, righteousness, and love have not passed away.
3. The real revelations of God's will within the Old Testament still occupy a specific place in the education and guidance of the world.
4. Christ taught through example that the principles pertaining to the rites and ceremonies of the Jews found in the Old Testament should be accepted as part of our whole spiritual development and practice.
5. The moral law is eternal and unchangeable in its obligations and sanctions.
6. Most of the moral law and precepts found in the Ten Commandments have been re-instituted by Christ in principle and explicit terms (Mark 10:19; Romans 13:9).
7. The Old Testament contains the historical dealings between God and man.
8. It contains predictions of the future state of the world.
9. It contains truth concerning the human condition.
10. It is holy and a source of spiritual delight to the child of God.
11. It is a guide to know the will of God and is a figure and shadow of the New Testament.
12. The New Testament came through and is rooted in the Old Testament.
13. All true believers must study all rites and ceremonies of the Old Testament to understand the New Testament. The Old Testament symbolizes the reality of the New Testament.
14. Studying the Old Testament strengthens one's hope in God.
15. It causes one to look for God's mercy.
16. It causes one to be steadfast in God.
17. It causes one to set his or her heart right toward God.
18. Approximately 35 percent of all the Old Testament prophecies have not *yet* been fulfilled.

CHAPTER 3
EARLY MIRACLES

When I study the Old Testament and read about the pharaohs, memories of my father flood my mind. My father, like the pharaohs, was going to have his way no matter what the cost and regardless of whom he hurt. If anyone had the spirit of the pharaohs, it was my father.

The spirit of the pharaohs is a spirit of control, domination, rebellion, and belligerence. Perhaps it is best summed up by the word *headstrong*. People like this must be broken. The Lord cannot save them unless they are broken. They must learn that when they butt heads with the Lord, they will lose.

I wish that my family would have known about my father's family history. We may have been able to find what kind of curses came through his family line.

My father always attacked my faith and relationship with the Lord. These attacks taught me to wait on God. And Satan continually accused me of not hearing the voice of God. Time and again, God had to let my father fall into a ditch to help him.

My Father's First Wife Murdered

My father was a man of integrity and morals until the murder of his first wife. The trauma of that experience changed him drastically in a terrible way. This change was evident in the way my father dealt with the man who murdered her. After my father had given this man a farm to help him get a start in life, he repaid my father by murdering his wife.

The fiendishness of the murder was so horrific and disturbing that it shook the whole nation. On May 23, 1918, the incident was reported in the Associated Press and national newspapers. The *Cordelle Dispatch* reported on the murder and wrote the following:

Mrs. Simmons was a small woman, but she was not frail. If there was the slightest resistance to the brute attack, there was no evidence left. The dining room, stove, and a table containing the cooking things in the small cook room were in their place and not disordered. If anything was thrown to the floor in a scuffle, it had been replaced by the fiend. Only two bloody table forks were found in the yard. The bludgeon with which Mrs. Simmons' head was battered to a pulp with was nowhere to be found . . . Further, Mrs. Simmons was attacked with forks. She was stabbed so often with the fork attack that the top of a pepper duster could not have possibly contained more perforations. The forks were both bent up in the attack so as to render them useless in a further assault of this character. This stabbing with the forks indicated that the murderer thought thus to reach her heart and end her life. But the bludgeon was apparently later used, and as many as five or six terrible strokes were plainly apparent in the different apertures in her head on the right side in the temple and over the right eye. Her sewing was still under the needle of her machine on the front porch of the house. Her shoes were in the room adjoining the kitchen. She laid in her stocking feet, her dress and underwear partially stripped away from her neck and right shoulder, but still pinned with two safety pins. About her throat were slight signs that she may have first been choked into insensibility, and around her, the blood from her body had flowed directly across the room. Her brains were shattered and scattered to the walls of the kitchen by the powerful strokes of the implement of death used by the brute.[1]

The untold shock of the horrifying experience of finding his wife murdered like this and seeing his first child crawling in the blood of her dead mother left unimaginable scars and baggage on my father that could not be healed in any way by man. No therapist or drug was going to fix the damage. After the experience, you might say my father went crazy. He tracked down the man, and the man shot at him, barely missing his head. The sheriff locked the man up, but the more my father and his brother-in-law thought about what happened, the angrier they became. They broke into the jail, took the man out, and killed him in a horribly brutal way. Yes, my father got revenge. But at what price? For many years after, he would wake up screaming from a nightmare, not knowing if it was his wife or the man he killed.

If only my father had gone to a Christian minister baptized with the Holy Spirit and empowered with the spiritual gifts of the Holy Spirit, then he could have found peace. It is the baptism of the Holy Spirit and the spiritual gifts that release the power of God to set people free. Remember that Psalm 55:22 says, "Cast thy burden upon the LORD, and he shall sustain thee: he shall never suffer the righteous to be moved."

The problem, however, was that my father was not saved. If he had been saved, this horrifying tragedy might never have taken place. If only he had walked in the arms of Jesus throughout all his life, this murder might not have seen the light of day, nor would he have had to carry the burden of it until he was seventy-five years old (when the Lord Jesus Christ saved him). If he had only confessed with his mouth the Lord Jesus and believed with his heart in his early life, he would have received divine help.

I am sorry to say that by the time I was born, the damaging effects of my father's past life had already taken a heavy toll on what remained of his life. After killing the man, my father could not lay it aside. Before that time, he never drank anything stronger than soda. He worked as a baseball pitcher and for the federal government. He began drinking when he left the federal government and started working for the state government of Georgia. What set him on the path of destruction can be blamed, in part, on his participation in cocktail parties after closing.

My Father and a Familiar Spirit

After the murder of my father's first wife (and before he married my mother), something strange and demonic took place in his life. It began very simply. He was traveling with his new horse and buggy by a cemetery at dusk. He stopped and unhitched the horse to give it a rest. The fact that he stopped near a cemetery was unusual. He was raised to fear demonic activity, instead of believing in the protection of the blood of Christ, the name of Jesus, the death of Christ, and the power of the cross.

At first everything seemed all right, but then my father saw something gray that resembled a small poodle. There were no dogs like that where my father lived in Georgia. Instead of fleeing the cemetery and this phenomenon of the supernatural, my father ran after the dog and tried to pick it up. I do not know how long he spent grasping at the apparition, but he couldn't catch it. Finally, the dog disappeared completely.

I believe the dog was a demon spirit because, after that night, my father was never the same. It was as if something unholy had possessed him. I believe that he became demon possessed.

Why would this apparition entice my father to follow it? For his destruction.

Do not the Scriptures warn all humanity about trafficking with demons and familiar spirits? (See Leviticus 19:11, 20:6; Deuteronomy 18:11; 1 Samuel 28:7–25; 2 Kings 21:6, 23:24; 1 Chronicles 10:13; 2 Chronicles 33:6; Isaiah 8:19, 19:3, 29:4.) My father chased this demon in ignorance, but others do it intentionally. The only protection against demon possession is the blood of Christ, the name of Jesus, the death of Christ, and the cross. The term "demon possession" is the best translation for Greek nouns referring to evil spirits indwelling people. The antiquarian grammarians defined these nouns only as this. Verbs referring to demon possession were defined by the antiquarian grammarians as "to have," or "to be possessed by demons." "To have" meant the same thing as "to be possessed by demons" in the Greek lexicons of the 1500s to the 1800s and beyond.

Doctor Jekyll and Mister Hyde

My father was as good as gold when he was not drinking, and he would help anyone who was less fortunate than we were. Yet when he drank, a force would take over his personality, and he would take on a split personality, like Doctor Jekyll and Mister Hyde. When he drank, he would brutally beat his children. He never knew when he needed to stop. It was quite easy for him to believe, "Spare not the rod" (Proverbs 22:15, 23:13, 29:15). He beat us so much when he was drunk that on occasion blood would flow from our backs.

So often, I remember my father's leaving the house to go to town. I wondered whether he would come back home drunk or sober. My siblings and I suffered so much that I often prayed to God that my father would die before he came home. I prayed this as a little child, innocent, and not saved by the blood of Christ. Later, I thanked God that He knew best and did not grant my petition. As I think back to those days, many families were dysfunctional according to the standards of today.

Daily Life

Let me make this statement: I don't believe in fighting. But I was taught how to fight by my father.

Because of father's first wife being murdered, he felt guilty that he did not teach her how to defend or take care of herself. So by the age of about six or seven, my sister Frankie and I each had a rifle. My father taught us how to shoot, handle, and care for guns. And we had a moral compass, which is significantly missing among children today. If we went into the woods to hunt, my father would hide and watch to see how we handled our rifles. If we shot in a straight line or got over the fence wrong, we would get a whipping. We were taught to never point the rifle at anything we did not mean to kill. After hunting, we were taught how to clean the rifle and how to clean and cook what we had shot.

In this setting, times were very hard. We loved eating fried squirrel with rice, but we would get tired of ham. The chicken was for Sunday dinner, and almost every Sunday there would be twenty people at our table.

I think about Frankie and my going to the woods to cut down trees for stove wood. The wood also would be used in the fireplace as well to warm in the wintertime or fire the tobacco barn.

My father did not allow us to cut down just any tree. He led us into the woods and showed us the kind of trees that needed to be cut down. Then he showed us to cut a notch out of the tree to make the tree fall the way we wanted it to fall. He would always point out that we needed to stand about three or four feet from the stump so we could safely see how the tree would fall. My sister always made sure her hand was on my shoulder, making sure I would not run but stay close to the trunk. This was necessary to determine which way the tree would fall so we could move quickly out of the way.

We used a crosscut saw. My sister Frankie was at one end of the saw, and I was at the other. If we were cutting stove wood, we had to learn how to split (splat) the wood to fit into the stove. Sometimes, we used a wedge. Since people can be killed cutting down trees, I don't understand how my father could let us go into the woods and cut down these big pine trees.

One night, I was watching the temperature in the tobacco barn, which is called cooking the tobacco. My mother was sick, but she did not allow me to stay at the tobacco barn alone. So we pushed the wagon under the tobacco barn shelter and put a mattress in the wagon so she could sleep.

About three o'clock in the morning, I began to get sleepy. We always had a clock set in cases like this. I set the clock to make sure that I would not sleep but maybe thirty minutes at the most. If I slept more than thirty minutes at a time, I could well set the barn on fire or ruin the tobacco. As I began to sleep, there came a noise like I had never heard in my life. I immediately jumped into the wagon on top of my mother. She sat up and listened to the same noise I had heard. She said, "Dot, my God, that is our neighbor's peacock." Let us assume that I did not go back to sleep.

Leg Burned and a Miracle from God

On one cold day when I was about five years of age, my leg was burned so badly that my parents thought I would never walk again. Since I was so small, it was hard for me to step over the hot pipes that were part of the process of cooking tobacco. On this day, I stepped over the pipe and bumped my leg against the hot pipe. The burn covered my whole calf and drew my entire leg up to my thigh. My mother did all she knew to do to help my leg recover. It seemed that I might only be able to crawl for the rest of my life.

Thank God, a preacher was running a revival close to our house and was blessed with the power of the Holy Spirit upon his life. He came into my house and prayed for my leg. In a few days, I was walking. God completely healed my leg.

Today I still remember that I would never get close to the fireplace. I still feel the fear that would come over me. No matter how cold I would be, I stood my distance.

Would you not think that my family, seeing this great miracle, would serve this loving God? Here I was, limping around and trying to walk with a homemade walking stick. And then I was able to walk entirely on my own. Yet they would not take the time to seek the miracle-working God. God even removed the fever that I had because of this accident.

David Smithers, an intercessor for Charles Finney, once said, "Until we reach for the impossible through fervent, faith-filled prayer, we will never fulfill our created purpose!"[2] And Corrie Ten Boom said, "Faith sees the invisible, believes the unbelievable, and receives the impossible."[3] Andrew Murray, a South African minister in the 1800s and early 1900s, wrote, "We have a God who delights in impossibilities."[4]

This incident was my first miracle, but thank God, it would not be the last one. Our God is still alive and working miracles.

Another Miracle

My foundation on how to fight and how to defend myself came in handy in the years that followed. Before the 95 Expressway was built, I regularly went down Dunn Avenue in Jacksonville, Florida, to enter Highway 17 to go to my job in Fernandina Beach, Florida. One night, though, things were entirely different. A small voice spoke to me, "Get your pistol." Three times I heard the voice of the Lord as I was driving, "Get your pistol." I stopped the car, drove back to the house, entered the house, picked up my pistol, and started again on my journey. Not knowing that someone had driven my car and left the passenger door unlocked, I began my journey again.

I stopped at a red light, ready to turn onto US 17, and immediately a man jumped into my car. All at once, my hand was on the pistol, and I put it to the man's temple. He jumped out of my car so fast that he almost got run over by another vehicle. I wish my father could have known his training saved my life.

Sometime later, I was watching TV, and I saw that the police had captured a serial killer named Otis Tools. I screamed. This was the man who had jumped into my car! He confessed to committing many murders, including the murder of six-year-old Adam Walsh.

I wish my father would have known this. My life was saved at that time, as it was many other times. I am glad that my father taught all the girls that if someone fought against us, we must finish the fight. If we did not finish it, he would whip us.

My father taught us the importance of Nehemiah 9:17.

> And refused to obey, neither were mindful of thy wonders that thou didst among them; but hardened their necks, and in their rebellion appointed a captain to return to their bondage: but thou art a God ready to pardon, gracious and merciful, slow to anger, and of great kindness, and forsookest them not.

We were taught that we must follow the leading of the Lord about anger, and like Him, we must be slow to anger.

When my husband and I were married in a church, I was so proud of my father. Before my wedding, I told him that if he were drunk, he would not walk me down the aisle. To my surprise, he came dressed in a nice suit and a tie. I was the only daughter who asked him to walk her down the aisle. The other girls were not saved when they were married and were only married by a justice of the peace.

My father looked handsome. I could see how my mother fell in love with him. That night when he took my hand, I saw a godly pride on his face looking down at me. I knew that even though I had to leave home to serve God, he approved of my life. How? He sobered up and gave me away. He also used some of his baby pine trees to decorate the church. Sometimes actions are more important than words. My father was not saved until the last five years of his life, but this was the first time I had ever seen any pride in his eyes toward any of his children. I felt his love for me that day.

CHAPTER 4
LIFE GROWING UP

Why was I chosen to stand in the gap for a family consisting of eight children, a mother, and a father? I was the baby girl, and it was the baby girl whom God chose to pray that her family would be saved.

Before the tragedy of his first wife being murdered, my father was considered a great man. I remember his working in Douglas, Georgia, on Saturdays selling groceries. He would catch a train home at midnight and bring all the essentials, including salt, sugar, flour, and other necessary things home to his family.

We lived on a farm during the Great Depression. It was especially important that almost everything we grew, we also were able to eat. My father made certain we were never hungry, even in the toughest times. My mother also helped us through the lean times. She knew how to can almost every kind of food. Since she was a great cook, she never knew how many she was going to have at the table for a meal. Therefore, she sought to have one hundred jars of everything during canning time.

Through the time of the Great Depression, my mother might look down the road and see a family with children walking her way. The husband or wife would tell my mother they were hungry, but they never begged. In every case, my mother told the family she would cook them a meal. Since there was no room in our small house, she would offer them the hayloft to sleep. She allowed them to open a bale of hay to sleep on and gave them bedding.

Since our home was between the highway and the railroad tracks, people would come from both directions. My sister once told me that no matter what time a family would come to our house—even during the early morning hours—my mother offered them cooked food. She would even pack them a lunch of maybe a biscuit and ham or bacon for each family member.

Uncle Frank

As a child, I was the runt of my family, and I was always into something. Regardless, my Uncle Frank loved me so much. He would not stay away long before he was sure to come to our house. He enjoyed spoiling me. He would sit me on his lap, place a cigarette between my fingers and teach me a bad word. He told my father not to whip me about it.

Then Uncle Frank was killed in a car wreck. My mother loved Uncle Frank and could not look at the place where he was buried without almost having a nervous breakdown.

It was very hard for my mother to correct me. Sometimes she would see me do something that reminded her of what Uncle Frank had taught me to do, and she would ignore my behavior.

One time, when I was three years old, I climbed in the window to see what was outside. I saw my father whipping my sisters because they had not shaken the peanuts correctly. I looked at my father and said, "S___, when I get big enough, I am going to beat the h___ out of you!"

Immediately he pulled me out of the window and whipped me. After the whipping, I ran a little away, turned, and pointed my finger at him, "One day I will grow up and beat the h___ out of you!"

He took his belt off again, and I ran under our house. When my mother missed me, she went looking for me. She did not know where I was. She thought that I might have run to the pond or the pine thicket. She finally remembered how I would run under the house at times when my father was playing games with me. She looked under the house and found me sleeping by the chimney. I woke up as she pulled me out.

Chilly Time

One chilly day at home, I lay down next to the chimney and fell asleep. My mother woke me up because my father was coming home. Sometimes, when my father was not drinking, he would come home with candy in three of his pockets. For Frankie, Bug, and me, these times were fun. My father would pretend that the candy was his and we would wrestle him. When we got the candy, I ran under the house. Daddy ran around telling mother we got his candy.

As I was the center of the fun, our relatives would always want me to go home with them. I was a mess and then some. I kept them on their toes as they tried to keep up with me. I was like a female Dennis the Menace. Thank God, only one of me was ever made; the world could not withstand another.

My Sister Ethel and Her Mother's Family

My oldest sister was the child of my father and his first wife. The family of my father's first wife stayed close to Ethel. My father and mother always made sure that all his first wife's relatives were welcome.

My sister Ethel married, and her first baby died at about age two or three. My mother began to worry about Ethel and her husband, Quitman, because of the death of their child. To help with the grief, my mother sent me off to stay with Quitman and Ethel. It filled the void for them.

Ethel lived in a big house with a living room, bedroom, dining room, and kitchen on the left side, and a bedroom, and a storeroom on the other. Not only did Ethel play hide and seek with me, but she also loved frightening me. I was always glad to hear my brother-in-law say, "Ethel, stop scaring that child."

Uncle George and Mary Lou

Uncle George would always come to our home and see if my father would allow me to spend time with his daughter Mary Lou.

Mary Lou was older than me and was a mess as well. She put me up to lots of mean things.

One day, while Uncle George was working, we found his cigarettes. She and I got them and ran to the outhouse. We each put a cigarette in our mouth and lit it. Boy! We were smoking and enjoying the cigarettes when Uncle George drove up and thought the outhouse was on fire. Mary Lou saw him, and we both threw down the cigarettes. Uncle George was not too happy, and both of us were punished.

Another time, Uncle George came home from work and was walking across the road to get a Coca-Cola. I hollered at him that if he did not buy some Crackerjack, he was a s___. He said, "My God, I had better buy you and Mary Lou some Crackerjack!"

I am writing all of this to let you know how far God had to reach down to pick me up. I am so thankful that I never got the habit of cussing or smoking. I cannot even imagine how God could reach down to the sixth child of a family, where the mother and father never read the Bible.

I want you to see just how cunningly Satan dealt with our family. Did he know that tobacco or smoking would one day cause cancer? Why was I the only child being taught to smoke at that time?

Later, two others of my family smoked. My brother Bug died of lung cancer. Did Satan know that God would one day save me and make me a witness to my family and my husband's family?

Some Kind of Faith

I have often said, "I don't know how I got saved coming from my family." I did see that they had some kind of faith. Even though I was small, I remember my father saying to my mother, "If we don't get some rain soon, we will lose the farm." Mother said back, "Roy, it will rain seven days before it is too late." She had faith in that.

When I grew older, we regularly picked cotton. If rain clouds began to form, we tried to get mother to quit picking the cotton so we could take what we had picked to the house before the rain. My mother would say, "It is not going to rain until we get this cotton picked and carried to safety." You know, it never did.

This faith had to come from somewhere. The Bible says, "So then faith cometh by hearing, and hearing by the word of God" (Romans 10:17).

D. L. Moody once said, "I prayed for faith, and thought that some day faith would come down and strike me like lightning. But faith did not seem to come. One day I read in the tenth chapter of Romans, 'Now faith cometh by hearing, and hearing by the word of God.' I had closed my Bible and prayed for faith. Now I opened my Bible and began to study, and faith has been growing ever since."[1]

Since I never saw Mother or Daddy open a Bible, this faith had to come from her youth. If she had ever been saved, no one knew. If she had become lukewarm or backslidden, no one knew either.

Living in the country, we never knew about what God was doing, except that He answered mother's words about taking care of the farm. Did the Holy Spirit have something to do with me as a young child getting out of bed on chilly mornings and following my parents to see the crops and learn about faith?

I only know one other person who had that kind of faith, and that was my husband.

In these days, I remembered only the Ten Commandments according to country people, as said by an unknown person many years ago.

1. Ain't but One God.
2. Honor yer Ma and Pa.

3. No tellin' tales or gossipin'.
4. Git yer hide ta Sunday meetin'.
5. Ain't notin' come before the Lord.
6. No foolin' with another feller's gal.
7. No killin', 'cept fer critters.
8. Quit yer foul mouthin'.
9. No swipin yer kin folk's stuff.
10. Don't be hankerin' fer it neither.

Country Entertainment

In the country, we had to make our own entertainment. We would get together with other children in the neighborhood. If a field of tomatoes was ready to be harvested, we would pick some and ride a horse to a little store and buy some bacon, bread, mayonnaise, and lettuce.

Never will I forget a neighbor named Mrs. Anderson, who would go to her kitchen and fry up the bacon. I can still smell it. We got around her table and ate. She always went with her daughter and me so we could go hunting or fishing with the boys.

One night, we were at her house ready to go fishing. We built up a big fire. A neighbor who owned the pond came down and said he did not want us fishing in his pond. I said, "That is okay," and we put the fire out.

Winter came—time for dove hunting. I heard some shooting on our farm, so I got on my horse and rode to the field. It was the same man who refused to let us go fishing in his pond and ran us off.

I said to him, "Do you think it's fair for you to hunt on our land and you not allow us to fish in your pond?"

He said, "No. I don't! I'll leave."

"No!" I said. "The bird will fly in and out. It's not going to hurt anything for you to hunt on our land."

The man replied, "Dot, you can fish anytime you want in my pond."

Watermelon Patch

All the neighborhood kids decided to invade another neighbor's watermelon patch like an army; the neighbor had no children. We said, "We are going to steal watermelons."

My father overheard our plans while we were talking up the courage to steal the melons. He went to the man and told him what we were planning on doing. He asked the farmer to take his shotgun and shoot over our heads. My father promised to pay for any watermelons that were destroyed.

About one in the morning we, including Mrs. Anderson, climbed over the man's fence. We found several big watermelons and picked them up. But before we got back over the fence, several rounds were shot over our heads. We threw two or three watermelons over the fence and tried to hide on the ground. We looked and saw that Mrs. Anderson was no longer with us. My God! We thought she had been shot. We crawled back to the watermelon patch and found her. She played us beautifully.

To teach us a lesson, Mrs. Anderson made us crawl all the way back to the fence on our knees. She continued to say, "He will shoot you." Well, we got over that fence in a hurry! I must say that the watermelons we stole were delicious, but we decided we would ask next time.

Incident of Stealing

One other time, I stole on the day we were cropping my neighbor's tobacco patch. We had eaten both breakfast and lunch, but working in a tobacco patch was back-breaking work. It did not take long to wear a person out, and we got so hungry.

The other neighbor at the end of the tobacco row had an apple tree. The apple tree was full of delicious red apples. We asked the man if we could have one, but he said no. My brother did not take that too well. He said that the man could have given one apple to his sister. The neighbor was so selfish that he could not give just one apple to a hungry child.

That night about twelve or one in the morning, my brother came to Frankie and me, woke us up, and asked, "Do you still want an apple?"

"Yes!"

"Get up and let's go get one."

Here were three kids going through their farm and through the field of our neighbor to steal red apples in the middle of the night. And we were quite prepared. We brought pillowcases to put the apples in. When we crawled over the neighbor's fence, his dogs went crazy. We learned to do two things at the same time here—watch for the dogs and pick up red apples. We stripped that man's apple tree.

Making sure not to be caught, we went home a different way. Thinking as we were going home, it dawned on us that we could not give our mother these apples to make apple pies since she would wonder where we got them. And another reason would be when she saw the neighbor, she would thank him for the apples. And we knew that this had better not happen.

So we thought and thought about what to do with all those apples. We decided to climb into the hayloft and bury them in the hay. We soon learned that a person could become sick of eating apples. We knew not to throw them away because my father would find them.

This experience taught all of us not to steal.

No Word "Can't"

We rarely experienced anything like play. Indeed, we knew very little about playtime. We had to work very hard. To help with the work, my father had one boy, one adopted boy, and the girls—but we girls were like boys.

If my father had written an English dictionary, he would have removed the word "can't." He despised that word. He refused to believe that we couldn't do anything. He would always say, "If there is a will, there is a way. So you had better find that way." I felt so sorry for my dad. He so badly wanted boys, and he and my mother had one girl after another. Yet, he forgot we were girls, and he worked us like boys.

While my father did not believe in slavery, he saw his children as slaves to work on his farm. His stubbornness and obstinacy let him have his way, regardless of whom it hurt.

No Slacking Allowed

My father always told us what to do on the farm. As he went to town, we knew how much work had to be done. If we did not finish every task, we would wake up with his belt.

While Coca-Cola Company continues to deny that, at one time, Coca-Cola had cocaine in it, the overall evidence points to the fact that cocaine was present in the original product. When my father mixed the original Coca-Cola with wine or whiskey, he became crazy. He lost it. When he didn't mix Coca-Cola with his wine or whiskey, he did not become crazy.

The last time I remember my father whipping me, he was drunk and beat me with a tobacco stick. It was one of the worst whippings I had ever received. It occurred after he told me to plow the watermelon patch, and I somewhat plowed it. My father had planted the watermelons in a rocky field, and there had been no rain for a long time. He should have been warned from Scripture about sowing in the rocky ground (Matthew 13:1–23). The fault was not mine; my father did not understand the biblical principle.

When I tried to keep the plow in the row, it hit a rock, and my plow got away from me. And it cut up some of the plants. So I quit. The word "quit" was like blasphemy for my father. That was another word that his children were never to say in front of him.

When he saw what I had done in the field, he picked up a tobacco stick and started hitting me with it. When he whipped me on this occasion, I refused to cry, and that made him angrier. He continued to hit me harder and with no mercy.

The blood began to run down my legs into my shoes. Thank God, my mother walked outside and saw what was going on. She ran to him, took away the tobacco stick, and shouted to him, "Roy, you are going to kill her!" And finally, he stopped.

I was a young teenager at the time. I warned him that would be the last time he would beat me or ever lay his hands on me again. The next day, he got the mule out and tried to plow the same patch. He failed. Even he could not plow it. He was very sorrowful over the whole incident and apologized.

The Plow and the Two Mules

When it was time to get the land ready to sow, I would hitch up two mules to a plow stock and begin breaking the ground. I do not remember how old I was, but I do remember I had to hold my arms above my head to hold on to the plow stock. Being so little, if I had happened to hit a root under the ground and I was unable to get the plow loose, I would have to find someone to help me get the plow unobstructed.

Being so little and so young, I was made to have my furrow (row) meet the other furrow I had already made.

One day as I was breaking the ground, our neighbor was coming through our land to shoot birds. He watched how my furrow lapped the other furrow and said, "I wish my boys could plow like this."

I thought to myself, *They would if my father whipped them right.*

When my father plowed the fields, he laid straight rows. You could look straight down the row from one end to the other. His rows were so straight, it was possible for a person to shoot a rifle down the row and hit a target.

We kids loved to impress him with our ingenuity. One day, I came home and hooked up my horse to the planter. My horse generally would walk fast, almost in a run, when hooked to the planter. Because my horse acted like this, I could almost catch up to where my father had put in fertilizer.

My father praised us when we did something that surprised or pleased him. For example, one day he brought some (what I call) "land plaster." This was a fertilizer that we put in the middle of the peanut bushes to cause the plants to make more peanuts. It looked like flour. He told us to get buckets. The buckets were very heavy. After all, we had to spread this land plaster across twenty-five acres of peanuts.

Daddy bought a tobacco sled, which had wheels. I told my sister, "I am going to the house and will be right back."

She said, "You'd better not take too long. Daddy will be mad."

I got the sled and took the sides off. Taking a mule out of the stall and hooking him up to the tobacco sled is not the easiest thing to do. And we had to put a number three washtub in front and one in the back to pour the fertilizer into. The peanut runner was not long enough for the wheels to hurt the plants. So my sister sat up front, and I sat in the back with our hands low over the peanut rows, putting the land plaster right where it did the most good. My father said, "I cannot believe how many bags you used." He bragged on us and told us he was going to give us money to go to a show.

More Cucumbers

My father was a smart farmer. While he did not depend on just one cash crop, he did make sure to plant cucumbers every year.

When my sisters, brother, and I came home from school, we hitched a mule to a wagon and went from one cucumber patch to another. If we wanted the best price, we had to pick the cucumbers when they were little. If my father found many big cucumbers in our sacks, we were whipped. Why? Because we lost money. And lost money might destroy our farm.

Sometimes, all we had to eat was the cucumbers since my mother was very sickly and unable to cook on occasion. Sometimes, we would pick the cucumbers, put them on the wagon, and carry them to the market in the dark. We had to put a lantern in the back of the wagon so a car would not run into us, but even with the light we stilled prayed that a car wouldn't hit us. We also prayed that a train did not come by and scare the mule.

When the cucumbers were being graded at the market, we went across the street to a store and were able to order RC Colas and MoonPies. I hope that

God has RC Colas and MoonPies in heaven. Those have always been delicious to me. And sometimes, we got a loaf of bread, mayonnaise, and baloney to make a sandwich. The baloney was always sliced thick. We would sit on the steps, eating, and watching the people grade the cucumbers. My father never complained about our eating baloney sandwiches and drinking RC Colas. He got the bill and asked us what we got. As long as it was food, there was no problem.

More Dangerous

If any Scripture verse proved to me that the Word of God is genuine, it is Psalms 91:11. "For he shall give his angels charge over thee, to keep thee in all thy ways."

Someone once said that the angels remain silent and refuse to work when we refuse to pray. If that is the case, my angels have always worked overtime in keeping me safe. Of all the children, I was the one who lived most dangerously.

I have no earthly idea when or why I got the attention of God. I remember early in my life, the Lord came and spoke to me. The Lord saw a little girl hiding in the pine thicket under a tent made of pine straw. He saw all the tears that I had shed. And all of this occurred when I was only about five or six years old.

I had very little hope to hold on to. I knew there was a cycle in my father's life, where he would go to town and come back drunk. And when he came back home, he fought the whole family, including my mother and all his children, regardless of how young or old the children were. He knew that we kids were not going to let him beat us without his having to fight us.

Being a little girl and continually scared, I heard that there was a God. I continually bargained with God, saying, "If you, God, are real, kill my father before he gets home." However, as I mentioned before, I am glad that God did not listen to that nonsense. Sometimes, he did not come home drunk and ready to beat us, but with candy in his pockets for us. My childish mind could tolerate his being around a while longer if he brought me candy.

I had no idea, even at this young age, that this was the beginning of a prayerful life, lasting eighty-five years at the time of this writing. I have cried not only for my family and my husband, but now in the ministry, there is so much more to pray for in these dark times.

Cases of Miracles

I remember a miracle that Dwight D. Eisenhower, our thirty-fourth president, wrote about that happened in his boyhood.[2] He was raised in a godly home and very poor.

He injured his leg while running home from school. That evening it started to ache, but he prayed and went to bed. By morning, though, his leg was painful. He went about doing his chores on their farm. Two mornings later his leg was so bad that he couldn't even walk to the barn. By noon, he had to go to bed.

Alarmed, his mother applied poultices and summoned the doctor. Dr. Conklin examined the leg and said he didn't think it could be saved. When Dwight heard this, he cried, "Don't take off my leg." The doctor said, "The longer we wait, the more of the leg will have to come off." Dwight called to his brother and said, "Promise me that you won't let them take my leg off."

His fever kept rising, and the discoloration crept higher on the boy's leg each hour. His parents, Ida and Jacob, were not yet convinced amputation was necessary. They were in a dilemma as to what to do. The doctor, getting impatient about their delay, told them they were responsible for the boy's life.

Then Ida and Jacob thought about faith in God and their minister, who believed in healing through faith.

The family decided on prayer as a new course of action. They rallied around Dwight's bedside; each member who was old enough took a turn in their twenty-four-hour prayer vigil over him. When the doctor returned, he immediately noticed a change in his patient's leg, the swelling was going down, and the discoloration was fading. His life was saved. Faith in God paid off in this miracle before their very eyes.

Abraham Lincoln and the Tears

President Abraham Lincoln learned the importance of tears when his son died at the age of twelve. According to Lincoln, he had not been a Christian for some time. He did not become a Christian when his son died, and his son's death was the severest trial of his life. But along with his son's death came the great battle at Gettysburg.[3] Lincoln saw grave after grave at Gettysburg. At that battleground, he gave his life to Christ.[4] With teary eyes, Abraham Lincoln told his friends that at last he had found the faith he had been longing to have for so many years. He realized, he said, that his heart was changed and that he loved the Savior.

Abraham Lincoln once said, "When I left Springfield, I asked the people to pray for me. I was not a Christian. When I buried my son, the severest trial of my life, I was not a Christian. But when I went to Gettysburg and saw the graves of thousands of our soldiers, I then and there consecrated myself to Christ. Yes, I do love Jesus."[5]

Immediately after the death of his son, the wife of Abraham Lincoln sought comfort with spiritualism. President Lincoln even allowed séances to take place in the White House, and it has been said that he attended one séance. No séance helped, nor was there any true communicating with their dead son.

A story is told that Lincoln stayed up all night and prayed, "If it is possible to let this cup pass from me." Ida Tarbell, an American writer, investigative journalist, biographer, and lecturer, described the condition of the President. He was experiencing deep human sorrow and divine comfort.

The full quotation about exactly what Abraham Lincoln said in reference to his son's death is here quoted from Tarbell's work:

> I have read, upon my knees, the story of Gethsemane, where the Son of God prayed in vain that the cup of bitterness might pass from him. I am in the Garden of Gethsemane now, and my cup of bitterness is full and overflowing.[6]

Sorrows bring us to the point of decision for Christ. Desperations drive us to Christ.

Frankie and the Hogs

Today's modern, caring mother would shudder to see how we kids lived in danger back in my day. My favorite play place—where I made my straw tent as a little girl—was right where the hogs would make their beds to have their babies. Pigs are dangerous, especially mama pigs. Yet no one gave a thought about where I was playing.

One time, a sow chased after Frankie. Another time, a sow ran after us when we had a terrible rain, and our pond was overflowing. The sow had given birth, and her piglets were in danger of drowning.

Daddy sent us down to be sure the pigs would not drown. The water was about to cover up the pigs. The only thing we knew to do in cases like this was to try to pick the pigs up and run them to safety.

But that old sow did not want us handling her babies. Frankie picked up one out of the water. The piggy squealed, and the sow ran toward Frankie. Then I ran and picked up a piggy. When it cried, that old sow turned to get after me. Frankie and I kept on with the same pattern until all the piggies were safe.

Uncle Jim and His Son

The next time God intervened in my life for protection was a Saturday when I was about four years old. My Uncle Jim's son drove a farm truck full of farmhands to town so they could buy their groceries. They bought ice at fifty pounds, along with their groceries, and put it all in the bottom of the truck. When they returned, my cousin pulled over to the side of the road so they could get off the truck and gather their belongings.

I was standing on the right side of the truck, watching them, and seeing the cars go by. For no discernable reason, I turned and made my way up to the front of the truck and somewhat laid my arm across the cab. Just then, a car doing eighty miles per hour hit the truck right where I had been standing.

Both the driver and two passengers in the car were killed, and another was put in a wheelchair for the rest of his life.

My sister came by and almost had a heart attack, thinking that I had been hit by the car. My brother-in-law came to see what had happened. He found me and carried me to my oldest sister, Ethel. She carried me home with her and made me a pallet by her bed. I could not sleep in a room by myself. I kept hearing the screams from the people in the car and the truck, replaying the entire scene in my mind.

People remarked that had I not moved, the car would have hit and killed me. Do I believe in angels? Just by a moment, my life was saved. I know the angels of the Lord moved me from that spot so my life could well be saved, and I could be used more for the Lord.

From this, I believe in the God of the miraculous; I believe in the gifts of the Holy Spirit. If God does not move and work, it is man's fault.

Thirty Minutes to Live

Once, when I was in the third grade, I had been feeling bad all day at school. The teacher thought I was pretending so I wouldn't have to do my work.

When I went home that evening, I still did not feel well, even though I was somewhat hungry. I had to pick up peanuts in one of our fields, and as I was picking up the peanuts for seed, I ate some. By the time mother had supper ready, I tried to eat, but there was a pain in my abdomen. The pain grew and grew. That night as I was lying down to sleep, my mother got into bed with me and put her finger on the spot where the pain was.

I was able to sleep a little that night. The next morning, my mother told my father to go to town to purchase mineral oil. Back in the days of the Great Depression and afterward, our medicine was commonly castor oil, Black Draught, mineral oil, and Epsom salt.

As the day went on, my father did not come back home with the mineral oil. He became drunk and didn't seem to care whether I lived or died.

Mother, watching over me, saw that my lips and fingernails were turning blue. She knew she had to get me to a doctor quickly. When the doctor examined me, he concluded that I was suffering from appendicitis and had only thirty minutes to live.

Immediately, the doctor called the hospital to set me up for surgery, and in thirty minutes I was having my appendix taken out.

As the appendix was being removed by the surgeon, it burst. We were told that if my appendix had busted in my stomach, I would have died.

My father was a drunk, and he tried to put the cost of that surgery on me. But I stopped him.

Years later, I left home, and he had to rent the farm out because he had no one to plow the land. He made a deal with the tenant. The tenant was supposed to plant twenty-five acres of cotton for my mother and take care of it. The tenant did plant the cotton but did not tend to it.

When my father went to see how the cotton looked, he was in shock. All he could see was big Jerusalem weeds, or Jerusalem thorns as some call them. The weeds had taken over the whole field. He came into our house, and I asked if I could clean out that cotton patch so that the farm could be saved. If I did not clean out that field, the whole farm was going to be lost.

The weeds were so high and thick that I had to plow between each row, turn around, and come back up. When I plowed the row and destroyed the weeds, my mother and my brother had to take them out of the field and put them at the end of the row.

In doing this massive work, I almost had a heat stroke. When my sister Ruby saw me, it scared her. She got ice water and put it on me to cool me off. She would not let us go back until it got a little cooler.

When the cotton sold, I asked Daddy, "Did it save the farm?"

He said, "Yes!"

Then I said, "Daddy, then I do not owe you anything. Do not bring up my surgery again. It is paid in full."

Riding Cows, Mules, and Horses

In my years of childhood, I truly tested one Scripture more than any other: "For he shall give his angels charge over thee, to keep thee in all thy ways. They shall bear thee up in their hands, lest thou dash thy foot against a stone" (Psalm 91:11–12). I can attest to the truth of this Scripture because there is no way in the world with my life that I could not have broken bones. I rode family cows, mules, and horses and received several scrapes, but never a broken bone.

If my dad had ever told us not to do something, it was to never ride a horse by ourselves. We did not listen. We wanted to ride cows, mules, and horses.

One day, my uncle brought a mule to my father to break.

Dad said to us, "Do not get close to this animal. He will hurt you. Your Uncle Saint cannot handle him. And he could do nothing with him."

That mule was very stubborn, and we were repeatedly told to stay away. My father was so concerned, he said, "That mule is a killer." My brother, Bug, looked up at me with a sly smile. Of course, the term killer meant the opposite to us. That term meant we *must* try the mule out. We could not wait for Daddy to go to town. We were determined to break that mule and be heroes.

It was wintertime, and we had been turning the land over to prepare to plant. That made the dark ground softer and caused the wheels of the wagon to go deeper into the soil. Preparing to break Uncle Saint's mule, we got another mule out of the stall and hitched her to the wagon with some bags of fertilizer. Each bag was fifty pounds, and they weighed down the wagon. Of course, that obstinate mule had another idea. He bucked, kicked, and tried to rear up. He continued his tantrum for some time, but eventually he gave up.

Though it was cold out, the mule worked up a sweat. We knew that we had to wash him down. Daddy could not see him like this. We got the wagon and all the fertilizer back to the barn.

At breakfast the next morning, Daddy informed us that he was going to begin breaking Uncle Saint's mule. He told us that we must watch out and stay in the yard in case the mule broke free and started to run.

My brother Bug looked at me with a broad smile. He said, "Sister, I don't think we have anything to worry about. Do you?"

Later, my daddy came back to the house and said, "I do not know why Saint could not handle that mule; I am not having any trouble with him." Because of all the work my brother and I did to break him, he became so gentle that a man working our turpentine barrels could use him without the turpentine barrels tipping over.

The man who used the mule to pull the sled to dip turpentine asked me to take him to the house and feed him. I said, "I will if you unfasten the hamstring."

The man did not know whether anyone had ridden the mule, but he put me on the mule's back. It was just the mule and me, and he tried to buck me off. Daddy was reclining on the porch and just about that time he looked up and saw me on the mule. He came running down the lane hollering, "Whoa! Whoa!" Daddy put one hand on the bridle and his other hand on me, and said, "Dot, don't you know that is a barbed-wire fence next to you?" I could tell he was scared. He took the mule and told me he would feed the animal. He forgot to whip me, and I did not remind him either.

My Other Time at a Hospital

One of my regrets is that I did not keep up with a family I met at a hospital in Augusta, Georgia. I was there for my sister Myrtle, and I heard someone crying outside my sister's room. I peered out and saw the wife of one of the patients. She was pregnant, and her husband had been near unto death. I asked her, "Can I help you?" She said that though her husband was doing better, he had given up hope. He was ashamed of ever leaving the hospital because of his condition. He had been badly burned and was disfigured. I told his wife to go home and let me deal with him. I am so glad that she explained how he looked, or I would have fainted.

The next morning, I talked with his doctors and went to visit him. I introduced myself and told him I was going to get him up out of bed so he could call his wife. In those days, hospital rooms did not have private telephones. He said, "I am not going out of this room."

I said, "Yes, you are. It is time you stop feeling sorry for yourself. You are going to call your wife and tell her you are doing well. Your wife is carrying your baby, and that is what is important." I looked him in the eye and said, "Do you want to help yourself into that wheelchair, or do you want me to help you?"

He said, "No! I am not going out of this room."

I said, "Okay," and I grabbed his cover. With his only good hand, he grabbed the sheet. I was finally able to get him out of his bed, and he called his wife. After that, I took him to the lunchroom and bought both of our dinners. As we ate, I talked to him about the baseball teams that were in the playoffs.

Later, I carried a TV into the waiting room. I told the people there that I would be bringing a patient into the room to watch television, and I explained just how he was going to look. I asked them to save two chairs for him: one for him, and the other for his good leg. He stayed all evening in the waiting room, watching baseball and talking to the people.

The next morning, the man told me what had happened to him. He, his uncle, and his cousin were stealing copper from electric power lines. They thought they knew how to handle active power lines safely, but when he got close to the lines, the electricity drew him into them. The power threw him around, and he fell to the ground. He was in so much pain that he crawled toward a lake and tried to drown himself. He could hear his uncle talking to his cousin, "We have to find him and kill him. If not, we will go to prison."

After they left, he was able to crawl to the highway. He was so burned that one finger came off, then another, and finally his thumb. He knew that if he could get on the road, someone would run over him. He was hoping that a vehicle would run over him and he would die. Yet, he awoke in the hospital.

He had passed out from the pain and, according to him, Jesus and Satan were fighting over him. He heard Jesus say, "He is mine!" And then he heard Satan say, "He is mine!" The patient was later told that a truck driver stopped just as the truck's front wheel was about to hit him. The truck driver called the police, and an ambulance arrived and took him to the hospital.

His pain was beyond imagination and so intense that he wanted to die. When the electricity hit his body, it surged out through his arm and his leg. He lost both.

He told me that he was called to be a preacher when he was a small boy. I said to him, "You can still preach with one arm and one leg."

I would like to know what happened to him. For a considerable time, I prayed that God would continue to be his Lord.

Sister Sue and the Train

Many miracles have occurred in my lifetime, but one that I want to bring up here is when I had to sit up at the hospital with my sister Sue, who needed surgery.

I was driving in the morning from Fernandina Beach to Jacksonville, Florida. Just as I was about to cross a railroad track, a car from somewhere went around me and stopped. I could not understand why he stopped, and just then, a train went flying by on the tracks. Had I not stopped, I would have been hit by the train. When I got home, I was shaking.

For thirty-three years, I worked in Fernandina Beach, and the Lord would tell or show me to slow down or go another way home. One night, after I had worked from four o'clock to midnight, I was driving along and I heard the Lord say, "Slow down." As I did, I looked up and saw a log truck hit a car. The car's battery flew up in the air and looked like it was going to hit my windshield. It fell right in front of me, just missing the front of my car.

If I had not slowed down, I could have gone into the ditch, collided with the truck, or had the battery smash through my windshield and hit me. God is good, regardless of the storms.

One day, my sister and her husband left my house and went to St. Mary's, Georgia. The Spirit was so strong, working on me to pray for them. I began to intercede with crying because God showed me that they would be in a bad wreck if He did not move.

About an hour later the phone rang, and my sister told me about the wreck that they were almost involved in. I said, "Let me tell you . . ." She said that a car came around them, ran into the back of a log truck, and logs broke loose and smashed through the car. She and her husband stopped just before hitting the car from behind. She said, "The brains of the man in the car were on the inside on the roof."

More History of Sue

My sister Sue and her husband learned the consequences of living ungodly lives. Her husband spoiled their daughter, and as parents they would pay for it.

Sue was a perfect housekeeper and cook. She and her husband had their own business. Both worked all day, went home, cooked a big dinner, and had guests almost all the time.

Both she and her husband also lived a rough life of partying. They were continually drinking and dancing. They went from bar to bar, always the life of the party. It was common for her to be so drunk that she fought others who were drunk. As I have always said, "Women, men, alcohol, and drugs do not mix well." Though she loved various types of alcohol and wine, she also took multiple kinds of drugs.

The style of her life finally began to take its toll. She had about fifteen surgeries. And she had a severe back problem because of a pinched nerve.

For years, she stayed drunk. She was either on pain pills or drunk with alcohol every day during that time.

One day, when I got off from work, I saw her drive up to the whiskey store with her grandson and buy a bottle of alcohol with him in the passenger seat. I was fearful of what lay ahead of her if she did not change.

I repeatedly cried for her. Tears continually flowed from my face as I interceded for her and her family. Psalms 84:5–6 reads, "Blessed is the man whose strength is in thee; in whose heart are the ways of them. Who passing through the valley of Baca make it a well; the rain also filleth the pools." "Baca" means weeping or making a well of tears.

When a person genuinely becomes an intercessor for his or her family, the person will live in the valley of Baca (the valley of tears). Someone once said, "In your trials, you will have Jesus going with you in the valley of tears. The Lord has chosen that valley to test you and never to destroy you." The valley of tears is always a temporary place and never a permanent residence.

Sue's family put my husband and me through so much hell. Every time they would get in trouble, the Lord would let me know, or they would call me. Sometimes, they would both be in separate hospitals at the same time.

Further, Sue carried a gun for six weeks, hoping she would see me so she could shoot me. That was not her. That was the demons who indwelled her. Thank God, He did not let her find me. I knew what was going on during this time. I repeatedly cried bitter tears over her and her whole family.

At My Mother's Grave

As I was standing at my mother's grave, I remembered her hard life and thanked God that, in the end, she met the Master, as my father did. Looking across the graveyard, I saw the grave of my sister Ruby. I could only remember how, for a long time, Ruby took the brunt of all the troubles in our family. Like my husband, Ruby was the troubleshooter for the family. I did not know just how much I would one day miss her.

When there was a problem in the family, Ruby and I were always called on, her more than me. The troubles took a toll on her life. Our mother was enough trouble to kill a thousand men and women—one problem after another problem followed our mother.

Some may say that troubles will make you stronger, but few truly know the nature of difficulties. They can destroy a person, or at least make that person weaker.

CHAPTER 5
INTRODUCTION TO PENTECOST

I had never been around Pentecostal churches. I had never seen what in the world went on there. I had never experienced the shouting, the strange utterances of tongues, the healings, the miracles, the casting out of demons, or the other manifestations of the Holy Spirit.

Aunt Hazel and My Cousin

The first time I ever experienced hearing these strange utterances of tongues, or ever listened to a shout of praise, was a shocking experience. As it happened, I spent one night with my Aunt Hazel and my cousin. Since they only had one bedroom, I (as a young teenager) had to sleep between them. About four o'clock in the morning, I was awakened by the strange and awful commotion of my aunt jumping, shouting, and speaking something weird, which I had never heard in my life. My hair stood up. I ran behind my cousin and said, "If she gets me, she has to get you first!" When Aunt Hazel began to calm down, she lifted her hands in the air, walked into the kitchen, and all I could hear her say was something like, "I thank the Ghost."

From childhood, my family and I would sit around the fire and, on occasion, hear all sorts of ghost stories. So, I was ready to leave that place. If there were not a door, I was prepared to make one. When she walked back into the bedroom, I heard her thanking the "Holy Ghost" and praising God for His visitation. As she was thanking the Lord, I was looking around to see if I could see the Lord too. Finally, the manifestation of the Holy Spirit subsided. My aunt said, "Kids, we can go back to bed now." I pointed my finger at my cousin and said, "This time you sleep beside her."

Often, I heard my aunt say that she wanted to leave this world, shouting and speaking in tongues. That is just what happened. God granted her desire.

The Ice-Cold Church

Once, John Wesley said,

The grand reason why the miraculous gifts were so soon withdrawn was not only that faith and holiness were well-nigh lost, but that dry, formal orthodox men began then to ridicule whatever gifts they had not themselves and to cry them all down as evil madness or imposture.[1]

Further, John Wesley said in one of his sermons,

The cause of this was not (as has been vulgarly supposed) "because there is no more need for them" because all the world had become Christian. This is a miserable mistake not a twentieth part of the world was then even nominally Christian. The real cause was that the love of many, of almost all Christians, so-called, had grown cold. The Christians had no more of the Spirit of Christ than the other heathens. The Son of man, when he came to examine his Church, could hardly find faith on the earth. The real cause why the extraordinary gifts of the Holy Spirit were no longer to be found in the Christian Church was that the Christians were turned heathens again and had only a dead form left.[2]

Smith Wigglesworth, a Pentecostal revivalist of the early 1900s, spoke about the lifeless and powerless believers: "Their lives are so parallel with the world's that it is difficult to discriminate which place they are in, whether in the flesh or in the Spirit."[3]

When I became saved, the church was cold, and there was no moving of the Holy Spirit. My conversion occurred in spite of this, because of a special moving of the Holy Spirit for me alone. What does this mean? Despite the condition of the church, God works on individuals to save them. So, if the whole church becomes backslidden, God still moves and convicts the individual, and an individual can still be saved. It may be that the corporate church is fallen, but the Lord still can work on each individual.

Sister Mae Terry

One night, I attended a Church of God, though not really by choice. A lady preacher, Sister Mae Terry, a Pentecostal evangelist, was the guest speaker. Her sermon was not a sermon made for itching ears (2 Timothy 4:3), nor was it a sermon filled only with empty words. Her speech was a sermon of power and dealt with the subject of hell.

The reason I went to the church was not to hear the sermon, nor did I have any concern about God. I went to the church to date a boy who attended there.

I thought some of the things going on—the shaking and speaking in tongues—were funny or at least strange. When I did go to the church, I always sat in the back row. I loved the back row. And I watched the doors. If the ushers closed the doors, I got up and opened one. The pastor knew that I was afraid. And of course, I was convicted of the Lord.

In these later years, it reminds me of a sermon preached by Jonathan Edwards. The sermon was called "Sinners in the Hands of an Angry God." When Jonathan Edwards preached this sermon, the hearers felt hell and its torments round about them. This sermon created so much conviction that hundreds ran to the altar to be saved. Jonathan Edwards would continue to preach this sermon to new hearers. The message never became old or outdated because it had the fire of God within it.

Just like the sermon that Jonathan Edwards preached so long ago, Sister Mae Terry preached a hellfire and brimstone sermon. I believed that the seat I was sitting on was on fire when she gave the altar call. Somehow, I found myself down at the altar crying out to Jesus to save my soul. The next thing I remember was that a woman was behind me praying, and she had her hand upon my back. Her hand felt like a warm iron. I turned around to see who she was, and realized it was the woman I had hated because of her having a sexual affair with my father. She had since repented and given her heart to the Lord, and here she was praying for me. That night, God burned away all the years of bitterness and hatred I had held against her. I became that new creation in Christ Jesus that Paul speaks of in 2 Corinthians 5:17. All the baggage I had in my life melted away. The effects of my dysfunctional family were washed away by the blood of Christ, which is far more than enough. If not, then salvation is an illusion.

That night, as a young teenager, I met and fell in love with Jesus. I knew nothing about that type of love and was not going to give it up, whatever the cost. If there were not enough tears already shed, there would be much more shedding of tears in the coming years for my son and my family. I had no idea how much I would need Jesus in the coming years. I could neither imagine the pain nor the anguish that I would also endure.

When I was saved that night, the people in the Church of God did not take it too seriously. They knew the type of family I was born into and concluded that I would never make it. Still, I want all the saints to know that the Bible says, "He which hath begun a good work in you will perform it until the day of Jesus

Christ" (Philippians 1:6). That has been proven in my life.

Sister Mae Terry's Revival

It was on special occasions that the power of the Holy Spirit would come into this ice-cold church. Sister Mae Terry came to town and held a revival at that church for a few weeks. She had the anointing and gifts of the Holy Spirit in her life.

I brought into the services a female friend whom, I didn't realize, was severely demon possessed. Sister Mae Terry came against the demons and cast them out. The demons left the church with violence. They went through an open window, hit a woman outside, and knocked her down. Sister Mae Terry had a rule. In cases like these, she told people that they must plead the blood of Jesus over themselves.

Another time, the anointing of the Holy Spirit was so powerful that the demons tried anything to stop it. They actually caused the Nicholls Church of God to catch fire. I'll never forget it. Of course, the members of the church saw what the demons were trying to do and put the fire out.

Life of Intercessory Prayer

When I was saved that night, I began a life of intercessory prayer for my family. At this time, no one in my family was saved. I was the baby girl and the only one standing in the gap for my family. Thank God for the next persons who were saved in my family—my sister and brother-in-law. She was a little older than I was. I have often wondered who prayed for our salvation.

I had very little or no experience with Christianity, serving the Lord, or anything supernatural coming from God.

My life can well be summed up by the hymn of John Newton, "Amazing Grace":

> *Twas grace that taught my heart to fear*
> *And grace those fears relieved;*
> *How precious did that grace appear,*
> *The hour I first believed!*
> *Through many dangers, toils, and snares,*
> *I have already come;*
> *'Tis grace has brought me safe thus far;*
> *And grace will help me home.*[4]

CHAPTER 6
MY HUSBAND'S FAMILY

We can learn a lot about humanity and the ways of God simply by looking at my husband's family.

While I was sexually pure before I married, and even before I was saved, the saving of my soul enforced my belief and conviction to remain a virgin until marriage, and to date boys who had found the same Savior that I had.

My husband and I refused to have sex before our marriage. We both waited. Still, on the day of our wedding, many in the church believed that I would not keep my salvation. And yet, I thank my heavenly Father that I did see people in the church who loved me.

Many times, I have said, "I married up and my husband married down." In many respects, I said that because my husband's family consisted of doctors, preachers, nurses, and other professionals. And his family was filled with great intercessors.

For example, my mother-in-law prayed her son JH, my husband's brother, through World War II. It was not unusual for my husband to wake up in the middle of the night and hear his mother in the outhouse, crying for God to take care of her son during his time in Europe. When JH returned from the war, he spoke of the several times he was in danger of death during some of the battles of World War II. Two or more times, he was caught behind enemy lines.

I remember the family talking about a holiday when Mrs. Roberts ran out of the house to the outhouse to pray. Anyone could hear she was in great distress and almost in a great panic. She was crying and praying, "Father, help my son, JH. Father, move for him now, Lord."

My husband, Elias, said that this went on for the rest of the night. The next morning, as she was cooking breakfast, she said that JH was in some trouble. When JH came home, she asked him about that particular time. He said, "Yes! I was behind enemy lines and had hidden in a hayloft. A German, checking the hayloft, thrust his bayonet between my legs and then close to my head." Another time while Mrs. Roberts was praying, JH was almost killed jumping out of a three-story window to get away from a German soldier.

Since he had been a medic during the war, JH was offered a position in a drug store. The owner offered to pay for his college in exchange for work, but JH had had enough of medicine. He had seen enough suffering and enough death. He struggled with shell shock, now called PTSD. Anxiety, nervousness, fear, and crying were always his companions, especially around two in the morning. Family members would get out of bed at this time and begin to pray for him.

When JH found the Master, the Lord Jesus Christ, his life was changed. Almost every night, he would pray and cry before the Lord. Finally, the Lord led him to change jobs and go back to college. He became a brick mason and outlived all his siblings.

Mr. Roberts Shot

My husband and I received a call to get home because Mr. Roberts, my father-in-law, had been shot. We lived out of town, and by the time we arrived at my father-in-law's house, the sheriff had already removed the yellow tape and all the investigating had stopped. Finding nothing that could help, we went to the hospital to see his condition. Thank God, the doctor told us that Mr. Roberts would recover. My husband asked me to go back to the house and clean up the blood. And it was everywhere: in the hall, the bedroom, on the wall in the living room, and on the windows.

I also saw that a window was propped half open with a stick. Somehow, my father-in-law had pushed himself out of the window and crawled under the house. I had to use Lysol to wash the bloodied wall, which still had several shotgun pellets and pieces of flesh in it.

My father-in-law refused to speak of what happened and never brought charges against the person or persons responsible. He carried to his grave the truth about what really happened and who was responsible.

I had been pushed into a situation where I was battling for the salvation of my husband's family and my family. Love will make you pray and fast for your own family. It took years of learning how to fight in spiritual warfare before victory could well be had. Prayer is not easy if you want results. And spiritual warfare will cost you everything if you want results.

Johnny Roberts

I wish I could say that Mrs. Roberts had won the spiritual battle over her family. For example, her son Johnny did not withstand the trials of life.

Johnny was saved just after my husband gave his life to the Lord. He married Evelyn, who became a preacher for the Church of God, and they lived across the street from us. Johnny and Evelyn did not have to wait long for their first child, a baby girl. She was the apple of her Uncle Elias's eye.

Johnny and Evelyn had three children. His oldest daughter could play the piano and sing. In fact, everyone in his family could sing. He was never mean or beat his wife. Nor was he evil to his children.

But, for one reason or another, Johnny did not retain his Christian faith. Soon after being married, he became rebellious, a drunk, and an adulterer.

Evelyn was under enormous pressure. Most of the time, Johnny worked as a shipping clerk, and she never knew if Johnny would come home after work, or if he would go drinking. He had been in many car wrecks. She had to work, and this pattern of her husband made things harder. She never knew what was going to happen to him. She could never depend on him. And during these times, he never permanently got right with God.

He began to womanize when he drank. He would find one woman and spend all the money that had been saved. Then he would beg Evelyn to forgive him. He would say to his wife, "Remember that Jesus has forgiven me." Repeatedly, this occurred. First, he'd commit adultery. Second, he'd asked his wife and the Lord to forgive him. And the pattern continued.

When his daughter was about two, the Reverend T. L. Lowery, a Church of God preacher, held a tent revival in Jacksonville. At one point, he stopped the service and said, "Some family member is going to kill himself." Our family ran to the front of the prayer-tent. When everyone else had got up and gone back into the other tent, my husband and my sister-in-law were left praying. The Lord had informed us all that the person who was going to kill himself was my husband's brother, Johnny.

After praying almost all night, we went home. About three o'clock in the morning, our telephone rang. Yes, Johnny had tried to kill himself by drinking poison. His little girl sat before him praying he would not die. As his little girl was begging, my husband grabbed a can of lard and began to cram it down Johnny's throat.

Johnny continued to scream, "Don't quit praying! Don't quit praying! When you stop praying, the flames of hell are burning my feet and legs. Pray! Pray!

The flames are coming up my body!" We all who were present in the room stood firm against the evil one and the flames.

After this, wouldn't you think Johnny would change? In just a few years, Johnny forgot all about the incident, and his old behavior of drunkenness and adultery came back with a fury.

Lust Drove Him

Johnny was so lustful about a particular woman that he drove to see her but wrapped his car around a tree. He broke his back and lost an ear in the wreck. When my husband arrived at the hospital, he was shocked by Johnny's condition. The doctors and nurses had not cleaned him up. They were waiting for him to die. My husband, Elias, called his father, who worked at the funeral home, and told him to come with an ambulance to carry his brother out of that hospital. His father called the family doctor and told him what had happened.

When the ambulance arrived to take Johnny out of the hospital, the nurse came running. We told the doctors and nurses we were moving him. They all said that it would kill him. My husband said, "If he stays here at this hospital, he will die." What the doctors and nurses did not know was that Johnny was going to see a married woman, and the husband of that woman was coming to kill Johnny. My husband spoke to the husband of that woman, "If you are going to kill someone, you should kill your wife."

As we carried Johnny away from the hospital in the ambulance to another hospital, we prayed all the way. When the doctor saw Johnny's condition and X-ray, he could not understand how he was living. His back was utterly broken. The doctor ordered a brace; but before the brace came, God heard the praying of the saints, and Johnny received a miracle. God completely and instantaneously healed his back.

The prayers of the saints do have results. The prayers of Evelyn, my husband, and me produced results. The prayers of repentance prayed by Johnny touched the heart of the Lord, and God healed him.

As a backslider, Johnny called upon the Lord, but it was the prayers of the Lord's saints that the Lord heard, not the backslider (Job 27:9; Proverbs 28:9; Isaiah 1:15; Jeremiah 11:11; Ezekiel 8:18; Micah 3:4; Zechariah 7:14). Psalms 66:18–20 reads, "If I regard iniquity in my heart, The Lord will not hear me: But verily God hath heard me; he hath attended to the voice of my prayer. Blessed be God, which hath not turned away my prayer, nor his mercy from me."

Therefore, prayers should be made with a pure mind, holy desires, and with a life free from defilement.

The prayers of backsliders and sinners are heard by the Lord if the prayers are of repentance and salvation. The hearing of prayers by God is itself a miracle, and that miracle is for the godly. God listens to the prayers of sinners and backsliders only about repentance and salvation. When sinners turn away from their sins unto repentance, then they are in harmony with the will of God. In other words, the only prayers that God will not hear are those prayed by sinners and backsliders who love their sins and will not give them up.

One commentator writes, "We know God does not listen to the cry of sinners, when, as sinners, they ask from the ground of their sin, to secure their sinful purpose."[1]

Further, God does not hear the prayers of His people because of their sins. They must cease doing evil and learn to do good (Isaiah 58:1–9; Jeremiah 11:9–14, 14:10–12; Ezekiel 8:17–18; Micah 3:4; Zechariah 7:11–13). God heard the prayer of Cornelius before he was saved because it dealt with repentance and salvation (Acts 10:4–31).

Still, one would think that Johnny would change his life for good this time. Not so. He still wouldn't repent. And years later, he had to be rushed to a hospital again. This time, his heart had built up so much calcium that it did not have space to beat. God once again came to his aid and brought him through the surgery.

But finally, God told his wife to let Johnny go. She got a divorce. Johnny married again. Years went by, and his second wife divorced him. He worked hard and tried to pay alimony. He worked all the overtime he could get.

Calcium Around the Heart and Aneurysm

More years went by, and he became sick again. He still had so much calcium built up around his heart. But this time, he had an aneurysm. His blood vessel blowing out was a death sentence. The doctors could not operate on his heart because of the aneurysm, nor could they operate on the aneurysm because of his heart.

Now what? He was in the hands of God. For so many years, he had abandoned God— the same God who had reached unto him, picked him up, and repeatedly healed him. When he was stable with the Lord, the Lord gave him the gift of discerning of spirits and other gifts. He had the most significant degree of the gift of discerning of spirits I had ever seen.

What about Johnny? Scripture says, "Such as sit in darkness and in the shadow of death, being bound in affliction and iron; Because they rebelled against the words of God, and contemned the counsel of the most High: Therefore he brought down their heart with labour; they fell down, and there was none to help" (Psalms 107:10–12). It is an awful thing to fall into the hands of an angry God.

He was given lots of time to repent and make things right with God. All I can say is what a shame that he did not do what God had called him and his family to do. Johnny died a lonely old man by himself.

My Husband's Baby Brother, Wallace

My husband's baby brother was more like a pharaoh than all others. He studied criminology, then worked as a deputy sheriff and was involved in the Georgia Bureau of Investigation (GBI). Wallace could have been anything in his life, but his life was all about self. He wanted his way, no matter whom he hurt. He not only divorced his wife, but he also gave up his children for the sake of self.

Wallace was a deputy sheriff on patrol one night when a speeding car flew by him. He chased down the vehicle and got it to stop. He walked slowly to the car, and the driver rolled down the window. Wallace asked for the driver's license and asked the driver, "Why were you speeding?" The driver replied, "Deputy, I don't know why I was speeding, or if I was." Wallace smelled a heavy odor of wine and noticed a brown paper bag with a bottle in it. He asked, "Have you been drinking?" The driver said, "No!" Wallace asked the driver to pass him the brown paper bag with the bottle in it. Wallace smelled and looked at the bottle. Sure enough, it was wine. Wallace said, "Look! You have been drinking wine!" The driver said, "No, sir! I was drinking water." Wallace said back, "But this is wine!" The driver said, "Oh no, Lord! The Lord has done it again! He turned water into wine."

Like the Earth Stood Still

One night, my husband was praying, and God showed him a vision in which his brother Wallace was going to be shot with his own .38 pistol within six months. He told a pastor about what God had shown him and sought immediate prayer for his brother. The pastor anointed a handkerchief for my husband to carry with him to Georgia.

The next morning, when I came home from work, my husband was standing in the kitchen, looking out the window. He said, "We will go to Douglas today."

When we walked into the sheriff's office, tears were running down my husband's cheeks. He told Wallace what God had shown him. My husband offered Wallace the handkerchief that had been prayed over the night before, in keeping with what the apostle Paul did. "And God wrought special miracles by the hands of Paul: So that from his body were brought unto the sick handkerchiefs or aprons, and the diseases departed from them, and the evil spirits went out of them" (Acts 19:11–12).

Wallace said, "Give me that handkerchief. I jumped down two flight of steps, getting away from a gun." My husband said, "No, Wallace. God said, 'You will be shot!'" Wallace put the handkerchief into his billfold. We left.

That day was the day the Lord God let the earth seem to stand still for us.

We drove two and a half hours one way. Then we went from the sheriff's office to my mother's house in the country and prayed for her and my sister, Ruby. During our prayers, Ruby said, "I hear the angels singing."

Then, going back through Douglas, Georgia, we arrived at the home of my husband's aunt. We prayed, and the glory of God fell. His aunt shouted and praised God.

Coming back to Jacksonville, Florida, we went to church. The pastor said, "God, let this day stand still for someone. It has been a long day." My husband raised his hand and said, "It was for me."

Wallace Shot

One hour before the end of the six months, Wallace was shot with his own gun. Coming in from work, I saw my husband standing, looking out through the window again. He had been crying much and looked up at me and said, "Last night, Wallace was shot in the chest. God spoke to me and said, 'Since you have given to Me both your life and your finances, I am giving back to you. Your brother will be all right.'" When my husband went to Douglas, Georgia, all his family was in a fury at the hospital because Wallace's wife had shot him. My husband told the sheriff there would be no charges brought against her. Why? Wallace had been beating his wife, and his mother did not raise her boys to beat their wives.

The family was not happy with the decision not to prosecute Wallace's wife. But my husband said to his brother, "Wallace, there will be no charges. God told me what you were doing."

Two days later, I was at work around three o'clock in the morning, when the Holy Spirit began to deal with me to go to the hospital immediately. When I got off from work, I quickly drove to Douglas, Georgia. I walked into Wallace's room just as he was trying to choke his wife. I broke that up. Our family had gone through enough. I said to Wallace, "If you cannot live with her, then divorce her."

When Wallace got out of the hospital, he came to our house. He said to my husband, "When I was shot with my own .38 pistol, I died. My spirit left my body. I saw the police officials and other friends saying, 'My God, it's Wallace. We can't get a pulse.' The ambulance came, and they loaded my body inside, but I rode along on top to the hospital. I knew the nurse that came running to get my body out of the ambulance. I heard the doctor pronounce me dead. I saw the doctor and nurses put a sheet over my head. But the hand of God came down from heaven and hit my body in the chest. A nurse walked by and saw the sheet move. She screamed, 'Wallace is breathing!'" According to what the doctor said, the bullet went between the two main arteries of his heart.

I wish I could say this experience made a difference in Wallace's life, but it did not. He became a devoted alcoholic, lost his job, got into trouble with the law he had once enforced, and finally committed suicide. He shot himself in the same way he had been shot years before.

He died in his sins like his brother, Johnny. All the other family members died with their family loving them. The Bible states, "Be not deceived; God is not mocked: for whatsoever a man soweth, that shall he also reap. For he that soweth to his flesh shall of the flesh reap corruption; but he that soweth to the Spirit shall of the Spirit reap life everlasting" (Galatians 6:7–8).

Did Johnny and Wallace go to heaven? I would be surprised to see them there. I have written this so that we can understand why two brothers chose the way of the world when their other four siblings went the way of God. Two of the brothers were even preachers. So, what happened to Wallace and Johnny?

As I write this, I remember my husband walking the floor and crying over the life of Wallace. If anything killed my husband, it was the suicide of Wallace. He could not ever get over his brother's death.

If we had known of someone who was familiar with how to break off the spirit of grief, my husband might have been set free from that fiery dart. We needed someone who was familiar with the practices of the ancient church, but at the time, there was no such person.

Wallace's life exemplifies Isaiah 24:9: "They shall not drink wine with a song;

strong drink shall be bitter to them that drink it." Also, Matthew 8:13 reads, "And Jesus said unto the centurion, Go thy way; and as thou hast believed, so be it done unto thee. And his servant was healed in the selfsame hour." My brother-in-law chose his life's path. Satan did not choose it for him. Wallace chose that path.

I will never forget the words of my husband about his baby brother. "My mother will never see her baby ever again."

Wallace and Johnny had the spirit of the pharaohs. They had known the way of salvation, but they finally turned away from it. And they hurt everyone in the family.

Another Tragedy

I am including this next story to illustrate the value of a praying family. That kind of family is priceless.

The only daughter of my husband's family was married to a physically abusive man. One day, as her husband was beating her, she was able to grab hold of a pistol. As they both fought for the gun, it went off. She said, "He pulled the gun up to his chest and pulled the trigger."

She was arrested and charged with her husband's murder. The case went to trial and she was found not guilty. When the verdict was read, God interrupted the proceedings by speaking through Evelyn. She began speaking in tongues. The judge sat back and said, "This is what set her free. I have been a judge for thirty years and never seen a more corrupt case than this one." The judge knew that the prosecutors were being bought off, the witnesses were paid to give false testimonies, and more. Yet most of the Roberts family were intercessors, who had been praying and fasting during the whole trial. We knew that this woman had lived through hell almost all of her life. And she had worked like a dog—chipping pines trees for turpentine, picking cotton, and raising her children. Through our prayers, she was set free to come home and raise her two children.

I wish someone in my life would have been saved and gone deep into spiritual warfare for me the way we did for Elias's sister and sister-in-law. Maybe my family would have accepted my being baptized in the Holy Spirit at first.

Elias's Brother, William

One night, God gave my husband a dream about his brother, William. The next morning, he said, "I have to call William."

Several years before this dream, William had been saved, had moved down to Florida, and gotten a good job.

My husband called him that morning and said, "William, I had a dream about you last night. I am going to tell you about it and put it in your hands. Last night, I dreamed that you and I were in a boat, and a big tidal wave came up and covered us. I was reaching for Ricky, my son. But I heard a voice say, 'It is your brother William. If he does not sell that boat and preach My Word, he will immediately die.'"

William did not say a word. He just listened to what my husband was saying. My husband was crying and finally was able to say, "I do not know all about this, but the dream was real and came from the Lord."

His brother said, "Elias, yesterday, I bought a new boat. I know you are of God, and you did not know that I had just bought a new boat. I will immediately sell that boat."

The next time we heard from him, he had retired from his job and began preaching in the Church of God.

I believe that John 5:24 speaks of William, "Verily, verily, I say unto you, He that heareth my word, and believeth on him that sent me, hath everlasting life, and shall not come into condemnation; but is passed from death unto life."

Can you see the difference between Johnny and William? One was humble while the other was rebellious.

As William preached the Word of God, the overseers gave him one church after another. Many times, the church buildings were not in good shape and needed repairs. William would fix up each building. I remember times he would preach in a building without any air conditioning. Finally, when the church began to recover, money would come in, and they would be able to purchase air conditioning. Then, William would be moved to another rundown church.

While he was not a theologian, William tried the best that he could. He knew Christianity 101 and preached a simple message. William's life reminds me of James 1:12–14.

> Blessed is the man that endureth temptation: for when he is tried, he shall receive the crown of life, which the Lord hath promised to them that love him. Let no man say when he is tempted, I am tempted of God: for God cannot be tempted with evil, neither tempteth he any man: But every man is tempted, when he is drawn away of his own lust, and enticed.

CHAPTER 7
FIRST EXPERIENCES WITH GOD

When my father-in-law was asked about his new daughter, almost immediately after my husband and I were married, he replied, "Elias became a millionaire when he married Dot."

I first met my husband when he came to our house. I was eight years old, and Elias was about eleven. He remembered how I was dressed: I wore a blue shirt and overalls, and my hair was cut short. This particular day, I was out in the yard playing marbles. Even at that young age, Elias told his brother, "I'm going to marry Dot." So, he watched me grow up.

Several years went by and we met somewhat on a blind date. My girlfriend asked me whether I would go out with her and her boyfriend to meet Elias. I agreed.

We all went to a theater that night and dated a few times. At first, I was not impressed at all with Elias. As girls do, I was already dating someone else. Elias had taken it for granted that we were going steady. He left town because he could not face my dating someone else. In the meantime, I met the love of my life, Jesus Christ, and I started going to that Pentecostal church.

That decision did not go well with my father. He was demon possessed, and the demons in him revolted against my decision. The demons knew that this was the beginning of a battle over my father's soul.

My only opportunity to attend church was with my Aunt Hazel. I started saving my lunch money at school to catch a Greyhound bus on Saturday evening to stay with her so I could go to church with her on Sunday morning.

On Sunday evening, I would catch the Greyhound bus to get back home. Where the bus driver stopped to let me off, there was nothing but woods and darkness. A lady looking out the bus window and seeing no houses or light, said, "I hope someone is meeting you."

I said, "Oh Yes! My Father will be with me." I did not tell her that the Father was my heavenly Father, not my physical father. The shame here was that my physical father was in bed drunk, not caring about whether I got home or not.

Many times, around midnight or one o'clock in the morning, I would quietly slip out of my bed and out the back door. I threw a headscarf over my head to keep my hair dry from the dew, crawled over a fence into a peanut patch, and walked far enough away from my house so no one could hear my long and deep groans of intercession. I did yet not know what was meant by this kind of groaning, travailing prayer.

Sometimes, I prayed so hard that it felt like my whole heart would burst out of my chest. At first, I prayed until I felt better. Later, I learned that I must pray until I prayed through and received an answer. In these early years, I began a life of prayer for my family's salvation, and whatever God put on my heart. It took forty-one years for my sister Sue to be saved. Regardless of the years, God was faithful.

God protected me through the nights walking in the woods. There were many times in those woods that fear would try to rise against me. One time, I heard a voice say, "Fear not." I just kept walking. I did not know how fast I was walking, but I just kept on walking through those dark woods.

Not only did I pray, but I also learned that I must fast. I learned the principle of fasting from a lady at church. She said, "I fasted five days for something. I did not know what I was fasting and praying for, but the Lord led me to fast and pray. And I followed Him and did what He demanded of me." I listened to every word she said. From that point, I learned to fast. I fasted one day and then two days with much praying accompanying the fasting.

I joined my Aunt Hazel through much prayer and fasting for our family. My sister, her husband, and Aunt Hazel's daughter and son-in-law all were saved roughly at the same time. Of course, Satan began to bring doubt against the works of God.

These conversions were the first fruits that came from my family. It took much longer for others in my family to be saved.

First Experience

Paul said as follows:

I knew a man in Christ above fourteen years ago, (whether in the body, I cannot tell; or whether out of the body, I cannot tell: God knoweth;) such an one caught up to the third heaven. And I knew such a man, (whether in the body, or out of the body, I cannot tell: God knoweth;) How that he was caught up into paradise, and heard unspeakable words, which it is not lawful for a man to utter. (2 Corinthians 12:2–4)

Just like Paul, I knew not in the body or out of the body how I underwent my first experience with the Lord.

The first experience I had with God occurred one Sunday morning at church. Many were down at the altar praying. I felt an urgent need to go to the Sunday school classroom. After I went to the classroom, a spirit of prayer came upon me, and I saw or experienced a vision. I had never been taught how to pray that way, nor ever had I experienced the moving of the Holy Spirit upon any person to pray in this way.

All at once I left the classroom and went up into a cloud. Jesus was with me, and we were sitting on chairs. The Lord told me about my family. He promised to save my family *if* (and there is usually an *if* with God) I would serve Him. He did not tell me about the battles that I would have to go through to see my family saved. He just gave me the results—if I would serve Him. He never told me the entire the cost.

I have held on to the written Word of God and this first experience with God for sixty years. Now, when I go to the cemetery where my family is buried, I look down at the graves of my father, my mother, my brother, my sister, and my husband, and I can say, "I will see you again." The circle will not remain broken. At my brother's funeral, I spoke and said, "I know that this is not goodbye, because I led him to the Lord."

Completely Trusting the Holy Spirit

I bear witness to the Scriptures and what they represent. I have experienced the power of the early church. No one can make me deny the gifts and power of the Holy Spirit that were given to me to fight for my family and for others. I learned to trust the Holy Spirit entirely, but it cost me everything.

Acts 2:4 reads, "And they were all filled with the Holy Ghost, and began to speak with other tongues, as the Spirit gave them utterance." And 1 Corinthians 14:2 reads, "For he that speaketh in an unknown tongue speaketh not unto men, but unto God: for no man understandeth him; howbeit in the spirit he speaketh mysteries." Lastly, 1 Corinthians 13:1 reads, "Though I speak with the tongues of men and of angels, and have not charity, I am become as sounding brass, or a tinkling cymbal."

In 1944, before the troops landed in Normandy, Dwight Eisenhower said, "There are no victories at bargain prices!"[1] And Amy Carmichael, a missionary to India, once said, "Satan is so much more in earnest than we are—he buys up the opportunity while we are wondering how much it will cost."[2] Dietrich Bonhoeffer, a German minister and theologian in Nazi Germany, decried what he called "cheap grace." According to him, such a thing as "cheap grace" can do nothing but produce a "bargain-basement salvation." Such salvation demands nothing from the Christians and will produce nothing either.[3]

The Holy Spirit became my teacher in many ways. The Holy Spirit helped me in school and helped me learn my jobs. My whole life was filled with missed days of school, but the Holy Spirit came in and helped fill in the gaps.

Further, I learned that the Holy Spirit was my Helper. The more experiences I had with the Holy Spirit, the more I wanted of God. Yet, my relationship with the Holy Spirit did not sit well with everyone. Most of the people I knew believed in a formalistic Christianity, devoid of power and life.

I did not know when I prayed and fasted for the baptism of the Holy Ghost, that I sparked a spiritual war. I had no idea that there are times of testing and times of warfare. My father had taught me quite well how to fight in the flesh, but I wish someone would have taught me how to battle spiritually.

My father refused to allow any "holy roller" or Pentecostal to be in his house or be a part of his family. I had never heard of "rolling" in the Spirit, but I knew about praying, fasting, and the baptism of the Holy Spirit. After all, we can, if we will pay the cost, move from glory unto glory with the Lord.

There was no way that I was going to give up any experience with the Holy Spirit. So, I gave up my father's house. I didn't think for one moment about it. Today, many would give up the Holy Spirit for the sake of sex or financial means and certainty. Few have the spirit of the early church, reformers, and revivalists. Yet I could not deny, reject, or denounce the movements, means, and methods of the Holy Spirit. Therefore, I gave up my father's house, and that was only the beginning. In a sense, I had to give up my whole family.

I quickly learned that after almost every movement of the Holy Spirit, there is a countermovement of Satan and his evil spirits. Therefore, I knew that demons in my father knew I would have to battle for my father's spirit and other members of my family. The demons were prepared. Indeed, they had prepared for years. The demons were present in my father and the lives of my family to try to prevent the fulfillment of the Lord's promises. This occurrence was just like that of the Promised Land, where the giants were already present before the Hebrews were led to take their inheritance (see Numbers 13:33).

Be careful about ever saying something like this when dealing with the moving of the Holy Spirit: "I will not do that," or "I do not want to see that."

The Holy Spirit will make a godly spectacle of Himself before men and women. The Holy Spirit rarely wants to hide what He is doing in the hearts of men and women. A clear example of that is found on the Day of Pentecost.

Holy Roller

In time, I heard of saints "rolling in the Spirit," but I had never experienced it. Then one night, a sister at church was rolling back and forth on the floor, and I said, "I do not want to do that."

Then, about sixty-four years after I had been saved, I was sealing away for twenty-one days in our church in Douglas, Georgia, to pray with some other women. During this time, the power of God came down and hit me. The power was so strong that it shook me and shocked those who were present. I was knocked out of my chair, fell, and screamed like I was having a baby. If that were not enough, I started rolling back and forth from the altar to a place where the Lord stopped me. The power of God would continue, and I rolled back and forth. This went on for about three and a half hours. The others who were with me stood silent and watched.

As the Lord was continuing to move upon me, I straightened out like a log. I never hit my head or my feet. Stationary now, my heavenly Father nailed me to the floor like a cross. I felt the crown of thorns put upon my head and the nail pierce each hand. I felt my feet being nailed. And when the Holy Spirit allowed me to experience in the spirit the sword piercing my side and the water and blood running down my side, I screamed.

In a finite manner, I was experiencing just a glimmer of what Christ did for me. I saw the agony and the suffering of the cross of Christ Jesus. And I bore witness with what Christ did on the cross.

In this vision, the Lord came and talked to me. After the Lord Jesus left, I was so weak and thirsty that the other intercessors gave me water, and I said, "I am hungry." And the intercessors gave me some food.

Immediately after that, I said, "Let us take communion." The intercessors and I took communion. I was too weak to go back to Jacksonville. That was the second time I had been slapped out of my chair by the power of God.

The Last Day

When I sealed away in Douglas for twenty-one days praying, the Lord spoke to me the last day. He said, "It was no accident that you sealed away to pray. It is no accident that I called those to be with you." Originally, when God told me to do the twenty-one days, my son said, "You could stay in the church, but you do not need to be alone." Thank God, I listened to him. As many as eight to twenty women stayed with me at a time during the twenty-one days. Again, the Lord spoke and said the last day, "There was no accident that you sealed away." Further, He said that He called those to be with me. The devil was working full force, but God's power steadily increased, and He continued to release more angels. The Lord knew our hearts for lost souls, and the pain over them going to hell. Even today, I feel if God does not save a soul each day, I will die.

A Son in a Car Wreck

After the twenty-first day of intercession with other ladies, Satan attacked one of the intercessors. He struck her son and made him have a car wreck. The intercessor received a call from the hospital, and a nurse said, "Come as quickly as possible." Immediately the intercessor and her husband left and went toward Jacksonville. However, they began to slow down when the intercessor remembered the word of the Lord that came the last night of our shut-in for praying and fasting. Because I rarely spoke during prayer, she said, "Dot never says anything, so this must be from God." The word was simply this, "I have heard your prayers, even to the domino effect. You have prayed for an intercessor's son who was in a hospital in Jacksonville, Florida. And he will be all right. I am going to take care of your families."

When the intercessor and her husband arrived at the hospital, their son had already been released. Because the car had been totaled, this was a great miracle.

Aftereffects of a Shot

Still again, Satan struck another intercessor that night. Her son went to a doctor and received a shot. Then he went to a party. He began to feel strange and funny. He thought he had better go home. As he was driving, he passed his driveway and ran into a ditch. A friend decided to leave the party but drove a different way than usual. He found the intercessor's son in the ditch and called for an ambulance. The medics were able to begin to work on him and finally drove him to the hospital. Both the doctors and nurses could not find any pulse, pronounced him dead, and covered his body up. Another nurse walked by and said, "This man is alive." God resurrected him!

There is a cost for successful prayer; there is a cost for touching the hem of the garment. If you have touched heaven, Satan will always counterattack. Too many people think they have prayed and touched the hem of the garment, but when there is no countermovement of Satan, something is wrong.

Brain Cancer

Another intercessor during this meeting of deep and intensive intercession received a phone call. The person on the telephone said that her grandson was in the hospital with cancer of the brain. Being upset as she was, driving up north, she said, "This is not what Dot said." During our prayer meeting, I had a prophetic word that God would protect our families for our obedience to be shut-in the church for twenty-one days of prayer. By the time she arrived at the hospital, the baby was all right.

If we believe the lies of the devil, his lies will become the truth or reality. We do not allow the circumstances of our lives to determine our view or faith. Smith Wigglesworth once said, "The faith of Christ never wavers. When you have that faith the thing [what you need] is finished."[4] That is, faith in Christ never wavers if faith has Christ as its object.

White Dove

As God was moving during this twenty-one day and night shut-in, people would come knocking or banging on the door to let them in for prayer. A couple came from Alma, Georgia. One of the intercessors praying with me said that she knew them and to let them in; they were her friends. The woman sat on the altar. While we were praying, she said, "Look! A white dove is flying around the inside of the church!" Immediately she was healed.

In this time, another message came forth and said, "You are like eagles soaring and searching for souls. Many times, I have seen your tears, and I have not deserted you, though some things have passed you by. You are My very heart, which has been through many valleys and many ditches. You have always pulled yourself up and kept going. The enemy comes in like a lion, and you have raised a standard against him."

Another word came forth by interpretation, "Your prayers were piercing My ears. I am pleased, and a great movement is needed to pull down and to build up." The Lord informed us that a greater lantern would be lit than what was lit in the late nineteenth century, and the beginning of the twentieth century through the Holiness and Pentecostal Movements. God said, "Did I not say when Mary Ruth Woodworth Etter [an evangelist in 1885 into the twentieth century] lit a light all over the world, that I will light a lantern that will be greater over the world?"

Yes, my life has been and continues to be a life of prayer. We need more people with the ability to pray like Etter. We must increase our prayer life to have that kind of anointing.

Holy Spirit and My Jobs

The Holy Spirit was my great Helper in finding and keeping jobs. In truth, I could do nothing alone. The baptism of the Holy Spirit, with the evidence of speaking in tongues, became the foundation of power for me during these times. The baptism of the Holy Spirit endowed me with the power to fight whatever problem arose.

Thanks be to God, He always provided me a job. The positions that God gave me, however, were not easy. There were always co-workers who wanted nothing to do with God. They refused to believe in God and refused to receive Christianity or Jesus Christ as the only means of salvation. Some of those who fought against me were even Christians. These Christians had been taught that the baptism of the Holy Spirit, and especially speaking in tongues, were of the devil.

I cannot imagine any Christian who would not want to pray directly to our heavenly Father in the languages of the Holy Spirit. These languages can well be human, heavenly, or even divine. The Holy Spirit, speaking through our spirit, can hit the mark of what is needed with just one word. Yet, on our own, we must pray and pray and pray to try to hit the target.

I know and live what is described in the hymn "It Was Alone the Savior Prayed".

Alone, alone, He bore it all alone;
He gave Himself to save His own;
He suffered, bled and died alone, alone.[5]

Warring Against Satan for My Job

After moving to Jacksonville, Florida, I applied for several well-paying jobs. I made a covenant with God that if He gave me a good job, I would not spend all my money on clothes to try and out-dress other women.

It is common to believe if God chooses a job for His child, the job will be problem free. How wrong that perception is. As I learned, God will make you a missionary wherever He plants you: in your school, college, family, and your occupation.

My first well-paying job was working for a meatpacking plant, though I quickly realized I had entered the devil's den—or the Roman Colosseum, as the devil saw it. My co-workers had no problem persecuting me for my beliefs.

God had given me an outstanding job making great money for the 1950s. It seemed that everything would be smooth sailing, but an important principle to learn from the Bible lay before me. I experienced similar problems to what the Hebrews endured as they tried to enter the Promised Land. God promised the Hebrew children a land flowing with milk and honey, but when they arrived, the land was already occupied by the enemy. To possess the Promised Land, the land of Canaan, they had to go to war. My Canaan—this new job—was occupied by the most evil, wicked people. They were in full possession of what God had promised and given to *me*. As soon as I was hired, a war broke out between the Holy Spirit and the wicked spirit in that meat processing plant.

During my first few days on the job, the union arrived on the scene. They hoped to improve working conditions and relationships between the bosses and employees and provide overtime pay and holiday pay. At the time, I did not know anything about unions, what their purpose was, or whether the Bible had anything to say about them. If my co-workers had taken the time to explain all these things to me, I would have had fewer problems. But I was unaware and uneasy about the union.

My co-workers brought me a union membership card to sign, and I immediately rejected it. As a baby Christian, I did not know if I should sign the card or not. My co-workers despised me because of my refusal to join the union, and their hatred of me was visible. There was a wrong spirit at work. I don't know if the spirit was the union itself, or a sinister spirit behind the co-workers. In time, I would learn spiritual discernment.

To make matters worse, some of the workers were stealing meat and anything else not nailed down. As a baby Christian, I was thrown into the devil's den, and I was pushed to steal. How could I be a Christian and steal? Either I was to be a Christian, or I was to be a thief. I could not be both. After all, light cannot be joined to darkness (see 1 John 1:5, 2:8–9).

It was not difficult to figure out who was stealing. I told my co-workers that I was not going to tell on them, but I would not lie for them either. That did not sit too well with them, and more and more strikes came against me. All hell was about to explode.

For fifteen months, my life at work was a living hell. Evil upon evil raised its ugly head against me. My Canaan—my Promised Land—was a living hell. God had put me there, and there was an absolute war. If I'd have had a choice, I would have quit.

Though the war was spiritual, it affected my physical world. My tires were cut. At night, people would call my home every thirty minutes. Co-workers threw rotten eggs at my car. They called me a "scab." I was not a replacement worker; I was a permanent worker.

The last straw was when the co-workers, mainly seven women, refused to allow me to sit in the lunchroom to eat. I knew I had to face my giant. I went to my boss and told him that I had had enough of this harassment. I would not start a fight, but I was not going to accept this treatment any longer. I told him that I would go to the lunchroom and sit in a chair with my back to the wall so that no one could be behind me. I would eat my lunch and stand up against these seven bullies. And last, I told him that if he wanted to fire all of us, then he should be around today.

The seven women, who were nothing but bullies, were waiting for me in the parking lot. They were there not to talk but to gang up on me and beat me almost to death. I knew it was possible that they could beat me so much that I could die since there were so many of them. Bullies are like this. They do not have enough guts to fight a person one-on-one.

However, I was prepared. My brother-in-law had taught me how to defend myself in such cases. I entered the parking lot and did not run. They thought I would run, but I did not. To face these bullies would be my Waterloo or my Jericho Victory.

The fight began. I struck two of my co-workers with karate chops. Just by these two karate chops, I showed the seven bullies that I was not hiding behind religion.

The first woman I hit was the daughter of a police sergeant. After the fact, he admired me because his daughter had always been overbearing. I kept on hitting the women with karate chops. One tried to hit me, but I ducked underneath her legs and came up with a huge karate chop to the back of her neck.

I kept my cool and my sanctification during the fight. I thought that no one hit me. I had done most of the damage. I was laughing.

Most of the women fled the parking lot, and I went home. I went to the bathroom to check myself out. When I pulled off some of my clothes, I saw a few bruises, especially on the chin. At that point, I lost it. I thought no one had touched me.

I got back in my car and drove back to the parking lot. With the state I was in, I was probably going to hurt the women badly, if not kill them. Thank God, only two other women were present, and they were in a car. They were not part of the seven bullies, but they had made trouble for me too. They knew I carried a knife to help peel hotdogs. One of the two threatened me with a gun. I said, "If you take that gun out, I will make you eat it." She did not pull out her gun, and they drove off.

I found out later that my boss had watched the entire fight. He told me that if they were able to get to my back, he would have called the police.

Rather than losing my job, the opposite occurred. Word went from one part of the corporation to another. The next day, I came in a little sore, but the others were beaten up. It was like they were grass and I had been the lawnmower. They were cut, beaten, and humiliated. One of the women said, "Well, I learned not to fight with Dot anymore. There is not enough money in the world for me to fight against her again."

This was the first and last fight. Before the fight, the police sergeant's daughter had been the ringleader of significant trouble at the plant, and the bosses did not know what to do about it. With one fight, I had finally put Mrs. Jezebel in her place, and their problems were solved.

The day after the fight, I was asked to go to the main office. The main bosses of the corporation were present. First, I was asked, "Who taught you to fight like that?" I explained. Then they wanted to know why I did not want to join the union. I said, "If I had just been asked politely or at least with respect, I would have joined the union. And if someone would have just explained the purpose of the union, I would have joined." One boss bought me a drink, and the other bosses shook my hand with thankfulness.

After the fight, we all became like a family. We became so close that when one person could not work and get her quota, we would fill in and make sure that she did.

Through this experience, I learned from the Lord just how to fight against sin. I became like Billy Sunday and his fight against sin:

> I'm against sin. I'll kick it as long as I've got a foot, and I'll fight it as long as I've got a fist. I'll butt it as long as I've got a head. I'll bite it as long as I've got a tooth. When I'm old and fistless and footless and toothless, I'll

gum it till I go home to Glory and it goes home to perdition.[6]

A few months after the fight, about four o'clock in the morning, I was called to go to the grandmother's house of the police sergeant's daughter. They wanted me to come to pray for her grandmother. I agreed.

When I walked into the grandmother's bedroom, it was like the room lit up. I knew I could not pray for her. I went into the kitchen and told the police sergeant that I could not pray for his mother, for the Shekinah Glory had fallen and lit up her room. I said to him that in two hours she would be with the Lord.

Two weeks after the death of his mother, the sergeant was admitted to the hospital. Again, the family called and asked me to go pray. I agreed and led the police sergeant in a prayer of repentance. Two weeks later, he passed away. The amazing thing about this story is the fact that this sergeant was open to talking to me about his salvation because he respected me. Why did he respect me? Because I had the guts to stand up to and fight his bully of a daughter. Yes, God can even use a fight to reach a lost soul.

I am amazed at how God can take conflict on a job and turn it for His glory.

Biggest Ulcer and a Patient

The stress from my job at the meatpacking plant caused me to have the biggest ulcer the doctors at St. Vincent Hospital had ever seen. I was near death when they admitted me. The doctors told me I had to lie flat on my back for fifteen days and could not eat anything but sweet milk and saltine crackers.

During my stay at the hospital, my nurse told me about another patient who was dying of cancer and was very difficult to deal with. The nurse said, "This lady ran three preachers out of her room today!" When the nurse left my room, the Lord spoke to me and told me to carry His gospel to her.

Because of the severity of my condition, I was not supposed to even sit up in bed. I certainly wasn't allowed to get up and go into the bathroom. If the ulcer ruptured, I would bleed to death in a moment. At that time, the hospital did not have an intensive care room for me. The staff put me in a room right next to the nurses' station and had blood waiting for me in case I needed it.

Sometimes, God demands you go to a quiet place to get away and pray. I prayed, "Lord, I am not qualified for this, but if You will keep the nurse from hearing me get up so I can go to the bathroom and pray, I will do it."

The next morning, I slowly got out of the bed. The nurses and a nun came running in and told me to get back in bed. I told them that God had healed me, and I had a job to do. The nun had her beliefs and I had mine, yet she said she would take the responsibility for my actions and let me go. After a few steps down the hall, I felt strengthened by the power of God. I felt so good I began to skip, and I skipped into the room of the cancer patient.

A nurse who had broken her foot was stationed in the room. When she saw me skipping in, she said, "You can bleed to death in a moment!"

I said, "The Lord healed me." She demanded an X-ray, and my healing was proven. The X-rays showed no sign of the ulcer. The doctors thought the X-ray machine had broken, so they sent me back to my room.

Consequently, I went down to the patient's room again and talked to the nurse. I told her, "The doctors and other nurses think the X-ray machine is broken. They are not fooling me. God has already healed me." The stage was set.

Just then, my doctor walked into my room and told me that the X-rays showed no sign of the ulcer. He said there was nothing the doctors had done that would have caused the ulcer to disappear. This was a miracle.

A nun had also come in about this time. The sister and I talked about the miracle. She said that this was the first big miracle she had ever seen. A young woman who had caused me trouble at work had also come to visit me. She was living a very ungodly life and was running from the Lord. As she heard about my miracle, the young woman ran out of the room crying and saying to the nun, "She can tell you something about miracles, Sister."

The sister told me about a special place in Spain where people can go to be healed. I said, "Sister, then God could not be a just God if He only healed in that place. For only the rich can go there. My Bible says that God has 'no respect of persons'" (Romans 2:11).

I told the sister, "I was lying in that bed, asking God just what I was going to do about this." I didn't feel qualified to talk to the cancer patient about salvation. I was trying to decide if I would obey God or not.

I decided to go. I walked into the cancer patient's room and began talking to the nurse with the broken foot about my healing. The patient was listening quietly to what I was saying. Then, I walked over to the patient and told her, "God wants to heal you so that you can raise your children. Today, you are to choose to live or to die. I give you until tomorrow to make up your mind."

The next morning, after I was discharged, I went back to her room and asked, "What is your decision?"

She cried and said, "I want to get saved, but I do not know how."

I said, "That is easy. Just repent. I will lead you into a prayer of repentance."

She prayed with me and accepted Christ, and God completely healed her. The cancer was gone! Thank God.

According to Greek grammar, to accept Christ is the same as receiving Him. Clement of Alexandria, a father of the early church during the second and third centuries, said, "Then we are made complete by accepting Christ as our Head and becoming ourselves the church."[7] Caesarius of Arles, a sixth century church father, said, "If you can accept Christ, you will be destined to reign with Him in heaven, but if however (God forbid it!) you choose the devil, you will be plunged with him into the underworld."[8] And lastly, A. W. Tozer once said, "To accept Christ is to know the meaning of the words 'as he is, so are we in this world' (1 John 4:17). We accept His friends as our friends, His enemies as our enemies, His ways as our ways, His rejection as our rejection, His cross as our cross, His life as our life and His future as our future. If this is what we mean when we advise the seeker to accept Christ, we had better explain it to him. He may get into deep spiritual trouble unless we do."[9]

Results of the Miracle

The story of how God healed me made a big difference in the workplace. It paved the way for a revival. God began to save my co-workers. Working in that plant became my victory rather than my defeat. I became the chief steward for thirteen years. God blessed the people with visitations, and He blessed me.

As time went on, I began to see the handwriting on the wall. The plant was going to close. So, I began to look for another job. I prayed and prayed. It was not just one prayer, but many that I prayed. Finding a good job during this time was almost impossible. But I believed in the God of the impossible.

I knew that I had to depend on God. The promise of the Father means nothing unless we pray. We must put the promises of the Lord into action by reminding God of His promises through prayer. God works in our lives according to our faith and our strength in our praying. Corrie Ten Boom once said, "Is prayer your steering wheel or your spare tire?"[10] If there are any inconsistencies in our lives, it is not God's fault; it is our own. Perhaps the troubles we face are because of sin, but many times they are because we do not pray. And if we do pray, we think prayer is easy. Really? Prayer is a task, a work, and a duty. It will take a person a lifetime to understand the complexities of prayer. Prayer is anything but easy.

I learned over the years to look forward and trust God and to look around and serve God. That is my life.

God Gives Another Job

I searched and prayed for another job, and the Lord finally answered me. The position was only part-time, but it was better than nothing. Sometimes, God makes small moves. Indeed, God sometimes takes only tiny footsteps.

I actually had two jobs at once. I worked on Saturdays in the meat department of a grocery store, wrapping meat. After that, I went to another store to work. I thanked God for those two jobs. I did not want any part of welfare.

I could have passed up these part-time jobs and held out for a full-time position somewhere "better." But that was not faith. One of the greatest hindrances for Christians is not believing when we pray. We should believe what we pray, and if something opens for us, we must step into it.

That little job in the meat department proved to be a big blessing for me. It provided discounted meat for my family. I was allowed to choose any meat that had turned dark from the bright lights shining down on the meat counter. The meat was still good. There were times when I carried home fifty dollars or more worth of meat for as little as ten dollars.

Mother and the Mental Hospital

The job also opened the door to help my mother. During that time, she was committed to a mental hospital where I volunteered. Committing her was one of the hardest things I ever had to do. My mother had tried to commit suicide, so my father brought her to me. I had worked closely with one of the doctors there. He told me there was one chance in a thousand to save my mother's life. He ordered a private room for her and told me that if there was any difference in the cost, he would take care of it.

My mother was in the mental hospital for several days until her system could be cleansed from the drugs she had been taking. She had never been a drug addict, and she never took any street drugs like heroin or cocaine. My mother had become hooked on pain and anxiety pills. And even this was not intentional. Her life was a living hell and utterly hard. No one should have to live such a life as my mother. Under such stress, she succumbed to temptations and fell into a deep cave of despair. It was only by her finding Jesus that she overcame despair and kicked her dependence on these drugs.

On a Sunday evening, I gave a party for the patients. The store I worked at closed on Sunday, which was a huge blessing. I was able to purchase at a discount all the hot dogs and hamburger meat that were beyond their sell-by date. Also, the managers gave all the sweets that were not sold. To see my mother come to me and enjoy herself with other patients was a gift from the Lord.

Another Attempted Suicide

Years later, while living with me, my mother tried again to commit suicide. One night, something strange took place. My mother's emotions went from one extreme to another. She screamed and groaned in torment and could not sleep.

After working all day, I stayed up all night to watch her. By early morning, I had finally fallen asleep when I was awakened by a knock on the back door. I knew that the lady I had hired to help me with my mother had arrived. But when I opened the back door to let her in, I was not prepared to face what I faced.

It was a cold morning, and a strong wind was blowing from the northeast. What I saw I will never forget. My eighty plus-year-old mother stood at the door, wet, and muddy from her head to her feet. She was freezing, and her lips were blue. I said, "Mother, what happened?"

She said, "I tried to drown myself. But every time I put my head under the water, an angel pulled it right back up." I knew immediately that some kind of miracle had taken place. There is no way that my mother could have climbed back over our bulkhead. The stones were just too slippery.

This is a clear example of Psalms 91:11–12. "For he shall give his angels charge over thee, to keep thee in all thy ways. They shall bear thee up in their hands, lest thou dash thy foot against a stone."

Immediately, I picked my mother up and carried her to the bathtub. I turned on the warm water and called the doctor. Thank God, we had a doctor who cared about my mother. He told us to take her to the hospital.

After several tests, the doctor discovered that my mother's medicines were unbalanced. They corrected her prescriptions, and that was the last time she tried to commit suicide. However, there was always tension in our home. We worried about what she may do and continued to pray and watch her carefully.

My mother was not saved. She sat in church for years, and all the while was on her way to hell. Just how many people are sitting in a church on the road to hell? Isaiah says, "Therefore hell hath enlarged herself, and opened her mouth without measure: and their glory, and their multitude, and their pomp, and he that rejoiceth, shall descend into it" (Isaiah 5:14).

A Door Opened for a New Job

God will remove any hindrance to His will, regardless of what the hindrance may be. Many times, I have seen God move despite people. I have seen Him repeatedly move the mountains that block His will (Matthew 17:20). If the mountains are not removed, there are hindrances, and the hindrances must be removed. In my case, God removed a hindrance to His will by allowing someone to die, which opened a door for me to receive another job.

When I was at this person's funeral, a personnel manager for a company was also present. She liked me and asked if I needed a job. She sent me an application for employment to fill out. At the time, I was still working part-time for the A&P Grocery store in the meat department. Since I was part-time, I was able to apply for this other job.

On the day of my interview, I almost had a car wreck. I had to slam on the brakes, and my car spun around in the road. I was so shaken up that I almost made a blunder on the test they gave me to see if I was capable and intelligent enough to do the job. I knew that day I had to depend on my Helper, the Holy Spirit.

I had to fight by the power of the Holy Spirit and go into spiritual warfare to get that job. I was praying, fasting, crying, and begging the Father for that job.

There is no guarantee that what a person is praying for is the will of the Lord God. If four people are praying about the same mountain, the Lord will only answer the prayer that follows His will (Matthew 17:20). This principle will be discussed in more detail later in the book.

In my life, I have learned that it is not the beginning that counts. It's the ending—the finish line—that counts. I began that job as a part-time worker, little and non-essential. God moved and made me an essential part of the company. Undeniably, the Lord took me from the tail unto the head. The Lord repeatedly fulfilled Deuteronomy 28:13 in my life as a Christian. It reads, "And the LORD shall make thee the head, and not the tail; and thou shalt be above only, and thou shalt not be beneath; if that thou hearken unto the commandments of the LORD thy God, which I command thee this day, to observe and to do them."

Knowing that Deuteronomy 28:13 is especially given unto the Jews, I still recognized that this is also a promise for Christians who have been grafted into the Abrahamic Covenant (see Romans 11:18–24).

Six months went by, and I heard nothing about the new job. My faith was being tested. True faith will stand through time and circumstances. All we must do is count the promise of the Lord as true and certain. Then God will stand with us.

I decided to put my faith into action. I put my faith on my feet. My feet were to become my faith in action. I dressed up with my best business suit and drove to Fernandina Beach. I asked to see the boss over the lab department.

When I walked into his office, I shook his hand and said, "I understand that this company is a good company to work for, and I am a good employee." I told him the reason that I was there, then asked him, "How long do you give a person to become a viscosity tester?" He told me that it generally takes six weeks. Prior to that, God had intervened and spoken to me to tell the boss, "I will work for free if I cannot learn that job within six weeks." These words got his attention. He hired me right then. One of the themes of my life is that I refuse to give up.

While another woman was applying for the job opening and scored higher in the chemistry part of the test than I did, I got the job by the intervention of God.

Troublemakers

In every church I attended, and at every job I worked, there have been troublemakers. Paul speaks of troublemakers in the church. "Now I beseech you, brethren, mark them which cause divisions and offences contrary to the doctrine which ye have learned; and avoid them. For they that are such serve not our Lord Jesus Christ, but their own belly; and by good words and fair speeches deceive the hearts of the simple" (Romans 16:17–18).

There are many troublemakers in the churches. They are very spoiled and selfish. Generally, they try to destroy the churches if they cannot get their way. As long as they get their way, there will be peace—a false peace—in the church. But if the minister rebukes them, or comes against them, all hell will break out. If the minister is not careful or smart, he will lose his church. It is the choice of the minister: fight, or compromise with the troublemakers.

There was a big troublemaker working in the lab where I wanted to work. This person messed up my samples and tried to get me kicked out before I secured the position. And I still had to hold on to my part-time job until I got the new job.

Oh boy, I did not want to begin this job as a tiger. I learned that trials and tribulations are great lessons. They prepare us for our walk with the Lord.

Looking back now, I see that all the negative experiences were for my training. Today we are often taught that God is the God of the positive. Christians today want everything in life to be positive. But how can we grow in our faith when everything is positive, good, and handed to us on a platter? It is impossible. In Genesis 1:2, the words "without form, and void" are negative words coming from the Lord. In our lives, there will be a mixture of positive and negative. Anyone claiming to be a Christian will suffer adverse life events. Indeed, for Christians, the negative events will overwhelm the positive events. Satan always congregates around the truly righteous!

During this time, Satan fought me on all fronts. He fought me at work, at home, and far away. He used my co-workers, my family, and my friends. There was nothing that Satan did not use against me. All evil was pouring against me, and I could only hold on to the Lord God and His Word.

Satan congregated around me so much so that all hell broke loose against me again. Satan struck against my son, my husband's job, and my family. For instance, my adopted brother was in so much trouble that they sent him to me to see what I could do with him. He knew how to steal anything. He was another Al Capone in the making. No one could help him. He truly was a lost cause, and he died a most horrible death. All of this was his choice; he chose his fate.

Satan enjoys attacking true believers. He hopes that, by attacking them, he can destroy their victory and promises before they can obtain them. Satan uses a manifold burden to try to make believers think their prayers are useless, and they should give up (2 Timothy 2:25–26).

A Test at Work

About three months into my new job, the first trial came when my boss told me that I was to come in on Monday during the day shift to calibrate the viscometer. Calibrating the viscometer had to be done correctly. One small mistake could cost the company hundreds of thousands of dollars.

Thankfully, not all the women co-workers were against me. Yet, some of the women did not measure my chemicals right. My boss could not understand this. He thought I was not doing the procedure right since I was a new employee. He was determined to figure out the problem. My boss told me to pour out what the workers had left for me. He placed the electric plugs into the socket so that the oven could stay at the right temperature. This was important because if the ovens didn't dry the sample at the correct temperature, the mistake would be disastrous to the final product. My co-workers kept pulling the oven's electrical plug out of the wall before my shift so my samples would be ruined.

From the cooked wood pulp, all kinds of products could be made, from polyester to cereal to ice cream. I was even the first person to figure out how to make plastic from wood pulp.

I was careful with my work. Calibrating the viscometer was very tedious in that you had to run it five times and use the average to get the T-zero. The T-zero had to be perfect. If the drop time was not close, it had to be washed out with sulfuric acid.

I carefully followed all the procedures, but my results were consistently not working out. Where I should have gotten a negative, I kept getting a positive. Such results did not make sense and cost the company more and more money. Because of this, one of the bosses pushed for me to be fired.

One day, I was doing viscosity testing, and my number three washer was crazy. It should have been a 9.72, but it was a 10.88. As my boss saw this, he began to slap the control sheet, laughing out loud, thinking that I was making a huge mistake. Then he went to the big boss.

I showed both bosses what I had done and how I had followed the procedures correctly. I repeatedly went over them with both bosses watching. I was doing it right. And they saw it, but the results were going crazy.

Then the plant siren went off, which meant something was wrong. The plant was going down, which meant that for the rest of the shift the workers would have nothing to do except clean up.

However, the old Dot had arisen when I checked the results. I got mad. On our control sheet, we had little blocks in which to write our answer, and one eight-hour period confirmed the eight hours before it. So, I wrote what I got in a big checkmark, which was 10.88.

The next day was Thanksgiving Day. Someone had altered the control sheet and had put a little mark on it. Whomever that was, he or she knew that I would get chewed out.

The office was closed due to the holiday. So, I knew I had lost my job when the big boss came into the lab on Thanksgiving Day. This boss was feared by everyone. He could chew a person out. Mistakes meant hundreds of thousands of dollars, if not millions, and he meant business.

The big boss said to me, "Mrs. Roberts, you had it hard working here. Could you look at that control sheet? Could you tell me what that washer should have been eight hours ago?"

I said, "Yes, sir! Around 9.72."

The big boss answered, "I was told that you had calibrated all of the viscometers since you have been here. Then you know how to back-calculate."

I said, "Yes, sir. That is right."

Then he said, "Why did you not put that 9.72 on the control sheet?"

Looking dead in his eyes, I said, "Because that is not what I get paid to do. I get paid to put what my answer is on the control sheet, and that is what I am going to do."

He replied, "Your honesty saved the plant more money than you could ever earn here."

No one knew that a pipe was leaking a wrong chemical into the product and ruining it. If the problem had not been detected, the whole product would have been rejected by the manufacturer.

The big boss told me if I had any problem, to tell them that I did not make the mess, I just ran the mess. And if they did not like it, they needed to see him.

Another Test at Work

Another time I thought I lost my job was when the scales were broken. The scales were an important part of our operation. Our company would have to hire a repairman to come fix them, and the delay could be hours or more than a day.

One day, I noticed the scales were broken, and I remembered how the repairman fixed them in the past. I sought to fix the problem myself. I sat down and took the scales apart, laying the parts on the counter. Wouldn't you know, of all the times that the boss picked to come into the lab, it was right then. He saw the scales torn down and I said, "You are not supposed to see this. Back out! Back out!" Surprisingly, he did back out!

I fixed the scales and ran the sample. To run the sample though I had to put it into a blender. My boss heard the blender going and brought another big boss in with him. They both sat down at the scales and tested the weights. The main boss looked up at the lesser boss and said, "She fixes these things. She would do a lot around here if we took the bits off." I saved the company time and money that day.

Once while I was working as a viscometer tester on the midnight-to-eight shift, the thermostat on the viscosity bath went out. It was three o'clock in the morning on a cold, rainy night. That bath needed to stay at a constant 25 degrees Fahrenheit. I knew where the boss kept the thermostats, but he was the only one allowed to handle them. I did not want to call the boss out of his bed at 3 a.m. to put a thermostat into the viscosity bath. So I handled it, and the woman working with me had a fit. She said, "Nobody, but nobody, touches that thermostat except our boss!"

As always, I paid her no attention and put the thermostat into the viscosity bath. The next morning, the boss came to examine the control sheet. I went and stood beside him. I whispered to him, "I might have got in trouble last night."

He whispered back, "What have you done now?"

I asked him to please check the thermostat over the viscosity bath. He checked, and he said, "Perfect. Thank you!"

God was laying a foundation for me. He had bigger plans for me than I could have never guessed. Where I thought they were running over me, God was using the circumstances to qualify me for two of the best jobs I would ever have.

A Revival at Our Plant

Going back to when I was first hired, I found out that I was the only one in the plant who was baptized in the Holy Spirit. I had my work cut out for me.

In 1975, God sent a prophet to Jacksonville by the name of Billy Joe Fain. In the meantime, at work, I had spent my spare time studying God's Word and anointing that place with oil.

Sitting at my desk and waiting for a sample to complete, I began studying on the Holy Spirit and made many notes. Time and time again, I asked myself questions about the Holy Spirit. I knew that the other women, my co-workers, were going to read my notes on the Bible. God was genuinely setting a plan in motion.

Billy Joe Fain came to Jacksonville, Florida, and brought in the anointing that was needed for my family to have a breakthrough and for my son to be healed. As far as we knew, no one in that city had enough of the Lord's anointing to bring about the miracle we needed.

One of my co-workers, who was well thought of, had a daughter who received the baptism of the Holy Spirit with the evidence of speaking in tongues at Fain's meeting.

My co-worker called me at work, very upset. She said that God had spoken to her daughter to give a sizeable amount of money to a prophet. She said that the Lord told her to take money that she was going to use on a down payment for a house and give it to this prophet.

My co-worker asked me, "What does he want with that money?"

I told her, "Go in your room, pray, and ask God." The next day, my co-worker told me that she lay in her bed crying. She told God that she loved her daughter more than anything in the world, and she did not want to come between God and her daughter.

My co-worker said, "The hand of God came out of heaven and slapped me out of my bed. A voice said, 'Take your hand off your daughter.'"

My co-worker had the following day off from work, so she went to Billy Joe Fain's revival. He prayed for her, and she received the baptism of the Holy Spirit.

The following Monday I was working the eight-to-four shift, and I heard the hallway door slam open, and in staggered my co-worker. She was drunk on the Holy Spirit and kept repeating, "Be not drunk on wine but by the Spirit, thus saith the Lord." The words came from Ephesians 5:18.

I couldn't believe my eyes. There was no way she would act like this on her own; she was always so dignified. I knew she would not stagger around quoting Scripture unless the Spirit had fallen upon her, and she was submitting herself to the movements of the Holy Spirit.

What I had been praying for had fallen upon the plant. The anointing came down like fire. Of course, I wanted the anointing to fall, but not like this. I said, "No, Lord. Don't do this. And do not do it to me."

People came from all over the plant to see what was going on with my co-worker. It was a sight. She kept on saying, "Be not drunk on wine but by the Spirit, thus saith the Lord."

A hush fell over the lab and offices. The Holy Spirit can come into a place as a lamb or as a lion, as a river or as a fire. He chose to come into our plant as a lion and a fire.

The movements of the Holy Spirit scared almost all the co-workers. One of the bosses came to me and said, "I do not know what you threw on her, but you had better take it off. She is going to blow herself and us up."

I replied, "I did not throw anything on her. But yes! If this is not of God, she will blow herself and us up. And I am ready to go to heaven. Are you?"

I had been praying for a revival to hit the plant where I worked, but also that it would hit Fernandina Beach and Jacksonville. Little did I know, God was pouring out a big dipper of His Holy Spirit all over the plant.

One by one, my co-workers received the baptism of the Holy Spirit. Besides this, people all over the plant were being delivered from demons. For a long time, I did not even know how many people had been saved, delivered, and baptized with the Holy Spirit. God is good!

Mrs. Jezebel and Her Husband

After a while, I was moved from my position as a viscometer tester into other various jobs. Mrs. Jezebel was my trainer. That was not her real name. I call her that because she had a spirit of Jezebel working through her. This spirit works through a person to hold others down, dominate, and control them. People with this spirit are overbearing and controlling. It is the same spirit that possessed Jezebel in the Bible (see 1 Kings 21).

In fact, many of my co-workers had the spirit of Jezebel. This particular Mrs. Jezebel was the worst. One day I caught her in the boss's office, telling him that I could not do the fact's tests. I lost my temper, pointed my finger at her and told her, "With God's help, I can do all things!" And I did.

I was greatly persecuted for the baptism of the Holy Spirit in my early life and the workplace. My father drove me from my home mainly because I was baptized with the Holy Spirit and spoke in tongues.

Regardless of just who it was, I was not going to let any job, any boss, or any Jezebel come between the Holy Spirit and me. I was not going to allow anyone to make me deny the Holy Spirit and His movements.

In fact, I told one of my little Baptist friends who had no mother that I would be her adopted mother. She saw just how hard it was for me to learn this job. She came to where I was in the back lab and prayed that God would help me learn the job. At that time, I believe the grace of God fell on me and gave me the gift of knowledge and the gift of wisdom. After that, there was nothing anyone could do to stop me from learning all the jobs.

Another time, this Mrs. Jezebel went too far. I grabbed her by the collar and shook her, but that did not hurt my reputation at all. The next day my counter was filled with Coca-Cola. Almost every person said, "Dot, if you must hit her, she will take out a warrant, but we will go in together for your bail. Don't worry!"

The morning after the incident, one of the bosses asked me if I felt better. I apologized to him. I told him that I was not a troublemaker, but I was not going to get run over either.

The husband of Mrs. Jezebel was a preacher. He had preached that Sunday night against speaking in tongues, saying that such practice was of the devil.

Here, we had a great situation. A preacher was preaching against speaking in tongues and claimed that such a practice was of the devil, while the wife of the preacher had her best friend speaking in tongues and coming into the workspace saying, "Be not drunk on wine but by the Spirit, thus saith the Lord."

The wife of the preacher, seeing this phenomenon, came home utterly miserable. She was questioning everything she had been taught. She was even questioning everything that her husband had just preached.

There was much of the Lord all over the workplace. The fear of the Lord even came home with Mrs. Jezebel so heavy that she could not sleep. She got out of bed, went to the coffee table, cried, and prayed. Her prayer was like this, "Lord if it is real, I want it." This was like my sister Ruby. She wanted anything and everything God had for His people. This preacher's wife received the Holy Spirit the same way that my sister Ruby received years earlier.

That night, the Holy Spirit fell upon the wife of the preacher and shook her badly. She began speaking in an unknown language that she had never heard, nor ever learned. She recalled that she felt as if her hair were standing straight up. She crawled to her husband's bed and shook him awake.

Her husband weighed over three hundred pounds. When he turned over, she was speaking in tongues, and he was so scared that he stood up in the bed. She took him by the hand and crawled back to the coffee table.

Immediately the power of the Lord hit him and shook him the way a hurricane shakes a tree. He had never known such power, and he knew he had to get help. He had to find somebody to explain this phenomenon to him—the baptism of the Holy Spirit.

The preacher did not fully receive the baptism of the Holy Spirit at the coffee table. He went to a Pentecostal preacher to explain this type of baptism to him. After understanding the baptism of the Holy Spirit, he received it later that week. He went back to his church and confessed what had happened to him.

I was introduced into the baptism of the Holy Spirit in the Pentecostal denominations, but here the baptism of the Holy Spirit jumped into other denominations. I did not know that I was entering the Charismatic Movement, which at that time was fresh and without the problematic doctrines of latter years.

It is a known fact that those who fight the most against the baptism of the Holy Spirit are often the ones who receive it.

A Psychic or Witch

I began to look at the workers at my plant as "my sheep." As I talked with them, I began to see some inconsistencies in how people interpreted the Scriptures. Some cut the Scriptures into two parts to prove a doctrine, and others were believing false doctrines. I asked some of them, "Where did you get that interpretation?" They explained that there was a lady who was coming into town to hold Bible studies in people's homes. I stopped at a little place called Yulee that night, and I said, "God, every step I take is of You. I bind that woman from bringing in false doctrine to my little sheep!" As time went on, I uncovered that the woman was in spiritualism.

Wonderful, I thought. I have a hard-enough time speaking to the living. We do not need to talk to the dead. God is the only One we should speak to. Speaking to the dead is necromancy.

Late one night, I was driving home and stopped at the railroad tracks, got out of my car, and prayed that this woman would be bound from coming over those tracks. I prayed she would no longer be able to come into Fernandina Beach to contaminate the minds and spirits of my little sheep.

After that night, she somehow got my phone number and called me. She wanted to meet me and some others for prayer. We agreed to meet at her house. During the prayer time, she said she saw my mother-in-law in the room. I said, "She better not be, she's dead and she can't cross back over!" David even remarked, after the death of his first son with Bathsheba, "I shall go to him, but he shall not return to me" (2 Samuel 12:22).

She replied, "Oh, you're the one holding up the service!"

I said, "Why, if we are of the same spirit?"

She backed up and said, "There's a dove flying around you. I can't touch you."

I replied, "Yes, I expect Him to be there. That dove represents the Holy Spirit."

She wouldn't touch me, however, the ones she did lay her hands on for prayer experienced dire consequences in the form of sickness and demonic spirits tormenting them. After that prayer meeting, we never saw the woman again.

Once the Holy Spirit came into the workplace, all the women, my co-workers, became the best of friends. Twenty years after I retired, one of the women I worked with met a man uptown who asked about me. She said, "You mean our protector?" He laughed. It was wonderful to have the opportunity to work at that plant for thirty-three years.

Clean up the Lab

One day, I was working on the fact's tests when my bosses came in to tell us that representatives from one of our customers were flying into Jacksonville. Apparently, the company was displeased with some of the products we produced. Our bosses told us that if we were not careful, we might lose this company's business.

The bosses told us to clean up the lab. At that time, I had been promoted to make all the chemicals that we used. One of the bosses saw all the praise and worship music we had in the lab and ordered me to put it all away. I knew in the Spirit not to put any of the praise and worship songs away. So I cleaned up my workplace in the lab. Just as I finished putting up all the chemicals that had been made, the representatives entered the building. I was the first employee to greet the president and vice president of this company that bought our products.

I took off my gloves and welcomed them. While the president of the company asked me some questions about what I was doing, the vice president noticed our praise and worship music on the table. He said, "I want to ask you something," and he pulled me away from the president and my boss to find out who was involved in the praise and worship music. I told him, "We all are. We pray over our products." I told him that I wanted to talk to him and the president. We went into the solution lab without my boss. There, I told the president and vice president about my son's testimony. I told them how my son had been born mentally challenged with severe brain damage and dyslexia. And I said to them that God had healed him and that he had jumped seven grades in school. They praised the Lord and walked with their hands in the air. It turns out that they both were Christians and baptized in the Spirit. They did nothing but praise the Lord for what He had done.

One of my bosses was walking in the hall and looked through the glass door wondering what was going on in the lab. He knew that if we lost this customer, we would close down for three months to a year. All our jobs were at stake, and he never knew what I would say or do. And here I was, by myself, talking to the president and vice president of this outstanding company. I can only imagine what was going on in my boss's mind. When the boss saw me talking to these men, it put him to praying.

When we came out of the chemical lab, the two representatives told our boss that they were ready to go back to the airport. They said that we could keep their business. After both left, our boss wanted to know what I had said. I just laughed and said that he would never know. We still had their business. Thank God!

Now, I want all to remember just how hard it was for me to learn this job. Yes, there were many times I left the plant crying. While the co-workers worked eight hours, I had to work ten hours to get my work done. I thought that my work was harder to accomplish because my tests were being sabotaged. Such things like this will put anyone to praying.

God will not just give a person a job. He will put a person where He can use that person as a missionary (see 2 Chronicles 19:7; 1 Peter 1:17).

Wine Not

The Lord repeatedly gave me good jobs, but I had to battle to keep them. Satan always brought his ambassadors of hell to fight against me. I fully believe Satan has ambassadors whose purpose is to pull people into hell.

Several times, I was required to attend work luncheons where they would serve alcohol. I refused to drink wine or any other type of alcohol. I watched alcohol destroy my father's life and my sister's life, and it was—and still is—an offense to me. My father was saved from alcoholism. There is no such thing as a sipping saint, and there are not—nor will there ever be—winebibbers in heaven. After all, Paul says, "And be not drunk with wine, wherein is excess, but be filled with the Spirit" (Ephesians 5:18). And Proverbs 23:20 reads, "Be not among winebibbers."

Satan loves to tempt us. My co-workers were always ordering a large jug of wine. After they poured wine into their glasses, they would intentionally set the jug of wine on the table right in front of me. Still, I refused to have a glass of wine.

My co-workers either did or did not understand my past. Regardless, they were tempting me to drink and become a drunkard like my father. I could not allow this to continue.

Finally, I'd had enough. At the next luncheon, I took control of the situation. When one of my co-workers set the jug of wine before me, I grabbed hold of that whole jug and poured every drop of wine into a nearby bush in the restaurant. I placed the jug back on the table and stayed quiet. I said nothing.

When one of the co-workers reached for the jug, he was surprised. There was no wine, not a drop. Others at the table also saw that there was no more wine. They all asked, "Where is the wine?"

I said, "The bush wanted a drink, and I poured it into the bush." That was the last time my co-workers ever put that jug by me. In fact, they never again drank wine at my table. By the way, the bush died from the wine.

Reflecting on this event now, I have changed my view about my experience. Today, I would have never bothered to even go to the luncheon. After all, Paul sets the prerequisite in such cases as these: "But now I have written unto you not to keep company, if any man that is called a brother be a fornicator, or covetous, or an idolater, or a railer, or a drunkard, or an extortioner; with such an one no not to eat" (1 Corinthians 5:11).

As time went on, I finally refused to go to the corporate Christmas party, remembering 1 Corinthians 5:11. My boss's wife asked, "Why do you not go any longer to the Christmas party?"

I said, "Because I love you and your husband too much to see you destroy yourselves by bringing a curse upon yourselves through drinking."

CHAPTER 8
MINISTERS WHO HELPED US

Smith Wigglesworth, a late nineteenth and early twentieth century revivalist, prophesied in 1936 that the established mainline denominations would experience a revival. He believed the Spirit of God would be poured out with the gift of the Spirit in a way that would surprise even the Pentecostal and Charismatic Movements.[1]

This prophecy was given to David du Plessis, who was the general secretary of the Apostolic Faith Mission. According to du Plessis, Wigglesworth had impacted South Africa even before his arrival. People had been hearing stories of the miraculous events and were captivated and interested in learning more. The example and influence of Wigglesworth on believers are still felt to this day.

I have felt this influence. A prophecy was given over my son's head when he was fourteen years old about a great revival, and that God was going to heal my son.

Similarly, the same man who prophesied over my son also said that God will bring the most significant revival with the greatest miracles, signs, and wonders that have ever been seen. Some have thought that either the Pentecostal or Charismatic Movement was meant. But something more significant is coming, even before the times of the Tribulation.

The man who prophesied over my son and spoke about a great revival was known as Billy Joe Fain.

Even before Billy Joe Fain came into our lives, God sent help through another man, Minister David Nunn. He was a national and international evangelist.

My life had been a living hell. I went from one disaster to another. No minister in Jacksonville, Florida, where I lived, could help me. Absolutely no one.

I heard about David Nunn, read some of his writings, gave offerings to his ministry, and heard his teaching. I knew that he had the anointing and the gifts of the Holy Spirit working through him because miracles and exorcisms occurred in his ministry.

One day, while I was at work, I decided to write to him. I could not find anything to write on, except stationary paper. I wrote my heart out on piece after piece of paper. I wrote to him what was occurring in my life, the family disasters, and every other thing that I could think of.

I mailed the sheets of paper in a large envelope to the Ministry of David Nunn. That was before 1975.

I thought I would never hear from him, but within a few weeks, Nunn wrote back and said, "You are fighting witchcraft!" Besides witchcraft, he said I was facing many evil spirits sent to destroy my whole family and me. He explained that God knew my condition and was sending help.

From this, I learned that one of my best friends was practicing witchcraft and throwing it upon my family and me. Her purpose was to see whose god was the strongest. In the end, she was saved, and Satan was defeated. I will discuss her more in another chapter.

W. V. Grant Sr.

Throughout much warfare and storms of life, God continued to send ministers to me to teach me.

One week, I went to hear a minister, W. V. Grant Sr., who came into Jacksonville to preach on the Battle of Armageddon. I was especially interested in this subject and had done a lot of research on it. I wanted to hear this man and what he had to say. When I arrived at the church that night, there were nearly two hundred people standing outside who could not even get in. All at once, a man took me by the elbow and led me through the crowd into the church. He sat me down in the second row, right on the aisle. I looked around the church to see if any older people were standing around, intending to give my seat to them, but something stronger than myself kept me in my seat. When the minister came to the platform, he said, "I said I was going to preach on the Battle of Armageddon, if the Lord let me. God changed my text when I came in the door of this church. It is for this young lady sitting right here. I am going to teach you how to pray tonight. God has called you to be an intercessor. He has called you to pray for other people. He loves someone else besides you and your bunch. He wants you to put your family on the altar and leave them there."

Billy Joe Fain

Who was this man? God sent Billy Joe Fain to Jacksonville, Florida, in the early 1970s. However, much of his story and testimony occurred before then.

When Billy Joe Fain was born, the midwife said, "Today, a prophet is born into the world."

Billy Joe Fain was born into a low-income family of nine children. They were so poor that most other girls and boys had more than Billy Joe and his whole family combined.

Living through the Great Depression and growing up in poverty, Billy hated being poor and wanted to go in the opposite direction. Even after witnessing miracles that occurred when his mother prayed, Billy went a worldly route.

Hot Bread

During the Great Depression, his mother worked for a rich family as a cook. From time to time, Billy rode with her and his father to the rich man's house.

His mother was ordered to cook the meals, but she was forbidden to eat anything. She was starving. But if she had eaten just a crumb, she would have been fired.

Utter hatred began to bubble up in Billy. He could not understand the reason for this, and the reason for God allowing this. His mother was hungry. Billy knew God is supposed to provide for His children. So why was this happening?

One day, Billy was waiting for his mother to come into the wagon. The food smelled so good, and Billy was so hungry. He went to crying and could not understand why he could not have at least a biscuit if God were so good.

He and his mother were riding home in their mule-drawn wagon, driven by Billy's father. Billy's mother asked, "If you could have anything to eat, what would it be?"

Billy said, "I want hot bread from the bakery with butter running down it!" The bread at the bakery was expensive, and it was impossible for his parents to buy it because of their lack of money.

His mother bowed her head and prayed, "Oh, Father, not for me, but for my child, give unto us fresh, hot bread with butter running down it."

As soon as she finished praying, Billy's father stopped the wagon. There was a box on the road right in front of their wagon. The father jumped out of the wagon to move the box. He picked it up and opened it, and surprisingly there was fresh, hot bread with butter running down it from the very bakery Billy requested. Billy persisted, "If you had prayed harder, we might have also gotten honey with the bread."

A great lesson was given to Billy: God is Jehovah Jireh—our provider. He was trying to show Billy the holy and honorable way of living and keep him from living a fugitive life of regret.

Bicycle

It seemed that no matter what God did for him, Billy always wanted more. He wanted a bike and other things that another child had. Billy said, "Well, I'm going to get these things some way. I'll get them for myself, and for others too." These words, little words, became seeds of destruction that led him into a life of crime, especially that of robbery.

In his neighborhood, a man had a recreation hall for all the children. This man was considered to be a good and moral man but looks can be deceiving. What most people did not know was the man had a back room in the recreational hall where he taught young boys how to be criminals.

As Billy went to this recreational hall, he discovered many boys had bicycles, and some even had automobiles at a young age. He knew something was going on. And he finally found out the whole story.

While his mother taught Billy the gospel and the moral way, there was something inside him that had a strong desire to become a criminal. And if he was to be a criminal, he wanted to be the best. So, he asked the man if he could come to his class to learn how to become a criminal.

The criminal classroom had blackboards and everything needed to teach the boys the art of crime. The boys even stole safes so they could learn how to open them in the classroom. Billy learned how to open safes, break into locked doors, and wire around burglar systems and alarms. He was taught how to use a gun, and which guns were the best to have.

Billy did his first criminal job when he was just twelve years old. He and three other boys drove up to the back of a place in an old '35 Ford. They found a large safe made of iron with wheels. They rolled the safe out the back door, but they were unable to get it in the car. They put a chain around the safe, through the handle, and pulled it behind the car. Of course, the iron wheels were knocking and rattling, and there was fire sparking from them as they dragged it down the road.

Regardless of what the four boys did, they were unable to open the safe.

However, the older boys at the recreational hall were able to do it. The man, whom they called "Pappy," took his portion of the money, which was almost the whole.

Pappy organized the boys into small groups and sent them out in pickup trucks. The boys were ordered to steal almost everything. Goods were easy to sell, especially during World War II.

Billy became known as a man with nerve. The other boys began to look up at him as a leader. And as time went on, Billy built a reputation as a criminal.

The Robber and a Gangster

As Billy grew older, he traveled from place to place to steal whatever he could. But his stealing increased in shape and size. He robbed poker games, stores, finance companies, insurance companies, banks, and almost any place that had money.

Even as a well-known robber and gangster with plenty of money, he still had the addiction to rob. He could not get enough money.

In one robbery, he took a gun with him and robbed eight men who were playing poker. These men were big criminals themselves. He had robbed the wrong place and thought his life had ended. Billy was only sixteen years old, but he lined up the eight men against the wall and took what they had.

After the robbery, a driver took him back to the train station so he could go back to Texas where he lived. However, two men were waiting for him. He did not know whether they were police or criminals.

Finally, he found out that they were part of the mafia. They took him to a large building where a man sat in a small office. As Billy stood there, he thought, *surely they'll kill me now.*

While fear gripped his whole soul, the man behind the desk started laughing and said, "Kid, what do you think you are doing?" It was impossible for him to answer.

Thinking that he was going to be killed, he jumped for the man's gun, but the man closed the drawer on his hand. Other men began beating him mercilessly.

The man behind the desk stopped the beating and said, "Kid, I like you." Not knowing what was going on, he said not a word. The other men took him to another office. Thinking that he was going to be killed, he was terrified.

The man finally came back and asked Billy to be his bodyguard. If he showed himself to be a valuable part of the gang, he would become this man's bodyguard. He became the man's chauffeur for a while and then became his bodyguard.

Crime Does Not Pay

Billy became one of the top forty criminals in the United States in the forties and fifties. In fact, he was on the top ten list of the FBI. Billy became famous and wealthy, but in the back of his mind, he knew that he would fall. Billy had a mother praying for him.

As time passed by, he owned at least three blocks of a large city. Billy had a reputation for using women, but he fell in love with a woman and married her. It was the first time he had fallen in love with any woman. In time, he and his wife had a child.

One of the greatest tragedies of Billy's life was the death of his child. He was unable to go to the funeral since the FBI was watching for him. There was an order to shoot and kill. Billy was so violent that the agents of the FBI could not believe that he could be caught alive.

Billy went into the woods near the cemetery and climbed the tallest tree he could find to watch the funeral. Afterward, he laid by his child's grave for the rest of the night and cried. When daylight came, he headed back to the woods.

He hated God for the death of his child and became so drunk that he tried to dig up his child's corpse. After digging for a while, he stopped. It was as if he had become temporarily insane. Grief can do that to a person who is also suffering from demon oppression.

Billy went back to work, though he was suffering from grief, drunkenness, and temporary insanity. He no longer cared about his life. He went into banks, shooting left and right and being fired upon by the bank guards and police. The interesting thing was that the shots were landing, but the bullets were not penetrating his skin. His shirts, which he was wearing, had holes in them, but still, the bullets could not penetrate his skin.

Further, various agents of the law chased him and shot at him with machine guns. Bullets were hitting his car and not him. In one incident, he was driving around a mountain with law officers pursuing him. His vehicle went off the road and careened down the mountainside, repeatedly rolling and tumbling. The first time, the car rolled, Billy was ejected from it. He landed on a shoulder or embankment with a lot of bushes. One FBI agent searched for him and came just a foot from Billy. It was death or life. Billy knew they had orders to shoot to kill. He then heard the agent saying, "No one could come out of this wreck and live." He and other agents left the scene. It would seem that God was protecting Billy.

It's important to note that Satan will use someone until he cannot use that person anymore and then double-cross him or her. During this period of grief, drunkenness, and temporary insanity, a man in Billy's gang turned on him. He told the police how to find Billy.

Soon after the death of his child, Billy knew what he had to do. He went to a church and asked the preacher to go with him to turn himself into the police. Billy was afraid that he would be shot.

When Billy went to the police department to turn himself in, there were guns drawn everywhere against him. There were enough government officials to capture a whole army.

Despite all this, his mother was still praying.

Sentenced to Ninety-Nine Years

Billy had done so much crime, that he had charge after charge against him mounting up to at least ninety-nine years of prison time. God was merciful, and the judge allowed the six sentences to run at the same time. However, this still meant that Billy got a life sentence with no chance of parole.

Billy's life in prison was difficult. Besides the fights, the guards used him when training the dogs to fight criminals. In one incident, the dogs tore his clothes off. When he looked up, a dog was coming at his face. When he covered his face, they got him in the back and the legs. They bit him all over. He fought them for a while but became so exhausted that his mind faded until he passed out. When he came to himself, the dogs were eating on him. He felt strength come back into his body, arose, and began fighting the dogs again until he nearly bled to death. One dog almost got a hold of his throat, until finally the guards stopped the dogs from killing him.

The prison sentence was not good enough for his mother. His mother went on a forty-day fast and sought the Lord to release her son. Billy's mother continued to ask God, "Where was His prophet?" After the fast, the Lord told her, "Go get your son. He has been freed."

She told her husband and the boys to hitch up the wagon and drive to the train station to pick up Billy. The Lord said to her that he would be on that train at that time. They did what she asked—more to please her than anything. They had no faith. The baby boy rode into town with them. They had no idea that his brother was going to be on that train. The train stopped, and his brother stepped off the train. The baby brother fainted. His mother, standing on faith, was home cooking lunch for her lost son.

Several conditions were set upon him to be released. He had to become a minister, give up all criminal activity, and make restitution for all that he had done. So, Billy Joe had to give up all the wealth he had gotten by stealing and serve God for the rest of His life.

1975

In 1975, there was a tent revival in Jacksonville. God told me to hear a minister at that tent. That night, the minister was called to pray for the people there. He said, "Lady, as I looked at you, all I can see is a ball of fire. You have got to pray for someone and lose some of that anointing. If not, you'll blow up." He said that a prophet was coming to town, and sometimes God only sent him for one family. I knew that he was for me.

At this time, Billy Joe Fain was on fire for God. His anointing was strong. He gave us words that have considerably come to pass.

In 1975, Billy Joe Fain prayed for my son and gave a prophecy. The prophecy said that God was going to heal my son, educate him, and move him into the direction of the ministry. God was raising my son to be a part of a Great Awakening.

Soon after, Billy Joe Fain faded away from our lives. He had done all that God wanted him to do. Regardless of what happened after 1975 or our times with him, God had his hand upon him. Sometimes, a prophet, or another type of preacher, comes into our lives just for a few years.

In the revival that we experienced with Billy and others, three noted experiences should be mentioned: a change of clothes, the Shekinah Glory, and angels unawares.

A Change of Clothes

One day, Billy came to our house to eat lunch. It was not unusual for preachers to eat at our house. During lunch, Billy looked at my husband and said, "Do you have an old pair of pants and an old pair of shoes?"

My husband said, "Yes."

Billy said, "Get them. I must give you my boots and my suit of clothes."

Elias said, "Your boots and your suit of clothes will not fit me."

Billy replied, "If God said for me to give them to you, they would fit." And guess what? The pair of boots and the suit of clothes fit perfectly on my husband. Even with boots and clothes, God can perform a miracle.

The Shekinah Glory

As everyone was praying and singing before the Lord, a manifestation of the Shekinah Glory as a mist occurred. It visibly covered the tent flowing around and touching my sister Sue three separate times. As the mist passed over the heads of the people, many fell out as if they were dead.

An Angel Unawares

One night, a man appeared in front of the tent. He spoke with such wisdom and had such a holy appearance that we were certain he was an angel. His appearance was beautiful. Why did he come? I had been studying about demons, even though I was not yet mature enough to handle the topic of demons. When a saint studies about demons, evil spirits will congregate around him or her. Therefore, the saint had better know how to fight them. The first thing I told the angel was that I was studying demons. He replied, "Why study demons? Study angels! They help the saints." I was dumbfounded. I had thought that studying demons was a mark of maturity. I learned so much from our conversation. The last thing I asked was, "Can we pray for you?" Appearing and acting like a man, he humbly bowed his head and accepted our prayer. Since then, this same man has appeared in two visions, proclaiming himself as an angel of the Lord and coming in the name of the Lord. From our conversation, I found out that he affirmed that Jesus Christ was born from a virgin, was crucified, and arose from the grave. He also proclaimed that Jesus Christ is God, and he accepted all the fundamental doctrines of Christianity. Remember Hebrews 13:2, "Be not forgetful to entertain strangers: for thereby some have entertained angels unawares."

Bud Chambers

In the midst of the revival being held by Billy Joe Fain and others, Bud Chambers came into Jacksonville and held a few services. One of his gifts from the Lord was music. He wrote many of his songs, worked in the prophetic, prayed for the sick, and cast out demons.

I will never forget the first night that my husband and I met him. He said, "The Lord demands that I go to your home!" That was not the first or the last time a minister had been to our home. My husband and I agreed and said that we would have dinner prepared for him when he came.

The strangest part was when we asked if he needed directions or to be picked up. The most amazing thing came out of his mouth, "No. The Lord will give me the directions to your home." When both my husband and I heard that, we simply gave one of our house keys to him and went home.

We went ahead and ate our dinner, prepared ourselves for bed, and went to sleep. When we woke up, Bud had found where we lived, unlocked the back door, sat down, and eaten dinner. After eating dinner, he drank the coffee we had prepared for him and wrote several songs.

He said, "What an anointed house you have. The presence of the Lord is throughout the house, and there are many angels present."

I will never forget as long as I live how Bud knew the directions of our home. No human told him and there were many miles between our home and the revival services. The Lord led him to our house. And what was more surprising is the fact that the Lord led him to our back door. The key we gave him was for the back door and not the front door. And neither my husband nor I told him that fact.

Minister and Fire Ants

I have purposely forgotten the name of another minister. While he did help us somewhat, the importance of meeting this minister was not what some would think. He taught us that it is not good for a minister to lie about money.

We invited this minister to our home where my husband and I cooked a great meal for him and his associates. And we had already made up our minds to help him and his ministry.

He and his co-workers went down to our backyard where there is a creek. The minister told us he had no money. Immediately after speaking these words, he stepped into a bed of fire ants. They entered through his shoes and began stinging his feet repeatedly. He had to pull off his shoes, and a fifty-dollar bill fell out of his right shoe. At that time, a fifty dollar bill was a considerable amount of money.

I merely said, "You did not have to lie about being broke; we were already going to give you an offering." We stood by our words and gave him an offering. God was testing us and testing the minister. We had been commanded to give to him regardless of what he did. Our hands were free of any blood or guilt. What he did after that incident was left up to him.

Al Edenfield

Another prophet that meant so much to our family was Al Edenfield. His full name was Alton R. Edenfield.

He was born into a Catholic home. Both his father and mother were alcoholics. They were Christian in name only, rarely went to church, and just knew about Christ. They never knew Christ until later. Therefore, Al did not have a godly heritage to lean on.

But God always has the means to touch us. Al had been watching an old Pentecostal woman walking up and down the road, waving her hands in prayer.

For a time, he went to her church and watched what was going on through a window. He had never seen anything like this. It was frightening, exciting, and bewildering. He saw people speak in tongues, fall, shake, and speak as if God Himself were speaking. The few times he went to the Catholic church, there was nothing like this.

He was still small. So when he went to the little Pentecostal church and looked through a window, he stood on an orange crate.

One day, as he was standing on an orange crate, looking through a window, he fell. Now his secret was out in the open. Church members came out and saw him there. Now that everyone knew what he had been doing, Al finally got enough courage to go inside the church.

That night, he got saved. He went home to tell his father and mother that he had received the Lord. But his father and mother took a broomstick to him and threw him out of their house. He had no place to go. The blood was running down his back, where his father and mother had repeatedly hit him. He remembered the old Pentecostal lady who lived down that street. He went to see if she would let him stay with her. She saw him, bruised and bloody, and opened her door and home to him.

Like some other sects, Al's father and mother had a funeral for him. To them, he was dead because he had received the Lord. Both he and the old Pentecostal lady watched the funeral from a distance. He knew that he could never go home again. He had no other choice but to join the Army. This was during World War II.

What Is in Your Pocket?

Shortly after Brother Al entered the Army, he was walking along the highway, thumbing a ride to church. A large vehicle pulled over and stopped.

The man driving the car asked him, "Where are you going, son?"

"I am going to church."

The man said, "Any soldier wanting to go to church, it is my honor to give him a ride."

A few miles down the road, Brother Al saw something move inside the man's pants pocket. He asked the man, "What is in your pocket?"

"It is a rattlesnake that we use at our church."

Brother Al said, "Whoa! I will get out at the next stop." Several years later he remarked about this experience, "If that were the only church out there, I would not have dared go through its door."

Can I See My Mother?

While still living in his hometown, Al heard that his mother was in the Catholic hospital, sick with cancer. He went to see her, but a Catholic nurse refused to let him in.

When Al got back to the base, he was down in spirit and weeping. The sergeant saw him and asked, "Al, what is the problem?" Al told the sergeant the story about his mother. The sergeant said, "Al, get on your best uniform and shine your shoes. Go back to that hospital to see your mother. If the officials refuse you entrance, call me. No young man who is going overseas should be stopped from seeing his mother. The Army will make sure that you see your mother."

Al prayed all night, dressed up, and went back to the Catholic hospital. He knocked on the door of the room where his mother was. The sister saw him and began to close the door. Al grabbed hold of the sister, and the power of God hit Al and the sister at the same time. The sister fell to the floor almost unconscious. She did not get in Al's way any longer. When she came to, she ran away from the power of God. (I thought she was a servant of God. If so, why did she run from the power of God?)

As Al walked up to his mother's bed, and she looked up at him. He said, "Mother, this is your son, Al. I am going to pray for you." Bloody fluid was running from her mouth. And there were tubes in her. Al took a washcloth and wiped her mouth. He picked her up and bowed down with her in his arms. Immediately, the power of God shook Al as he prayed for her. When he had finished praying, he put her back into bed. As he walked to the door to leave, he looked back and saw just one teardrop run down her cheek.

In all the years that he knew his parents, neither of them had ever said that they loved him. Never!

Before Al left for Europe to fight in World War II, he heard that his mother had been completely healed. As he was leaving town, he took a small piece of brown paper, wrote a letter on it, and addressed it to his mother and father. He wrote, "Whatever corner of the world I am found in, I will be praying for you and father." He wrapped the paper around a lump of coal and threw it out the window of a moving train. Only in his later years, did he hear that his parents received it and kept it.

He excelled in the Army and became a driver for a sergeant. He was able to stay at the sergeant's home before he went overseas.

During War World II

While in war, other soldiers made fun of Al because he spoke in tongues. When the campaign began, the sergeant, who never made fun of Al, always wanted Al in the Jeep with him and always wanted him speaking in tongues. Why did the sergeant not laugh at or criticize Al's speaking in tongues? Because his own mother spoke in tongues.

During the fighting, Al heard soldier after soldier screaming in pain and dying. He crawled out of his foxhole, even though the sergeant said, "I will shoot you if you go." Al was willing to take that chance.

Al crawled from soldier to soldier. Many were dying; others had their arm or leg missing. He led them in a prayer of repentance. How many soldiers were saved by the persistence of Al's going from foxhole to foxhole will only be known at the Judgment Seat of Christ.

Brother Al often said, "If I could have anything in heaven, I would like to see all the soldiers I witnessed to on the battlefield."

One night, God spoke to Brother Al, "You are going home tomorrow. Your Jeep will be hit, but I will be with you. You shall not die."

The next day, a shell struck close to the Jeep and blew it up. Brother Al did suffer from that explosion. He became paralyzed and was unable to walk any longer.

Not only was most of his body paralyzed, but every hair on his body was burnt off. To make matters worse, he would be arriving home with no one to take care of him. His parents had still disowned him. Al was on disability. He was in a wheelchair and unable to walk or move any part of his body, except one hand and arm.

The same old Pentecostal lady who had taken him in as a child now greeted him as he came home, and again she took care of him.

Al, You Are Called to Preach

In the meantime, God called Al to preach. The old lady had no problem with this and his condition. She said, "Al, you can preach from a cot." So he began one of the most significant ministries that I ever had a part of participating in and ministering unto the Lord.

Brother Al began his ministry by preaching on Zacchaeus in the tree (Luke 19). Six weeks later, he still had Zacchaeus in the tree, and he was never able to preach him down. The power of God came down so powerfully that people ran to the altar and submitted to conversion and became saved.

Meanwhile, the military people heard that a disabled soldier was preaching. They filled the church and ran unto the altar for salvation.

Brother Al became a prophet. He prophesied that God would heal a mentally disabled young man, and that took great faith. Further, he prophesied that the same young man would jump seven grades in school. Both prophecies came to pass two years later. My son was healed from a mental disability, including dyslexia, with brain damage, and jumped seven grades.

Kathryn Kuhlman

Several well-known evangelists are indebted to Brother Al's ministry, especially in the prophetic and healing gifts. And even today, one massive ministry owes much to Brother Al, for the minister's wife was saved and baptized into the Holy Spirit in Al's services.

Immediately after returning home from World War II, God opened several doors for him to minister. He went to several churches, preaching and praying for people. Many people were healed and received miracles during these times, and yet Brother Al was still in his wheelchair.

He had to have help to take a bath, to use the bathroom, and he had a catheter bag. It is impossible for any saint to be in such a condition and not have the devil speak to him or her, denouncing God. How many whispers did Satan speak about God when Brother Al was living in such a shameful condition? And what made it worse was the fact that God was healing and performing miracles for others.

One day, Brother Al was rolling down the street and had heard about a woman preacher in town—Kathryn Kuhlman. He thought, "I wonder what

Mrs. Jezebel is up to." He did not think that much about Kathryn Kuhlman.

Brother Al made up his mind to go to her service. He rolled into the auditorium and sat where he could well see what would be going on.

After a lot of singing, Kathryn Kuhlman finally came to the platform. She preached a wonderful sermon. As God began to move in the service, she looked in Brother Al's direction and said, "You are a servant of the Lord, aren't you? Rise up and walk in the name of Jesus Christ!" Immediately Brother Al arose out of his wheelchair and repented. He never needed that wheelchair again. But the healing was not yet complete. As Brother Al proved himself, the healing continued to be more and more complete.

Brother Al did say, "Since that time, I have been walking ever since."

An Elderly Couple and Biscuits

Brother Al walked as he preached, but he still had to use crutches. At least he was able to go to the bathroom by himself and no longer needed a catheter bag.

As Brother Al went from church to church, he had to go to home after home to invite the people to the services. His services included singing, preaching, and praying for people.

In the winter, Brother Al was required to go from home to home even when it was very cold. He was warned not to go to one particular house because he would be treated horribly. Of course, Brother Al did not allow difficulty to bother him.

In the mountains, he slowly walked with his crutches in the snow. He was cold, and he did not have very warm clothes.

He came to a home where an elderly man and woman lived. He knocked on the door. The door opened and immediately shut. Again, Brother Al knocked on the door. The door opened, and the man said, "We are not interested." And he closed his door again.

Brother Al, not believing in the word "can't," knocked again. When the elderly man opened the door, Brother Al put his foot into the door and begged the old man to allow him in from the cold. The old man allowed Brother Al entrance.

While Brother Al had gone through much embarrassment due to what happened in World War II, he was a very clean man and believed in a spotless home. If he saw a hair in his food at a restaurant, he would most likely faint.

The home of the elderly man and woman was not clean. They rarely had anyone in their home.

As Brother Al and the elderly man talked, the man said, "This is the first time a minister has come to our home."

For better or for worse, the time that Brother Al had come to their home was when they were having dinner. Now dinner to them was merely coffee and biscuits.

The elderly man begged Brother Al to stay and eat with them. He said, "Stay and have vittles with us." He tried his best not to eat with them. He could not see how he could eat what they had. His stomach was very weak due to the consequences of World War II. But he finally agreed.

Neither the elderly man nor his wife understood the word "water" when it came to how to clean their hands.

The elderly woman had had the coffee on for hours. It was repeatedly boiling and had turned into something like oil or black tar. The ashes coming from their wood stove covered every place in their home, especially the kitchen. Everywhere Brother Al sat, there were ashes. And everywhere he looked, there were ashes.

The elderly woman began to prepare the biscuits. Her hands were very unclean, and her nails were filthy. And ashes were falling upon the biscuit dough. The more he saw the ashes fall upon that dough, the more his stomach turned. And ashes fell upon the butter too. He prayed, "O Lord, let me find a door!"

Of course, the elderly woman picked out of the dough a large piece for Brother Al and said, "This one is for you." Internally, Brother Al was having a fit. But he knew that regardless of his stomach, the spirits of this elderly couple were more important than his stomach.

As she baked biscuits, Brother Al talked and talked to the couple. He told them his testimony of how he had survived World War II, how God had delivered him from a wheelchair, and how God is the only answer for all people.

At last, dinner came, and coffee was served. The elderly man poured and poured coffee into a coffee cup for Brother Al. It took a long time for that coffee to be poured into that coffee cup.

The biscuits came out of the stove. Brother Al admitted that the biscuits smelled good. But before he could stop the elderly woman, she slapped butter with ashes into his biscuit. His stomach turned over and over. Brother Al hated butter.

He did not know whether he could drink that coffee and eat that biscuit, but for the sake of this elderly couple, he would try. The more he chewed the biscuit, the bigger the biscuit seemed to become. He drank coffee to wash that biscuit down, but that made things worse.

As he was finishing the biscuit, the elderly woman prepared another large biscuit for him. She said, "This big biscuit is for you." "Oh no," Brother Al thought.

If there is a crown for drinking black tar coffee and eating biscuits with ashes in them, it is here. If there is ever a person who could be a martyr for drinking coffee like this and eating a biscuit-like this, it is Brother Al.

It is hilarious when we understand the temperament of Brother Al, who always checked for hair in his food before he would eat and never would have eaten a biscuit with ashes in it unless God demanded it. And he could not stand butter.

The black tar coffee and the biscuit with dirty butter and ashes in it became an instrument for bringing two elderly persons into the arms of Jesus Christ.

When the dinner ended, Brother Al invited the elderly couple to his service, and they agreed to go the next day.

Brother Al was concerned that they just might not come to his service. He prayed and prayed. The service began. Brother Al had the singers sing, sing, sing, and sing. The singing continued going on in this service. He did not want any preaching to occur before the couple showed up. Nor did he want any altar call before they came. And last, he did not want any moving of the Holy Spirit until they could come. He sought the Holy Spirit to wait.

As the singers were becoming exhausted, the church door slowly began to open. The elderly couple slowly came through the door and sat down in the back.

Brother Al preached a hell and brimstone sermon. He preached that this could be the last call. So much conviction was in the church, almost everyone was crying, weeping, and repenting. There was a run to the altar.

These two elderly people left their seats, moved slowly to the altar, and Brother Al led them into a prayer of repentance. Both changed from darkness unto light. Both were saved. At the end of their lives, Brother Al performed both of their funerals.

His Mother: Possessed and Insane

As Brother Al was preaching and praying for people, he had very little connection with his family. He knew his mother had been healed, and that they had received his piece of brown paper. But he had lost touch with them.

A word came from his family that his mother had gone insane and that she may have to be put into a mental hospital.

He immediately went to his mother's house and found her utterly demon possessed and insane.

For a considerable amount of time, he tried to help keep his mother in her home. He sat with her and tried his best to resolve the situation. It became apparent that he must do more.

The situation became so severe that Brother Al had to handcuff his mother to the bed and sleep in the same bed with her, praying and rebuking the demons. This went on for days, if not weeks.

All that Brother Al had would not help. He sought that God would deliver his mother, but it was not time.

Finally, he had to put his mother into a mental hospital. She stayed in that place for months. Her mind was utterly gone; evil spirits were speaking through her, and she acted like an animal. All dignity had gone. She was throwing her feces all over her room. She was eating her flesh, and the staff ordered that all her teeth be pulled out.

Brother Al sought the Lord to go to the hospital to pray for her. The Lord said, "No! It is not time." This tore into Brother Al. He was praying for people and casting out demons, but he could not help his own mother.

In this case, the insanity came from demons and did not come from some mental disease or defect. Her condition was mainly due to her disobedience. When God had healed her in the past, she still had not made things right with God and had not made things right with her son.

Brother Al was at a particular church and heard the Lord say, "Al, it is time. She has had enough. Go set her free. Go to the mental hospital, and I will heal and deliver her." God was about to do His part, but Al had to do his part too.

He left the revival and drove quite a long way back to his town where he grew up. He went into the mental hospital and sought the doctors and nurses to let him see his mother. Of course, the doctors and nurses did not believe in demon possession.

The staff of that mental hospital finally, and reluctantly, allowed him to see his mother. She had become so violent that the staff had to put her in a padded cell and put restraints on her.

Brother Al, walking in the power of the Lord, told them, "Release my mother from those restraints." This occurred before he entered the room. As soon as he came into the room, his mother, without restraints, violently ran toward him and tried to kill him. She was wild like an animal. She wanted him dead. Of course, it was not her. It was those demons.

But Brother Al was up for the task. He immediately leaped forward and laid his hands upon her. He said, "Release her in the name of Jesus Christ." As soon as those words came out of his mouth, the power of God hit his mother, the demons fled, and her sanity came back.

At that moment, as what happened to Paul, she was instantly saved and delivered (Acts 9:1–43).

Before that deliverance, she looked at Al with so much hate, but after the deliverance, she looked at Al with so much love. She could finally say, "Al, I love you." When the demons left, and her sanity came back, she said, "Hi, Al! What am I doing here?" just like Jesus.

Sometime later, Al's father was also saved. In the end, Brother Al did both of their funerals.

Ex-Lax and the Brownies

Brother Al married and became a pastor of a small church, where he helped as many as possible.

Brother Al was to hold a service. The church did not have indoor plumbing, and there were no indoor bathrooms. Everyone used an outhouse.

As Brother Al was preparing to preach, he thought that it might be good if he went to the bathroom ahead of time. He went to the outhouse and sat down to do what comes naturally. Like every other church, his church had its crazy kids—those kids who love to play pranks. One kid took a switch from a tree and went with the others toward the outhouse. The kid began to hit the outhouse, and the switch entered the outhouse like a snake.

Brother Al, thinking that this was a snake, left the outhouse with his pants still down. Everyone saw him with his pants down while all the kids were rolling on the ground with laughter.

If embarrassment could kill, it would have killed Brother Al. He took the prank well, but it was the wrong timing. I would not doubt that his sanctification left him for a time. And how could he preach and pray for people when his mind was still on the outhouse incident?

He did not treat the kids horribly. He refused, at least for a time, to lower himself to their level of pranks. Time, of course, did change.

Both Brother Al and his wife could not allow these kids to get away with this. They needed a lesson.

It was time for a seasonal party. Both Brother Al and his wife thought and thought about how they could teach the kids a lesson.

They concluded that Ex-Lax and brownies were the answer. They prepared the brownies and added Ex-Lax to one batch for the kids who loved pranks and left the Ex-Lax out of another.

The kids loved the party, and they loved the brownies until about halfway home. The driver stopped the car, and all the kids ran into the woods, where they did what was natural. And the only thing they had to wipe with was the old fashion toilet paper, corncobs.

Do not prank a prankster, and do not do any evil against a minister.

The Nude Beach and the Preacher

More and more, the Lord blessed Brother Al. What meetings he had. I am a personal witness to these meetings. Sometimes he prayed for everyone. Other times, he only prayed for a few. And his style of preaching was unique. He told story after story and would make people roll with laughter.

As God was blessing him, and he was invited to a church to have a revival, the pastor of that large church did everything right for Brother Al. The pastor and his staff treated a man like Brother Al with great respect and reverence because he and his staff saw the giftings of Brother Al and his office.

The pastor set up Brother Al in a lovely hotel. He supplied Brother Al with good food and took him to several good restaurants. The pastor especially knew the consequence of mistreating a person like Brother Al, as long as such a person is in the will of God.

Brother Al ate a delicious meal, took a wonderful bath, and went to sleep in a beautiful bed. In the morning, a worker at the hotel knocked on the door with his coffee and breakfast.

Everything was going well until he pulled back the curtains. The pastor and his staff had booked Brother Al at a hotel with a nude beach.

All Brother Al could see on the beach was nude bodies. One person after another was nude on the beach. He could not believe it. His eyes saw things that once seen cannot be unseen unless God delivers that person.

People say that young people are the ones who are the sexual problem. But Brother Al observed that this was not the case. Almost everyone on the nude beach was middle-aged or elderly. According to Brother Al, gravity affects our bodies terribly. Everything seems to sag or drop.

He saw that age makes little difference to the power of lust. Elderly men, either half-dead or almost dead, were on the beach completely nude. What a sight. And, according to Brother Al, whenever young women came by, these near-dead elderly men became alive again. They walked as fast as possible to catch these young women.

Upset, Al called the pastor. The pastor did not know about the nude beach there and raced to Brother Al's rescue. I wonder if the pastor thought Brother Al might go down to the beach and exorcize demons.

Before Brother Al went to another hotel, he and the pastor checked the beach. And from then on, Brother Al was always careful about where he stayed and when he opened the curtains.

Brother Al and a Convention

Somehow—only God knows—Brother Al was invited to a convention. Brother Al had been against women preaching, but his experience with Kathryn Kuhlman taught him that God could use women to preach and proclaim His gospel.

During one particular convention, a man was preaching against women, trying to prove that women had no part in the gospel and no part in the proclamation of the gospel. If that be the case, no woman could even teach Sunday school.

The man had a contrary spirit; his preaching was unsound and belligerent. As the minister was preaching, with no anointing present, he shook his leg and said, "I feel the anointing in this place so much so that I can run a mile." Brother Al and some women stood up and said, "Obey the Spirit! Obey the Spirit! Obey the Spirit, man! Run!"

Some people believe that women have no right to teach or preach in the church, based on 1 Corinthians 14:34, which states, "Let your women keep silent in the churches, for they are not permitted to speak." The problem with this thinking is that it binds women from serving in any capacity within the church. In other words, any woman would not be allowed to do anything in the church, including taking care of children and singing. We must understand the history of the Corinthian church and especially the Greek grammar used.

Brother Al and the Prostitutes

Brother Al was in a city holding a revival for several days. The anointing was going outside the church and touching people on the street.

One night, Brother Al was praying for souls to be saved. The anointing began to pull people from the streets. Three scantily dressed prostitutes walked into the church service.

Rather than allowing the Holy Spirit to work on them, the ushers wanted to escort them out. But Brother Al said, "No! I have been praying the prostitutes into the church services." When the altar call was given, the three prostitutes ran to that altar. Brother Al took his coat off to cover one of them and others followed suit. According to Brother Al, the tears began to flow from these prostitutes with much repentance. Their cosmetics were running everywhere. The prostitutes were saved that Friday night.

According to Brother Al, the mascara was a sight; the prostitutes looked like raccoons in the face. The mascara was black, and it just kept on running down their face, and as they tried to wash it away, the mascara covered their whole face.

Their clothes were very tight and short. The clothes were what some women call "hooker wear." During the process of their deliverance from evil spirits, the prostitutes did not disgrace themselves by showing anything. The power of the Holy Spirit restrained their clothes and refused anything to be seen that was not appropriate. For example, while the breasts of the prostitutes were partially visible, these women pulled their clothes together so that no breast or a part of a breast could be seen. Shame came back to them.

If only women and men in the church could learn what these prostitutes learned, they would experience the change that Jesus Christ gives the saints. Too many times, I have had to throw covers over women who enter the presence of the Lord inappropriately. They have no idea the judgment that they can receive from the Holy Spirit if something is not done.

Being in the presence of God demands appropriate clothes. Peter Cartwright, during the Second Great Awakening, said, "The moment we saw members begin to trim in dress after the fashionable world, we all knew they would not hold out."[2] In other words, one of the critical things he looked for was clothes. He could tell if someone was going to lose their awakening (conversion) when he or she changed back to the clothes of the world, especially those that were tight and short.

Furthermore, in his autobiography, Peter Cartwright mentions a group of women who became awakened (converted) when they met the Lord Jesus Christ in 1806:

I traveled in the state of Ohio in 1806, and at a largely-attended camp meeting near New Lancaster, there was a great work of God going on; many were pleading for mercy; many were getting religion; and the wicked looked solemn and awful. The pulpit in the woods was a large stand; it would hold a dozen people, and I would not let the lookers-on crowd into it, but kept it clear, that at any time I might occupy it for the purpose of giving directions to the congregation.

There were two young ladies, sisters, lately from Baltimore, or somewhere down east. They had been provided for on the ground in the tent of a very religious sister of theirs. They were very fashionably dressed; I think they must have had, in rings, earrings, bracelets, gold chains, lockets, etc., at least one or two hundred dollars' worth of jewelry about their persons. The altar was crowded to overflowing with mourners; and these young ladies were very solemn. They met me at the stand, and asked permission to sit down inside it. I told them that if they would promise me to pray to God for religion, they might take a seat there. They were too deeply affected to be idle lookers-on; and when I got them seated in the stand, I called them, and urged them to pray; and I called others to my aid. They became deeply engaged; and about midnight they were both powerfully converted. They rose to their feet and gave some very triumphant shouts; and then very deliberately took off their gold chains, earrings, lockets, etc., and handed them to me saying, "We have no more use for these idols. If religion is the glorious, good thing you have represented it to be, it throws these idols into eternal shade."[3]

There was no church service on Saturday night, so Brother Al rode around the city and prayed. It was early evening, and there on a street corner stood the three former prostitutes, dressed provocatively. They were—if I may say—ready for business, but something was amiss. They had had no offers of money. Indeed! There had been no Johns yet. It was as if a sign hung over them saying something like, "Not for sale any longer." Thank God.

When Brother Al recognized them, he immediately stopped and picked them up. He taught them that the Word of God speaks about the need for living a godly life once a person is changed. The former prostitutes did not know they could not go back to their old lifestyle.

Well, to be sure, the spirit of Jezebel is always in a church. Three church women saw Brother Al pick up the three former prostitutes, and they could not wait to call the pastor and tell him what they saw. As Brother Al once said, "No one can cut you up to pieces with their tongues like those tongue talkers can!" Of course, no genuine saint who spoke in genuine, Holy Spirit tongues would do what these three church ladies did. They used their tongues to gossip and spread rumors to destroy and corrupt other people.

Though they were wrong, the three church women believed that Brother Al was sinning in picking up the hookers. Their gossip hurt the revival. Brother Al committed no evil, but he was penalized because of doing what God demanded.

The three former prostitutes told Brother Al that prostitution was all that they could do. They did not have any money to buy new clothes or means to try to get another job.

When all these details came to the church's attention, the three church women were rebuked by the pastor. The pastor's wife and others gave the three former prostitutes money to help them start a new life and went with them to purchase new wardrobes. The pastor, his wife, and the church did not merely buy a dress for each prostitute. Oh no! They went out and bought them whole new wardrobes—everything they would need to go into the world and find a new type of occupation. The wardrobes included everything that was appropriate and modest. They purchased underwear, perfume, and other necessities for these prostitutes.

In time, one of the prostitutes became a minister of the gospel and was used mightily by the Lord. From then on, several ladies of the church made it their mission to go out into the streets to rescue prostitutes and drug addicts. In such cases, it is far better for ladies of the church to go out and minister to prostitutes rather than men.

In truth, the three former prostitutes left their old life on the floor of the church and never picked it up again. They experienced the awakening (conversion and change), which is regularly spoken of by the early saints and the revivalists.

Jesus and the Overall Preacher

As God blessed Brother Al, something changed. The anointing began to leave him. He became more and more settled in just playing church. He decided to become like most other Christians, with no power or anointing from the Lord.

His divorce from his wife helped fuel this. She had cheated on him, and he went from one state of depression unto another. He wondered whether serving

God so heavily was worth it.

Brother Al was very successful in his ministry, and his small church in Florida turned into a very large congregation.

He continued to hear about a minister in Alabama who always wore overalls and held services in a tent. There was little pride in that minister. Few would even like that minister in their churches.

Like Peter and John, the overall-wearing minister did not care about money, ego, pride, reputation, prestige, or status. He could not care less about any of these things. He knew what he was in Christ Jesus. And few know that.

Brother Al packed up his little dog and drove to Alabama to find the tent meeting. Yet, he was very famous during these times and did not want to enter the tent and be recognized.

He slowly came closer and closer to the tent and stopped to hide behind a tree. The overall preacher began his service. When he took the platform and began to preach, he immediately stopped, looked in the direction of Brother Al behind that tree, and said, "Al Edenfield, God knows you. Come from behind that tree and come in. The Lord desires you to know something about your life."

Brother Al was scared, but he came forward. The overall preacher spoke the words of God unto him. They were not beautiful. There were no words of prosperity, nor were there words of mercy or grace. The words were that of judgment and warnings if he did not go back to his first love. As long as Brother Al lived, he refused to say everything about what that overall preacher said to him. We asked about the words given to him, but he never spoke about it once.

To say that Brother Al was shocked cannot even describe his state. He ran back to his car, got in with his small dog, drove home, crying and upset, and did not pay attention to the speed limit.

The Lord Jesus Christ appeared in his car on the passenger side. Even the stillness of Al's small dog indicated the presence of the Lord.

What Jesus said was not good. It was warning after warning. Brother Al must change and go back to his first love. He must leave that large church and go back to his roots, where he could regain the anointing of the Lord.

There were several great miracles here. But the greatest miracle was how Brother Al reacted to this. He was driving his car with his hands raised, his eyes closed, and speaking in tongues. He did not know where he was. And even more, the car drove itself by the power of the Lord to Al's home, parked itself, and the engine turned off. When Brother Al came to, he was parked in front of his home. This is just like Jesus.

Brother Al and a Little Boy

One of the numerous things Brother Al suffered throughout much of his life was constant troubles with kidney stones. The kidney stones would move from his kidneys to his bladder. It was common for the kidney stones to be very large and interrupt his ability to urinate. He would take hot baths and drink vinegar with water to help, but sometimes it was almost impossible for them to pass. He would scream from pain when the stones were passing.

After he had rededicated his life to Christ, left the large salary and church, and went back to his first love (Christ), he had problems with a lack of funds. It was common for him not to have money to go to the hospital or even a doctor. His congregation and others did not understand that it was their responsibility to help him.

Brother Al went from being blessed from God to being blessed from the devil and the world, and then being attacked by the devil. So the devil continued to attack his funds. Remember that wealth or prosperity is not a prerequisite of faith or obedience unto God.

Brother Al was visited by cancer more than once. He was truly sick, but still, he had to go to churches to preach and pray for people. He had said on the radio that he would pray for people himself. A young boy who was dying of a brain tumor was listening, and something about what Brother Al said made that young boy have faith.

The young boy sought his mother and father to carry him to the revival. Both agreed, and they brought him to the church. That night at the service, Brother Al was sitting on the altar singing. He had a beautiful voice.

When the young boy came into the church, he received the worst news. The minister announced that Brother Al was too sick to pray for anyone, so others would be doing the praying.

The pastor and his staff prayed for others, but when the young boy came forward, he refused to allow the pastor or his staff to pray for him or even touch him. The young boy ran to Brother Al and said, "You said on the radio that if we come down to the church tonight, you would pray for us and we will be healed. So I want you to pray for me." Brother Al was bound. His own words now trapped him.

He moved slowly to the dying young boy with tubes in his head. The young boy knew this was the time for his miracle. He knew if he did not have Brother

Al pray for him, he would die.

Brother Al began to pray for that young boy, who would not receive no for an answer. The power of the Lord hit the young boy and instantly healed him. Then the power jumped on Brother Al and instantly healed him. The faith of the young boy was enough for both him and Brother Al. Sometimes, it is not the faith of the minister that counts, but the faith of a child.

Brother Al and the Wheelchair

A disabled man in a wheelchair came to Brother Al's services, and would always wheel himself down to the front for prayer. If there was little anointing present, he would wait for prayer. However, if the anointing was strong, he would leave the prayer line and go back to his seat.

The man did not want to give up his disability check. Brother Al became very disgusted about that. He knew that the man did not want to be healed because he would lose his government handout.

Every time the man came to the prayer line, Brother Al was hit with the wheels of that old wheelchair. Time and again, Brother Al prayed, and nothing happened.

Finally, the man came to the prayer line when there was a little anointing. His wheelchair hit the feet and legs of Brother Al for the last time. Brother Al pushed the man in his wheelchair from the prayer line back to the place where he had been sitting and said, "Until you make up your mind to be healed, do not come back up here."

Brother Al and the Coffin

One incident occurred when Brother Al was sick with cancer. He was going to a church to preach the gospel. He arrived and found out that the church had been celebrating Halloween. Of course, he did not approve of that.

He was on the first floor of the church, and there were many decorations for Halloween, one of which was a coffin. As Brother Al was walking by the coffin, a voice spoke out of the coffin and said, "You are next." He ran up the steps and continued to say, "I rebuke you, devil! I am not next."

Christmas and Cancer

In another circumstance, Brother Al got the worst news imaginable. He had cancer *again*, and it was very aggressive. The doctors could do very little for him.

They began chemotherapy treatment, which made him very sick.

Though his cancer continued to be very aggressive, he still went to various churches, preaching and praying for people. Here was Brother Al, sick with cancer, preaching and praying for people, and God was healing and performing miracles. But Brother Al stayed sick, very sick. He was even stinking badly. He had to wear adult diapers, which was very embarrassing to a man who believed in cleanness. Bloody fluid came from his body. How many days did he cry before God? Only God knows.

One December day, around Christmas, Brother Al went to a large church and preached. He still had cancer. Bloody fluid was again coming from his body, and he still smelled terrible.

Somehow, Brother Al was able to preach and pray for people, and God did move. But Christmas was near, and no one in the church wanted Brother Al with them for Christmas. The Lord noticed their behavior toward Brother Al.

A pastor sent Brother Al to a very nice hotel, away from everyone. There Brother Al was—alone and sick, taking care of himself in that hotel room. He called room service and had food and beverages brought up, but he was alone during the worst time of his depression.

He reviewed his life, and I am sure Satan sent evil thoughts his way, probably something like, "Your God has abandoned you. Look, He does not love you. He has left you alone to die."

Brother Al cried and cried. But there is an explanation—an answer to the *why*. Brother Al, like Paul, needed circumstances that would keep his pride in check. God had done much for Brother Al, and it was easy for pride to take hold of his life. Remember what Paul said: "And lest I should be exalted above measure through the abundance of the revelations, there was given to me a thorn in the flesh, the messenger of Satan to buffet me, lest I should be exalted above measure" (2 Corinthians 12:7).

His time in that hotel room was wonderful for him. It broke his pride. Like him, many of us need to be repeatedly broken.

Soon after this experience, a day came when he was preaching and praying for people, the Lord looked down upon his servant and touched him the way He had touched others. God restored his health immediately. It was not just a healing, but an instantaneous healing, which is called a miracle.

My Experience with Brother Al

In 1976, I met Brother Al in a church where he was preaching and praying for people. He was in his late 60s or 70s, and the power of God was still present with him. He retained his humility, not by choice, but by necessity.

I knew him for years and saw many manifestations of God's power in his services, heard many stories about his life, and saw the hand of God upon him.

He lived in Florida and was a servant of God who helped bring into north Florida a great revival. Many of those who worked with me came to the Lord by his ministering.

My husband and I opened our home up for Brother Al and became close to him. Time and time again, he would come to our home, starving. He rarely ate at the homes of people, and rarely ate anything that anyone prepared.

Brother Al taught us a lot about the occult and how to survive the ministry.

Where we lived, it was not common for a preacher to have the anointing in the 70s. God moved and brought Brother Al with great anointing for many reasons, but one reason was to pray for my son that he may be healed. It took a large amount of anointing to touch and heal my son of mental retardation.

The Old Buzzard

One night, while Brother Al was in a revival service in Jacksonville, I was sitting behind a wife, her son, and her husband. The wife had driven from another city in her car, and it had broken down.

The husband and son had come to fix the car so that she could get back home. However, she refused to go until she could hear a prophet speak.

While Brother Al was preaching, he said, "God does not ever embarrass anyone, but he is going to permit me to say this: There is an old buzzard sitting in this service. He has his wife thinking that they are living on pauper street. He makes his living by hauling something on a pulpwood truck. He has told his wife that he had to have a transmission put in his truck. You old buzzard, you just put your neighbor in a fence."

What Brother Al did not say was that the Lord God had told him that the old buzzard was committing adultery with the woman, his neighbor.

The wife hit the old buzzard and said, "That is you!" Thank God for the men in the church service. The old buzzard was going to jump on Brother Al for being exposed, but the men got around Brother Al and escorted him out of the service.

The next night, the wife, her husband (the old buzzard), and son came back to the service. That night, Brother Al was having a Pool of Bethesda service, based upon John 5. That type of service provides a portable pool put in the church and allows the people to walk into the pool and then out of the pool if they can get out. The waters are anointed with oil, and people pray over that pool all day before any person can enter it.

I have personally seen the waters troubled, and people fall in the pool, or outside the pool. Others shout and shake throughout the pool and outside the pool. I have seen many healed, baptized in the Holy Spirit, received miracles, and delivered from demons in such services.

During this service, I was sitting behind the wife, husband, and son as Brother Al called for a line to be formed for people to step into the pool. The father said to his son, "You go ahead and get into it."

The son replied, "No!"

Then, the father said again, "You get in there." Finally, the son obeyed and went to get into the pool.

I was right behind the son in the line, and I was praying that the power of God would hit him hard.

The power of God did not disappoint me. It came down. The son was knocked and bounced up in the air about three feet, and then he came down and went right back up again in the air.

After this, Brother Al asked the son, "Is it real?" The son was crying and was repeatedly saying to his father, "It is real! It is real!" The whole family became saved.

A Blind Boy and a Seeing-Eye Dog

One night, a blind boy came to a service with a seeing-eye dog. The boy went in the prayer line with his dog.

Immediately, the boy received his sight. Afterward, the young boy gave his seeing-eye dog to another. The one to whom the boy gave his dog was also healed. For a long time, every blind person who received that dog was healed entirely and regained their sight.

Regardless of how we can understand this miracle, the truth was that the anointing that night also fell upon the dog, and every blind person who had that dog regained their sight.

Brother Al and Foods

Brother Al was always concerned about poisoned or spoiled food being offered to him. Because of that, he rejected many cakes, other desserts, and various types of meals.

He learned the hard way that he could not just accept the food of everyone, especially from women. On several incidents, he became sick after eating the food offered him. From city to city, he had special homes where he would eat.

We were blessed to be one of those homes. Every time Brother Al came into Jacksonville, he came to our house to eat and have fellowship.

I have great memories of his coming to the back door, and the table filled with all his favorites, especially chicken and dressing.

When he came to our home, it was common for him to throw away cakes, other desserts, and various cooked food given to him by other people. He threw all these foods into our trash can.

Much can be done to food. Poison can be put into food; the food offered to a minister can well be spoiled. And besides these two examples, spells can be placed upon food.

Brother Al warned my son about witchcraft and food. He advised him to be careful about what he eats and where he eats.

If Brother Al went to a restaurant, he tried to find a table with one of the chairs being at the back of the wall. He always wanted to see what was coming toward him.

He taught us the importance of the eyes in spiritual manners. He taught us that demons could be seen in a person by looking into the eyes of that person.

Supporting God's People

Can you imagine the reward the old Pentecostal lady would receive for what she did for Brother Al? After taking him in as a child, she took him in again, severely injured after World War II.

It is important to note that the old Pentecostal lady taught Brother Al the Bible. Like her, I hope that God will remember all the many meals of chicken and dressing I made for him.

It was a great honor to have a man of God who knew what trials and troubles were. It gave me hope that in the end, victory will come. In his old age, God did not forsake Brother Al. He went to a home for retired preachers, where he lived for the rest of his life among his contemporaries.

Like Paul, Brother Al went home but not without scars from all the trials and troubles of his life.

CHAPTER 9
TEACH ME TO PRAY

I was very naïve when it came to prayer. Like others, I thought prayer was easy. As I've said, prayer is far from easy; it is a work and a task. And it will take a lifetime to learn how to pray effectively.

To touch the hem of the Lord requires precise and successful prayer. It requires constant, repeated, and persevering prayer. We must continue to pray on a subject until we have prayed through and received assurance that the answer of the Lord God is on its way.

Like the apostles, I sought the Lord to teach me how to pray. We see this in Luke 11:1, where one of the disciples said unto Jesus, "Lord, teach us to pray."

Hard Knocks

Over many years of learning to pray, I went on a journey from hard knocks to common sense. Within the first few years of public ministry, I went crazy praying for every person I could find, taking their burdens to the extreme, draining myself, and almost going to the point of mental and emotional breakdown.

However, I began to notice something in Scripture that caught my attention. I learned that Paul himself ran from a battle, for a time, until God moved (a critical word: moved) him to go into battle. When the time was right, God moved upon Paul, and the fight was won.

I am referring to the incident in Acts 16, where the damsel was possessed with the pythonic demon, and the demon kept running after Paul, harassing him. Finally, God moved upon him, and Paul stood against the demon.

I realized that if apostle Paul avoided this battle until God moved upon him to stand his ground, and command that evil spirit to be exorcized from the damsel, maybe I needed to stop running into battles that God did not want me to get into. Maybe I, too, needed to wait until God moved upon me to become engaged in a battle that He alone commanded me to fight with the authority of Christ and the power of the Holy Spirit.

I learned that not every battle is for me to fight. I also realized that people have their own battles to face, and sometimes, I am not allowed or ordered by God to fight for them or with them.

In 1 Corinthians 6:9–15, Paul, being very honest, after listing various kinds of people who are excluded from eternal life if they do not change, said, "Such were some of you" (1 Corinthians 6:11). I asked my son, "What would be the best way to translate this phrase of 1 Corinthians 6:11?" He said there are three ways of translating the Greek here that are better than how the King James Version has translated it:

1. "These things are what some of you were."
2. "These dreadful things were some of you."
3. "These detestable sinners were some of you."

According to my son, the neuter form of the demonstrative pronoun in the Greek text points out a horrifying view about these practices. Paul regards all the vices listed as horrors or monsters. By the simple phrase "such were some of you," Paul is entirely pointing back to the vice list and saying to each sort of former sinner at Corinth, "Some of you were fornicators, some of you were idolaters, some of you were adulterers and so on; but now you are washed, sanctified, and justified."

John Owen says it quite well. "Hell can scarce, in no more words, yield us a sadder catalogue. Yet some of all these sorts were justified and pardoned."[1] John Calvin, in his commentary on First Corinthians, writes, "The simple meaning, therefore, is this, that prior to their being regenerated by grace, some of the Corinthians were covetous, others adulterers, others extortioners, others effeminate, others revilers, but now, being made free by Christ, they were such no longer."[2] Charles Hodges, in his commentary on First Corinthians, says, "The idea being, 'Some were impure, some drunkards, some violent, etc.'"[3] Calvin, Owen, and Hodge understood "some" as distributive in nature. Repetition is meant.

In the Corinthian congregation, a good variety of such former immoral persons was to be found. Paul points out a contrast between their present state and their past. Their moral condition made an uncompromising demand to leave all the past sins and deeds and never practice them again. Their sinful lives are in the past. So their moral lives are monuments of the power of the blood.

To Paul, such debased sins are so strong that only some can submit to the call of God and receive the redemption wrought by the blood of Christ Jesus. Paul acknowledges the power of these debased sins to create defiance against God within the majority of those who practice them. Few ever want to change.

Paul divides the Corinthian church into ten main categories of former evildoers. Out of each sinful category at Corinth, only some denounced their particular sins, came out of that category and were changed. The majority of former sinners in the Corinthian church had come from these ten categories.

Paul clearly tailored his vice list of 1 Corinthians 6:9–11 to the needs of the Corinthian community he addressed. In Paul's vice list, the absence of a sin does not give a license to commit it. Any sin not mentioned in this list is still understood as an evil practice. The sins that afflicted Corinth considerably were mentioned. The sins that did not dominate Corinth were understood as still present, but very little problem for that city.

Paul's emphasis here is a warning. Only some who practice a particular abomination will be saved and delivered from it. In such cases, the blood of Christ can only reach a few. Why? It is not because the blood is insufficient; it is not because the power of God is impotent. Instead, the response rests with the majority of these types of sinners never wanting to be saved. So I learned that I must pursue after those sinners who wish to be saved and changed from their sins.

Then, again, I remembered the parable of the sower, and within that parable, the four grounds (Matthew 13:18–23). The seeds were broadcast throughout the ground and landed on four types of ground. Out of the four types of ground, the seeds grew consistently and in a sustained manner in only one type. The other seeds were destroyed, or their plants were destroyed. But the seeds that grew on the good ground significantly produced. I learned for this to happen, people must cultivate their lives. So I learned not to focus on uncultivated land, but on land that has been cultivated by prayer, obedience, faith, consecration, dedication, the fruit of the Holy Spirit, the power of the Holy Spirit, and the authority of Jesus Christ. Some will accept Christ, but others will not. People must have their ground (lives) cultivated (prepared) to receive Christ. But they must also have that ground cultivated to have their prayers answered, and to be healed, delivered, and have prophetic words come to pass.

What is Prayer?

One of the most significant statements about prayer was by Tertullian, a father of the early church in the third century, in his book on prayer:

> Only prayer is that which prevails with God, but Christ has willed that it works no evil. He has bestowed on it all the virtue of goodness.

Therefore, it knows nothing except how to call back the spirits of the dead from the very path of death, to transform the weak, to heal the sick, to purge those who are demon possessed, to open the doors of prisons and to release the chains of those who are innocent. Also, it washes away faults, repels temptations, quenches persecutions, comforts the fainthearted, delights those who are high spirited, leads travelers, calms the waves, paralyzes robbers, feeds the poor, rules over the rich, raises up the fallen, props up those who are falling, and sustains those who are standing. Prayer is the wall of faith; its arms and missiles are thrown against our enemy who watches over us on all sides. And so, we never walk defenseless. By the day of our station and by the night of our vigil, we must be mindful. Under the arms of prayer, we guard the battle standard of our general; we must wait in praying for the trumpet of an angel. Likewise, all angels pray; every creature prays; cattle and wild beasts pray and bend their knees; and when they come out of their dens and caves, they look up toward heaven with no idle mouth and make their breath vibrate rapidly after their own manner. But then the birds too raise out of the nest, lifting themselves up toward heaven, and instead of hands, they spread out the cross of their wings, and say something that may seem to be like a prayer. What, therefore, is greater than the office of prayer? Even the Lord Himself prayed; to whom must be the honor and virtue unto the ages of the ages![4]

The first sentence about prayer by Tertullian, "Only prayer is that which prevails with God," as explained by my son, refers to the wrestling of Jacob with God through an angel (Genesis 32:24–32) and Matthew 11:12: "And from the days of John the Baptist until now the kingdom of heaven suffereth violence, and the violent take it by force." Further, the prevailing (wrestling) cannot mean that a person can make God do anything against His will. Instead, the idea is that only prayer can move God to change His will and plan about a circumstance if God so wills. For instance, there was a struggle between God and Moses about the Israelites. God had decided to destroy the Israelites and choose another people as His chosen people because they made and worshiped the golden calves. According to Jewish sources, there was more than one calf; there were thirteen golden calves.[5] But by intercessory prayer and fasting, Moses tugged on the heart of God and changed the mind of God about the Israelites. Therefore, God did not destroy them (Exodus 32:9–35).

The possibilities of prayer are always found to be in alliance with the purposes and will of God. Prayer can only change the purposes of God if God allows it (Matthew 26:39; John 18:11; Judges 10:13; 2 Kings 20:1; Jonah 3:4).

Accordingly, while the practice of prayer is widespread, there are very few Christians who know how to pray and how to receive results from their prayers. Indeed, we are often unable to grasp the fullness of prayer. We think too little about prayer or that it is just words. We do not know the power of prayer when our words are united with God's will.

Today, the belief that God will answer our requests is almost non-existent. If we pray thinking we will not receive anything back, we should stop praying. We are defeated before we begin. And if people do pray, their prayers easily become a selfish practice, where the self is exalted rather than selflessness. Today, there is very little submission and humility.

It is sad, but our prayer life has become the prayer life of a young granddaughter. For instance, "An elderly gentleman passed his granddaughter's room one night and overheard her repeating the alphabet in an oddly reverent way. 'What on earth are you up to?' he asked. 'I'm saying my prayers,' explained the little girl. 'But I can't think of exactly the right words tonight, so I'm just saying all the letters. God will put them together for me because He knows what I'm thinking.'"[6]

In truth, prayer must have holiness, dedication, determination, perseverance, obedience, integrity, commitment, simplicity, purity, humility, and faith interwoven into it before we even begin to pray.

Sometimes, a prayer might be prayed only once. Other times, a prayer must be repeatedly prayed before an answer is given. And other times, the results of our prayers will be long and drawn out. That requires continual prayer over many hours, days, or years.

For example, George Mueller, a Christian evangelist in the 1800s,

> began to pray for a group of five personal friends. After five years one of them came to Christ. In ten years, two more of them found peace in the same Saviour. He prayed on for twenty-five years, and the fourth man was saved. For the fifth he prayed until the time of his death, and this friend, too, came to Christ a few months afterwards. For this latter friend, Mr. Mueller had prayed almost fifty-two years! When we behold such perseverance in prayer, we feel that we have scarcely touched the fringe of real importunity in our intercessions for others.[7]

Prayer may need to go on for decades to see the complete fulfillment of its results.

And a century earlier, in 1727, twenty-four men and twenty-four women of the Moravians begin to pray each, one hour a day in scheduled prayer. This prayer vigil continued an astonishing one hundred years; when an intercessor died or became too sick to continue, another one took his or her place. Results of their prayers included the greatest missionary movement in the world until that time, the massive movement of God's Spirit in the First Great Awakening in 1734 and the founding of America in 1776.[8]

In one special instance of continual prayer, until the Lord moved, Reverend Harry E. Bowley, a Pentecostal revivalist and pioneer, and Reverend Lawrence, another Pentecostal revivalist and pioneer, faced one of the greatest times of their lives. A man named Joe French had died, and they knew to pray for his resurrection. They fell on the floor of their room and stayed there in agony of soul and spirit for at least three or four hours in continual prayer, rebuking death, and speaking life upon Joe French. They did not stop praying intensively until there came a knock at the door, and a woman said, "Hallelujah! Joe's alive." The words of Reverend Harry E. Bowley are worth noting: "God can do things when people pray." The man whom they prayed for was saved and began preaching the gospel and giving his testimony to many people.[9] Most Christians would have allowed the man to die, and God would have been robbed of a great testimony of His grace and power.

For approximately two thousand years, the Spirit and the bride continue to say, "Come" to the Lord Jesus Christ (Revelation 22:17). This simple prayer is the only recorded prayer of the Holy Spirit. And that prayer focuses on the coming of the Lord for His saints (1 Thessalonians 4:15–18). If the Holy Spirit continues to pray in repetition over the coming of the Lord, we should follow His example in certain circumstances.

Prayer has many facets and many means. Many definitions of prayer can well be used to define prayer, and some of them are as follows:
1. Prayer, at its very foundation, is a conversation between God and us, communion and unity between God and us, and a relationship with God.
2. Without prayer in the life of a saint, there cannot be any relationship with God.
3. Therefore, without prayer in the life of a saint, that person cannot be a saint.
4. Prayer is crying out to God from your heart.
5. Prayer is intermingling with God.

6. Prayer that is of God will consist of the prevalence of truth, faith, obedience, purity, simplicity, and the gift of grace at its very simplest forms.
7. Prayer is like a spiritual gun. This holy gun comprises three things: faith, the name of Jesus, and the promise from God. Faith is the barrel of that gun, the name of Jesus is the trigger, and the promise of God is the bullet.
8. Prayer is recognizing the presence of God, talking with God, listening to God, identifying with God, and knowing God.
9. Prayer becomes an act, a practice, and a way of life that will lead those who pray to know Christ. If not, prayer is not true.
10. Prayer is used to express everything that we are in Christ (Matthew 7:7–8; John 16:13).
11. Only by prayer can we experience a relationship with God.
12. Our life of prayer determines or regulates the value, quality, and state of our spiritual life with God.
13. Prayer is entering and enjoying the presence of God.
14. Prayer can unleash the power of God on our behalf.
15. Prayer can open the many passages of God's blessing into our lives.
16. Prayer is the means by which God accomplishes the various things that He wants to see in our lives.
17. Prayer can open many opportunities for God to move and bless our lives.
18. Prayer is the originator and channel of devotion; the spirit of prayer is the spirit of devotion to God.
19. Prayer and devotion are united like body and spirit.
20. Prayer is not repeating void formulas or void repetition of words (Matthew 6:7).
21. Prayer is the work of the Spirit who uses our organs of speech for instruments of the divine praises. In such cases, every stop and pause of those instruments is the conclusion of a prayer.
22. Prayer is a great duty, and the most significant benefit and privilege of a Christian.
23. Prayer is the primary instrument whereby we minister to God.
24. Prayer is the ascension of the mind of God and petitioning for such things as we need for our support and duty.
25. Prayer is a theoretical and practical representation of a Christian's life

and dedication unto God.
26. Prayer is an act of religion and divine worship.
27. Prayer distinguishes religious phenomena from all those that resemble them from the moral sense.
28. Prayer seeks all that God is, and we give Him all that we have or all that we can give.
29. Prayer confesses the power, grace, and mercy of God.
30. Prayer is an intense emotion and intense aspiration.
31. Prayer is the most perfect and divine action of which a saint is capable.
32. Prayer celebrates the attributes of God.
33. Prayer confesses God's glories, reveres His persons, implores His aid, and gives thanks for His blessing.
34. Prayer is an act of humility, respect, and dependence, expressed in the prostration of our bodies, and the humiliation of our spirits.
35. Prayer is an act of charity when we pray for others.
36. Prayer is an act of repentance when the prayer confesses and begs pardon for our sins.
37. Prayer is an act of grace and mercy.

Necessities of Prayer

1. We pray because we love God and want a relationship with God.
2. We pray because we must depend on God rather than upon ourselves (Colossians 3:4).
3. Only by prayer, do we obtain the comfort, ease, endurance, potency, determination, and other supplies we need for every part of our Christian life.
4. Prayer is as necessary unto our spiritual life as breathing is essential for our natural life.
5. We must pray to stop, hinder, or resist temptation (Matthew 26:41).
6. Without prayer as a weapon in our lives, it is impossible to stop, hinder, or resist temptation.
7. By prayerlessness, we become weaker and weaker in our spiritual life.
8. By prayerlessness, we finally become lukewarm or backslidden.
9. By prayerlessness, Satan can gain an advantage in our lives.
10. We must pray because we need God, and we need salvation from Him.

11. We must request God into our lives so that He will work.
12. If no Christian prays, Satan controls and dominates the affairs of men and the issues of the church, and the judgment of God will eventually come to pass.
13. By prayer, we beseech God to reach down and touch multitudes to be saved, who otherwise may not be saved.
14. The necessity of prayer is grounded upon the commandment of God to pray (Colossians 4:2; 1 Thessalonians 5:17).
15. Prayer is necessary for what God wants to happen in the world of men (Daniel 9:2).
16. We pray to spend time with God.
17. By prayer, we identify with God (Galatians 5:16).
18. By prayer, we gain strength to resist temptation.
19. By prayer, we can get right with God.
20. By prayer, we can find forgiveness, mercy, and grace.
21. By prayer, we learn the will of God.
22. By prayer, we learn the authority of God.
23. By prayer, we offer sacrifices to God.
24. By prayer, we can release the authority and power of God.
25. Without prayer, all our knowledge, our libraries, and our education become useless.
26. Prayer makes a person a saint.
27. Prayer determines the status of a saint.
28. Prayer moves God in the world if He wants to be moved in the direction that is being prayed.
29. To a prayerful man or woman, God is present in realized power.
30. Prayer is the established and singular condition of God to move ahead His Son's kingdom.

People, Please Pray and Pray Right

Christians pray for numerous reasons, and many of these reasons are unbiblical, even selfish. Christians pray because it might work. Or we pray because our mother, father, or grandparents may have prayed. We remember in the back of our minds that, if all else fails, pray. For many, if not most, prayer has become the last choice when there is no hope. Instead, it should be the first hope and first practice.

As Christians, we know that we must pray and should pray, but we may still not understand what prayer is in the first place. Or why God wants us to pray about our needs. Or why God needs our prayers to be fulfilled. Indeed, most Christians have forgotten the task and duty of prayer. And in so doing, we have forgotten the weapon of prayer.

Our Call to Pray

Genuine prayer unlocks the entrance for God to work in our lives and the nations of the world. Without prayer in our lives, there is no submission to God. For prayer and submission are united together. It is impossible to submit to God without prayer; it is impossible to really learn how to pray without submission. And prayer is the means by which Christians submit everything to the Lord God.

Further, genuine prayer calls God to come forth and work for us in our lives and in the things that affect us in our lives. By obedience to His commandments, and placing our cares, troubles, trials, and thoughts on Him, we put those things under His sovereignty and power instead of our own. When we pray and believe in the power of prayer, we reject our independence and learn to submit and depend upon the Lord (1 Peter 5:6–7). By doing this, we learn dependence upon the Lord God.

Many years ago, I personally heard Lester Sumrall saying that he refused to give counseling. He saw that it never helped. Instead, he led people to Jesus Christ, told them to pray, set them there before His feet, and walked away. Lester Sumrall had much success in this way of taking people to Jesus. And this was primarily when the anointing of God was present.

Another example is the case of Daniel. During this time, the condition of the Israelites was awful (Daniel 9:1–2). God had not moved; He promised that the Israelites were to experience only seventy years of captivity. God had not fulfilled that promise for His people; it appeared that the captivity was to continue, or something worse was to occur. It was possible that the Israelites were to be destroyed, if not rescued. But when Daniel stood up in prayer and fasting—he stood and prayed alone—remembering the promise of God and reminding God of that promise, God began to work for Daniel and the Israelites. Though God knew about the promise and what the problem was, He was waiting for someone to pray and care enough about that promise and problem to pray.

Many problems in the world go unsettled because Christians refuse to pray as God directs them to pray. Then we blame God when He is not at fault. We have just not prayed.

What if Christians had become proactive about Hitler or Stalin? The evils done by them might have become non-existent or greatly reduced just by the prayers of the saints. Too many saints focus on themselves and not on the divine plan. When the self rules prayer, prayer becomes useless to the kingdom of God.

Furthermore, in genuine prayer, we declare and confess that God can take care of us in all our circumstances. In prayer, we must confess our sins and our condition before the Lord as we pray.

In prayer, it is key to come before God with repentance, thanksgiving, and humility. We come before God as repentant men or women, bowing ourselves before the Lord God and His sovereignty. In so doing, our condition is right to receive answered prayer, and our spirits are allowed greater fellowship with the Lord.

Lord, Teach Us to Pray!

After living daily with Jesus and learning so much at His feet, his disciples asked, "Lord, teach us to pray" (Luke 11:1). This petition came from men who had seen the robust results of Christ's praying. They sought after a more in-depth experience in prayer than they had experienced in their own lives. It takes years to learn prayer, its importance, and the various ways of praying.

Beginning to Pray

1. We must begin to talk to God.
2. We must acknowledge God as our Father.
3. We must acknowledge Jesus as our Friend, Helper, Lord, Intercessor, Master, and Savior.
4. We must recognize the Holy Spirit as our Comforter, Helper, Intercessor, and Guide.
5. We must know just who we are in Jesus Christ.
6. We should pray unto the Father in the name of Jesus Christ (John 14:6; Hebrews 10:19).
7. We must confess our unconfessed sins.
8. By confessing our sins, the blood of Jesus Christ cleanses us and allows us entrance into the presence of God.
9. We must "enter into his gates with thanksgiving" (Psalm 100:4).

10. We must thank God for forgiving our sins, for coming into our lives, and for making us His children.
11. We must ask God for whatever we need.
12. We must thank God and praise Him for His answer.
13. We must also spend time asking for His Spirit to help us to pray and to pray for us as an intercessor.
14. We must also pray that Jesus will be our intercessor.
15. We must talk to the Holy Spirit.
16. We must tell the Holy Spirit what we want Him to know (Romans 8:26).

Preparations for Prayer

1. Our inner man must be prepared to have fellowship with the Lord God by confessing our sins (Psalm 24:3–5; Mark 11:25–26; Hebrews 10:19;1 John 1:6–9, 3:21–22).
2. Without preparing our inner man, it is impossible for a Christian to enter the presence of God and have fellowship with Him.
3. We must be determined in what we are petitioning God.
4. We must have a direction to our prayer.
5. We must focus ourselves on one subject at a time.
6. We should have a specific prayer.
7. Our prayer must proceed from the right perception of God.
8. We must have faith in what we are asking the Lord.
9. We must ask according to the will of God.
10. We must know what the Word of God says.
11. We must renew our minds with the Word of God (Romans 12:1–2).

Common Patterns of Prayer (John 16:23–26)

1. Prayer is addressed to the Father. So the Father hears and answers the prayers.
2. Prayer is sent through Jesus. So Christ permits, acknowledges, accepts, receives the prayer, and sends it to the Father.
3. Prayer is collected, influenced, and sent to Jesus by the Holy Spirit.
4. There are exceptions to this typical pattern of prayer.

Keys to the Prayers of the Ancient Church

1. Prayers were grounded in the Bible itself.
2. Prayers were formed by phrases and words directly from the Bible.
3. Prayers emphasized the holiness of God.
4. Prayers expressed a spirit of reverence to God.
5. Prayers stressed the Trinity.
6. Prayers were more collective than individual, which reduces self in prayer.

The Model Prayer

1. Prayer begins with a statement and a testimony to God and with the reward of faith (Matthew 6:9–13).
   a. We are reminded of our duty to God.
   b. We are reminded to obey, fear, and give reverence to God.
2. "Hallowed be thy name" means that His name is to be holy, sacred, and to be esteemed. It is universally recognized that God is to be blessed by every man and woman in every place and time because of the memory of His benefits falling upon all mankind.
3. "Thy Kingdom come" has reference to petitioning the rule of God over and in our lives.
   a. This also denotes a cry that His reign will be hastened upon the earth.
   b. It is a cry, "How long, O Lord, holy and true, dost thou not judge and avenge our blood on them that dwell on the earth?" (Revelation 6:10).
   c. It is a cry that the long foretold millennial kingdom would soon come.
4. According to this model, the phrase, "Thy will be done in earth as it is in heaven" means that we pray for His will to be done in all the universe.
   a. We want God's will to be done on earth the way it is done in heaven.
   b. We make a petition.
   c. After that, He supplies us with the substance of His will, and the capacity to do it, so that we may be saved.
   d. This phrase also denotes that we must perpetually petition in

Christ for our whole life and everything we need.
5. "And forgive us our debts as we forgive our debtors." This phrase deals with clemency for sinners.
   a. All the sins of infirmity, invasion, sudden surprise, and those great sins that were washed off from our spirits and the stain taken away by the blood of Christ are meant here.
   b. It is repentance again of all sins, including past and present.
6. "And lead us not into temptation." He prays that the saints of God will suffer not to be led into temptation.
   a. This will be done through spiritual warfare, being watchful, being careful, and ever ready.
   b. It also means not to be overcome by temptation.
7. "But deliver us from evil."
   a. Deliver us from the assaults or violence of evil, from the wicked one, who not only presents us with temptations, but heightens our concupiscence, makes us imaginative, fantastical and passionate, and makes the lust active coming against us, and our appetite for that lust complete and ready to receive it.
8. "For thine is the kingdom, the power, and the glory, forever."
   a. These things we pray for must be for the honor of His kingdom, for the manifestation of His power, and the glory of His name and mercies.

Guidelines of Prayer

1. We must depend on the Holy Spirit.
2. We must meditate on the Lord Jesus Christ, and His Word, and petition in our prayers what we need.
3. We must realize who we are in Christ (John 16:24–26; Colossians 3:17).
4. We must know how God hears us (John 16:24–26; Colossians 3:17).
5. We must remember that we are the saints of God, and His children (John 1:12; Galatians 3:26; Revelation 1:6).
6. We must believe and expect that God will answer our prayers (1 Peter 3:12).
7. When we pray, we must forgive those who have hurt us (Mark 11:25).
8. When we pray, we must ask for forgiveness (Luke 18:9–14).
9. We must remove all hindrances (Matthew 5:23–24).

10. We must accept the answer of God (2 Corinthians 12:7–9).
11. We must do something for God (John 15:16).
12. We must be right with God and right with others (Psalms 139:23–24).
13. We must listen to the Lord (Psalms 46:10).
14. We must trust the Lord (Proverbs 29:25).
15. We must pray and pray again (James 5:13–18).
16. We must fast (Daniel 9:3–4).
17. We must accept correction, chastisement, reproof, and pruning from God (Hebrews 12:5–7).
18. We must live a holy life (1 Peter 1:15–17).
19. We must meet the conditions of God (Isaiah 55:6–7).
20. We must pray in agreement (Matthew 18:19–20).
21. We must recognize the presence of God (Matthew 6:5–6).
22. We must put God first (Matthew 6:10).
23. We must thank God for answers to prayer and for our salvation.
24. We must tell God how great He is.
25. By thanking God, we will increase our faith.
26. We must worship God.
27. We must submit completely to God.
28. We must ask for daily provision.
29. We must pray the Word.
30. According to Romans 10:8, the Word of God must be in our spirits and our mouths when we pray.
31. When we pray, we should notice that God desires to meet, fulfill, and keep His promises.
32. Then, we should use the Word of God, continue reminding God of His promises, and keep asking God to fulfill His promises.
33. We must plead the glory and honor of God's name (Psalms 106:8; 2 Samuel 7:26).
34. We must plead the nature of God, which means His glory, majesty, power, and other divine attributes (Isaiah 16:5).
35. We must plead our sorrows and needs (Psalms 35:11–13).
36. We must remind God of His answers to our past prayers (Psalms 27:9, 78, 85:1–7).
37. We must quote a promise and show our assurance in receiving an answer.

38. We must quote a fulfilled promise as a reason for praise.
39. We must find a particular verse of Scripture to claim for the situation.
40. We must pray the Word of God over our needs.
41. We must pray the Word of God into the lives of people and ourselves.
42. We must pray the Word of God into situations, trials, and other types of troubles.
43. We must be in one accord with the Father, the Lord Jesus Christ, and the Spirit.
44. True prayer begins at the Father; true prayer will always be answered. Why? It is the will of the Father to answer it. It comes from the Father.
45. Unanswered prayers are prayers that do not originate from the Father.
46. We must ask God for definite things that we want (Psalm 37:4).
47. We should pray in such a way that we will know afterward what we prayed for, and we will recognize when the answer to our prayer is manifested.
48. We must allow God to lead us to pray for others rather than praying our wills.
49. We must thank God for the results of prayer, even if we have not seen them (Philippians 4:6–7).
50. We must pray with thanksgiving.

Two Main Rules for Prayer

1. We are bound to pray for all things that concern our duty, and all that we are bound to labor for, such as glory and grace, the necessary assistance of the Spirit, spiritual rewards, heaven, and heavenly things.
2. We are bound to pray for both spiritual and temporal blessings. We may lawfully testify our hope and express our desires by petition.

After We Pray

1. We must stand firm.
2. We must take firm control of our thought life.
3. We must think on positive things (Philippians 4:6–9).
4. By praising God and confessing the applicable truths of the Word,

we must cast down every thought and every imagination that is contrary to our prayer.
5. We must use the Word.
6. We must wait on the Lord.
7. We must be confident in mind.
8. We must keep speaking what the Word says on the issue at stake (2 Corinthians 4:13; Hebrews 10:23).
9. We must act in line with our faith and our confession (James 2:17).
10. We must continuously meditate upon the promises and the Word of God.
11. We must emphasize the greatness, majesty, and holiness of God.
12. We must expect the prayer to be answered.
13. We must live in expectancy when we pray.
14. If we expect nothing, we will receive nothing.

General Types of Prayer

1. Worship (1 Chronicles 16:10–12; John 4:23)
    a. In prayer, as we worship the Lord, we must worship Him in spirit and truth (John 4:23).
    b. In true worship, we bow down and submit our spirits unto the Lord God.
    c. In worship, we express love and admiration to God.
    d. As we worship God, we submit to the love, will, and moral law of God.
    e. In worship, we should hear the voice of God.
    f. We are responding to God's glory.
2. Confession (Romans 10:9; 1 John 1:9)
    a. In the confession of sin, with our mouths, we tell God our sins.
    b. In the confession of the Word, with our mouths, we tell God what He has said in His Word.
    c. We are responding to God's holiness.
3. Thanksgiving (1 Chronicles 16:34; Ephesians 2:15–19a; Colossians 3:15, 4:2)
    a. In this type of prayer, we thank God for what He has done for us, both blessings and those blessings not yet seen.
    b. It is natural and correct that we should thank God (1

Thessalonian 5:18).
4. Supplication (Matthew 26:42; Acts 1:14)
   a. Supplication is pleading concerning sins, in which one who is sorry for his present or past evil deeds asks for pardon (Matthew 26:42).
5. Praise (Psalm 92:1, 100:4; Acts 16:24–26)
   a. As we praise God, we declare the good things about God, both about His nature and His actions.
6. Petition (Ephesians 2:15–19a, 6:18–19)
   a. As we petition God, we are asking Him for the things we desire.
   b. We are commanded to ask God.
7. Intercession (Daniel 9:1–21; Philippians 1:19)
   a. The practice of intercession, also known as intercessory prayer, does not focus on self or our desires. Instead, it focuses on the needs and wants of other men and women.
   b. Intercession involves all other types of prayers.
   c. As intercessors, we stand in proxy or "in the gap" between God and other people seeking God's favor for them.
8. Waiting (Habakkuk 2:1)
   a. As we wait on God, our spirits are silent and wait for God to move or speak something by His Spirit.
   b. We must wait patiently on God.
   c. Through waiting on God, we practically express unto God that the will of God will be done in this world, not our own will.
   d. As we pray, we should not always be talking, but we should talk and listen.
9. Warfare (Psalm 149:6–9; James 4:7; 1 John 4:4)
   a. This is a prayer directed against the powers of darkness.
   b. We announce against Satan and his forces the written judgment by reading the Scriptures of judgment against them (Psalm 149:9).
   c. We command Satan and his forces to be bound, to be loosed, or to leave their positions of authority or influence in the name of Jesus Christ (Matthew 16:19; Mark 16:17).
   d. We rebuke the forces of evil (Zechariah 3:2; Malachi 3:11; Matthew 4:4–10; Luke 4:4–10; Titus 4:2; Jude 9).

    e. We resist the onslaughts of evil (James 4:7).
    f. This is another form of intercessory prayer.
    g. Warfare prayer is not for the untested (1 Timothy 3:1–7).
10. Praying in Tongues (Acts 2; 1 Corinthians 14:2, 15; Jude 20)
11. The Prayer of Faith (Matthew 21:21–22; Ephesians 6:18)
    a. The prayer of faith is shades of all these prayers; the prayer of faith is that which gets results; it is the prayer that begins with the Father and ends with the Father.
12. Ministering Prayer (Psalm 40:1; Acts 13:2)
    a. We need times of waiting on God and ministering to the Lord.
    b. We need times when we are not asking for anything, not petitioning, but ministering to Him.
    c. This type of prayer, where we minister to the Lord and wait on Him, is something that can make the impossible possible.
13. Imprecatory Prayer (1 Corinthians 16:22; Galatians 1:8)
    a. There is no more significant example of an imprecatory prayer than 1 Corinthians 16:22: "If any man love not the Lord Jesus Christ, let him be Anathema Maranatha." It is impossible to forget the cries and prayers of the martyred saints mentioned in Revelation 6:10, which shall be done in the future: "How long, O Lord, holy and true, dost thou not judge and avenge our blood on them that dwell on the earth?" In Revelation 6:10, the martyred saints will manifestly make an appeal to the divine court because of the gross miscarriage of justice that will be done against them.
    b. Imprecatory prayers are based upon God hearing the cries of His people and acting to shield and to deliver them for the sake of fulfilling His promises.
    c. In such prayers, we repeat Scripture, reminding God of what He already promised for the sake of His saints, or simply petition God, and it is God Himself who decides.
    d. Further, such prayers mean absolutely nothing, if not done in the inspiration of the Lord. The Lord is the One who breathes it, the One who inspires it, and the One who desires it. The saint simply repeats it.
    e. In the early church, the legitimate imprecatory prayers were uttered fundamentally for blatant violation of the moral order

and the moral law, and often in a public forum with appeal unto the Lord God.
f. Jesus Christ, in life-threatening circumstances, uttered woes and imprecations against the most evil forms of unbelief (Matthew 11:20–24, 23:13–39; Mark 11:12–14, 20–21).

Prayer and Church Tradition

Within church tradition, the variety of orthodox ways to pray is almost limitless. Very few of the ancient authorities denounced such variety. Most held that since very few apostolic forms of prayer existed, Christ, as well as the apostles, only intended to give the saints a starting point, and allow them to change their ways of prayers as the Holy Spirit directed.

What would be most noteworthy today about the variety of prayers that was sanctioned by the church was that the church prayed to Christ, as well as to the Holy Spirit, and not just to the Father through Christ and the Holy Spirit. But the church understood that the Scriptures that stated not to ask Christ anything were dealing with Christ's humanity, and not His deity (John 16:23).

The church understood that since Christ is just as much God as the Father is God, then they have the right to address their prayers to Christ, not as a man, but rather as God. Since all three persons are God, by addressing one, all three persons are addressed. So by addressing Christ as God, the other persons are also addressed. Scripture gives several examples of saints praying to Christ (Acts 1:24, 7:59, 9:10–16; 1 Corinthians 16:22; 2 Corinthians 12:8; Revelation 22:20).

My Experience with Prayer

Out of all prayers, I pray the prayer of petition more than any other prayer. It was the prayer that I understood first. The prayer of praise should be the first prayer used by us. And only after that should we petition. Praise causes us to enter the very throne room of God and sets everything in biblical perspective and relationship.

Apostle Paul prays a prayer of petition:

Wherefore I also, after I heard of your faith in the Lord Jesus, and love unto all the saints, cease not to give thanks for you, making mention of you in my prayers; that the God of our Lord Jesus Christ, the Father of glory, may give unto you the spirit of wisdom and revelation in the knowledge of him: The eyes of your understanding being enlightened;

that ye may know what is the hope of his calling, and what the riches of the glory of his inheritance in the saints, and what is the exceeding greatness of his power to us-ward who believe. (Ephesians 2:15–19a)

Besides the prayers of petition, I pray many warfare prayers and prayers of intercession.

Leonard Ravenhill, a well-known minister and author on prayer, once said, "A sinning man will stop praying. A praying man will stop sinning."[10] Ravenhill also said,

> The true man of God is heartsick, grieved at the worldliness of the Church, grieved at the blindness of the Church, grieved at the corruption in the Church, grieved at the toleration of sin in the Church, grieved at the prayerlessness in the Church. He is disturbed that the corporate prayer of the Church no longer pulls down the strongholds of the devil. He is embarrassed that the Church folks no longer cry in their despair before a devil-ridden, sin-mad society, "Why could we not cast him out?" (Matthew 17:19).[11]

And he said, "A man may study because his brain is hungry for knowledge, even Bible knowledge. But he prays because his soul is hungry for God."[12]

Furthermore, Ravenhill nails the main problem with the modern church:

> No man is greater than his prayer life. The pastor who is not praying is playing; the people who are not praying are straying. We have many organizers, but few agonizers; many players and payers, few prayers; many singers, few clingers; lots of pastors, few wrestlers; many fears, few tears; much fashion, little passion; many interferers, few intercessors; many writers, but few fighters. Failing here, we fail everywhere.[13]

John Wesley once said, "I value all things only by the price they shall gain in eternity."[14]

Charles Finney said as follows:

> If Christians were not such cowards, and absolutely disobedient to this plain command of God, one thing would certainly come of it—either they would be murdered in the streets as martyrs, because men could not bear the intolerable presence of truth, or they would be speedily converted to God.[15]

Charles Finney also said as follows:

I have never known a person sweat blood; but I have known a person pray till the blood started from his nose. And I have known persons to pray till they were all wet with perspiration, in the coldest weather in winter. I have known persons pray for hours, till their strength was all exhausted with the agony of their minds. Such prayers prevailed with God.[16]

Matthew Henry said as follows:

The prayers and supplications that Christ offered up were, joined with strong cries and tears, herein setting us example not only to pray but to be fervent and importunate in prayer. How many dry prayers, how few wet ones, do we offer up to God![17]

Learning About Prayer

From many years, I learned just what our prayers must consist of:
1. We must pray in the name of Jesus Christ (John 14:13, 14, 15:16; 16:23–26; Romans 1:8; Ephesians 5:20; Hebrews 4:14–16; 1 Timothy 2:5).
2. We must pray by the will of God (Matthew 26:39; 1 John 5:14–15).
3. We must pray with understanding (Matthew 6:7; 1 Corinthians 14:15–16).
4. We must pray with our whole heart (Jeremiah 29:12–13; Matthew 6:5; Luke 22:44).
5. We must pray in faith and not in doubt (Mark 11:24; James 1:5–8).
6. We must pray concerning God and with great humility (2 Chronicles 7:14; Luke 18:9–14).
7. We must pray with repentance (Genesis 18:27; 2 Chronicles 33:10–13).
8. We must pray and forgive others (Matthew 6:12,14–15; Mark 11:25).
9. We must pray and live a faithful life (James 5:16; 1 John 3:21–22).

Greatest Prayer Warrior in American History

Sometimes, history is rewritten, and some facts are forgotten. Secular writers and historians love to ignore Christians and their works. In the history of America, there is no more magnificent prayer warrior than Father Daniel Nash, a companion of Charles Finney (1775–1831).

At the age of forty, Nash became a pastor at Stow's Square Congregational-

Presbyterian Church, Lowville Township, in upstate New York. During his first year as the pastor, a revival sprang forth, and seventy people were saved.

By 1822, his services were no longer needed in the church. The church members believed that Father Nash was too old to be a pastor and fired him. Besides this, there is little more known about him. Nevertheless, his praying has not been forgotten. Nash's prayer ministry makes him a great hero in the ministry of revival.

Through the infirmity of an eye disease, the Lord led Nash to become the personal intercessor of young Charles Finney. In time, the enemies of Finney feared and hated the prayers of Father Nash more than anything else.

Father Nash was known to prophesy and work in the gifts of the Holy Spirit. For example, there remains a prophecy that he gave over several young men who resisted the moving of the Holy Spirit in the Second Great Awakening. From his prophecy, we can see his determination, faith, and strength in God. In Father Nash, there could not be any compromise.

Charles Finney, who was a witness of the incident and the prophecy, wrote,

> The next Sabbath, after preaching morning and afternoon myself–for I did the preaching altogether, and Brother Nash gave himself up almost continually to prayer–we met at five o'clock in the church, for a prayer meeting. The meeting–house was filled. Near the close of the meeting, Brother Nash arose, and addressed that company of young men who had joined hand in hand to resist the revival. I believe they were all there, and they sat braced up against the Spirit of God. It was too solemn for them really to make ridicule of what they heard and saw; and yet their brazen-facedness and stiff-neckedness were apparent to everybody.
>
> Brother Nash addressed them very earnestly and pointed out the guilt and danger of the course they were taking. Toward the close of his address, he waxed exceeding warm, and said to them, "Now, mark me, young men! God will break your ranks in less than one week, either by converting some of you, or by sending some of you to hell. He will do this as certainly as the Lord is my God." He was standing where he brought his hand down on the top of the pew before him, so as to make it thoroughly jar. He sat immediately down, dropped his head, and groaned with pain.
>
> The house was as still as death, and most of the people held down their heads. I could see that the young men were agitated. For myself, I

regretted that Brother Nash had gone so far. He had committed himself, that God would either take the life of some of them, and send them to hell, or convert some of them, within a week. However, on Tuesday morning of the same week, the leader of these young men came to me, in the greatest distress of mind. He was all prepared to submit; and as soon as I came to press him he broke down like a child, confessed, and manifestly gave himself to Christ. Then he said, "What shall I do, Mr. Finney?" I replied "Go immediately to all your young companions, and pray with them, and exhort them, at once to turn to the Lord." He did so; and before the week was out, nearly if not all of that class of young men, were hoping in Christ.[18]

In addition to this, Father Nash had great faith in God and determination. He refused to give up. When he prayed, he believed that God would hear his prayers and finally answer them, one way or another. Father Nash did not stop praying on a particular subject until God answered his prayer. After that, he only reminded God of His promise.

Father Nash prayed daily. His prayers were prayed with great struggling and weakened health. Throughout his intercessory ministry, he paid many prices that God would move in His power during the Second Great Awakening. There were many results of such a type of prayer. The power of God was highly manifested in the revival and the cities; men and women were saved, people glorified God, and there was a continual opening heaven.

Following Paul

In my journey, I have learned much from Paul when it comes to prayer. I learned to pray as Paul did; I learned to commune with God as Paul did; I sought to seek the Holy Spirit as Paul did. Following what Paul did will cost a person everything. As I heard many times, a prayer that costs nothing will get us nothing.

In Acts 9:11 and Acts 16:13, we learn how to pray in the very school of prayer as founded for the church by Paul. We owe much to Paul, and that includes how to pray to get results.

Paul and Barnabas established every church with prayer and fasting. Both made a habit, a business, and a life out of prayer. Paul's greatest spiritual trait was a strong tendency to pray, regardless of the circumstances, and regardless of the cost.

Paul knew quite well that a Christian who did not pray did not live for God.

And a praying saint was a praising saint (Acts 20:36–37).

In Colossians 2, we see Paul was so burdened down and in a spiritual conflict that he wrestled in prayer against Satan, who was seeking to lead these believers astray. Paul knew how to overcome Satan—through prayer and the Word of God (Ephesians 6:17–18). This is also true of the ancient church. He longed to see the saints united in Christ and enjoy the riches of blessing in Him.

According to ancient Christian sources, the prayers of the ancient saints rallied against all the forms of magic, witchcraft, and all the forces of evil; nothing evil could stand against their prayers. There is no comparison between the church of today—at least in modern, wealthy nations—to that of the ancient church.

According to the early church, a person can arise in their prayers to a life of perfection of prayer in their lives.

It is possible today for the saints of God to work in such a perfect form and method of prayer that nothing can stand in their way, nor withhold from them the blessings of God. And this journey of prayer should start with Jesus, or at least Paul.

Paul and Silas

Acts 16:24–26 reads,

Who, having received such a charge, thrust them into the inner prison, and made their feet fast in the stocks. And at midnight Paul and Silas prayed, and sang praises unto God: and the prisoners heard them. And suddenly there was a great earthquake, so that the foundations of the prison were shaken: and immediately all the doors were opened, and every one's bands were loosed.

For the sake of Christ, and the preaching of the gospel, both Paul and Silas were arrested at Philippi (Acts 16:24). The imprisonment of Paul and Silas was because Paul cast out the spirit of python from a damsel (Acts 16:16–18). The young damsel, possessed of the pythonic demon, continued to harass Paul as he went on his way, proclaiming the gospel of Jesus Christ. The pythonic demon spoke through the young damsel these words: "These men are the servants of the most high God, which shew unto us the way of salvation" (Acts 16:17). The article "the" is not present in the text and Acts 16:17 should be written as "*a* way of salvation." The pythonic demon, speaking through the young damsel, lied, and said that Jesus Christ is only *a* way of salvation rather than *the* way of salvation. According to the view of my son, the difference between heaven and hell can be the presence or absence of the definite article "the."

By Paul's casting out that pythonic demon, various consequences took place. For example, besides being imprisoned, they were beaten.

Despite being in an awful state, they could still sing a song of victory. From Paul and Silas came a song of victory, which issued out of the blackness of a dark dungeon. Such a song of victory went through the walls of the prison, beyond the roof, into the clouds, and finally entered heaven itself and the throne room of God.

The song of victory was unto God. Paul and Silas were ministering to God, not asking for deliverance, but worshiping Him because of who He is.

All Christians must have the right attitude, behavior, and motive when dealing with terrible circumstances. Both Paul and Silas had the right frame of mind. They held that they were living in victory, regardless of their circumstances. Why? Because of their relationship with the Lord and having knowing-faith—knowing that God would move. There was no positive mental attitude here, no positive confession. Both Paul and Silas were not living in disobedience—they were right in God's will. And still, they were imprisoned.

The earthquake that shook the foundations of the prison at Philippi was in answer to the power of intensified prayer. This earthquake saved Paul and Silas and showed the pagans just who God is.

Paul and Silas understood the road to victory. In this case, the way to victory must begin and end with devotion. Paul and Silas saw that devotion is a necessity when one is in difficulties. To Paul and Silas, devotion is the deathblow to challenges and problems of all kinds.

We do not need counseling, but we need to release the power of God within a situation. This is done by entering the presence of God, and that is done through devotion.

From Acts 16:16–26, we learn that circumstances are no criteria of character. And doing good does not necessarily produce equal results. Further, the righteous are non-resistant in their method of meeting persecution. The ungodly are permitted great freedom.

God moved at the last minute only when Paul and Silas were lifting prayers and praises. God will not act unless we act first. And we must act first with prayer. The results are manifold.

Smith Wigglesworth said, "First thing every morning when I get out of bed,

I jump out; I don't just drag out, but I jump out. And when my feet hit the floor, I say, 'Praise the Lord,' and I praise God every morning."[19]

Limits on Prayers

Prayer begins to decay before us, and the perfection of prayer begins to be lost when we interject our wills, passions, and desires above the mind and will of God. Therefore, prayer has limits and can well be undone due to our attitude and our volition entering such a holy place of God's presence.

It is clear that this also happened to Paul when he prayed that the angel of Satan, who had been allowed by the Lord to buffet Paul for his own good, might be removed, saying, "And lest I should be exalted above measure through the abundance of the revelations, there was given to me a thorn in the flesh, the messenger of Satan to buffet me, lest I should be exalted above measure. For this thing I besought the Lord thrice, that it might depart from me. And he said unto me, My grace is sufficient for thee: for my strength is made perfect in weakness. Most gladly therefore will I rather glory in my infirmities, that the power of Christ may rest upon me" (2 Corinthians 12:7–9).

Paul was praying contrary to God's mind and will. And he was praying beyond the ability for God to move. For God will not move against His will, His character, and His advantages. He bids us that we must have the full and undoubting confidence of the answer, only in those things which are not for our benefit or temporal comforts but are in conformity to the Lord's will.

When we sometimes ask for things opposed to our salvation, we are most providentially refused.

Looking also to Jesus, we see a limit on prayer. Scripture reads, "And Jesus said unto them, Because of your unbelief: for verily I say unto you, If ye have faith as a grain of mustard seed, ye shall say unto this mountain, Remove hence to yonder place; and it shall remove; and nothing shall be impossible unto you" (Matthew 17:20–21).

If there are four persons praying that the mountain be removed, one on each side of the mountain, just whose prayers will be answered? The person whose prayers follow God's sovereignty, His will, His omnipotence, and His nature. And this is also true for our faith as well. Faith, which has no power, must line up with the object of that faith: God Himself.

Praying beyond God's ability to answer is praying a prayer that draws from God the answer, "I am sorry, but I cannot or will not do what you ask." Many teach that there is nothing that God cannot do, but this is wrong since He cannot lie or sin. If there were no limit to what we can pray about, then we would be God and God would be our servant.

In studying prayer, we forget that prayer works in the best interest of everyone concerned. The ability of God to answer us should not be a worry or concern but a blessing. For by this, we know that God will answer according to His will and not ours, as John says in 1 John 5:14. These boundaries have been determined by God's grace, God's sovereignty, God's will, God's power, time, and especially free will.

God gives man the choice to obey or not obey (Deuteronomy 11:26; 1 Samuel 15:22).

Godly Restrictions on Prayer

Like all spiritual weapons, prayer can never be used as a weapon against God. All the weapons are to be used against the powers of Satan and his forces (Matthew 10:1; Mark 3:13, 16:17; Luke 9:1, 10:19; John 16:8–11; 2 Corinthians 10:5–7; Ephesians 2:6–7, 6:10–18; Colossians 1:13, 2:14–17; Hebrews 2:9, 14; 1 Peter 2:9,14–15, 5:7–8; James 4:7; 1 John 3:8).

In prayer, God is the Master while the saint is the servant. Prayer cannot make us the master of God (1 Samuel 23:10; 2 Samuel 7:20–26; Isaiah 42:1, 49:3–6, 52:13, 53:11; Ezekiel 34:23–24; Zechariah 3:8; Matthew 8:19, 9:11, 10:24–25, 12:38, 19:16, 22:16, 20:28, 22:36, 23:8, 23:10, 26:18; Luke 22:27; John 13:13–14; Galatians 4:7; Ephesians 2:6–7, 6:9; Colossians 4:1; Titus 1:1; Jude 1:1; Revelation 15:3). This is clearly seen from the Greek.

Prayers cannot make God act for our benefit and in the way we wish. If that were the case, then the saints would be able to manipulate God. God would subsequently and invariably be dethroned, and the universe would have many gods. As such, prayers cannot be universal laws or formulas that even God must obey. The heathen believes prayers are like that.

If God moves when we pray, it is because we are praying according to His will in a situation, and God wants to move in that situation before we even prayed; He is only waiting to see if we will join in the battle. Remember, God will not fight in spiritual warfare for us until we enter the fight. For example, God did not move for Daniel until Daniel began praying and fasting (Daniel 9–10).

Conditions of Prayer

In Mark 11:20–26, Jesus uses the fig tree to teach us that there are conditions of prayer.

The first condition of prayer is that we must have faith in God, even if God is silent. A Jewish Holocaust victim said, "I believe in the sun even when it is not shining. I believe in love even when I am not feeling it. I believe in God even when He is silent."[20] Smith Wigglesworth said about faith, "I am not moved by what I see. I am not moved by what I feel. I am moved only by what I believe."[21]

The second condition of prayer is expectancy. A person must believe and expect the answer to his prayers.

The third condition of prayer is forgiveness. This is a critical condition of prayer; a condition that is stressed time and again by Jesus (Matthew 5:23–24, 6:14–15, 18:32–33). It does no good to pray unless one forgives.

The fourth condition of prayer is that prayer must be in the dominion of Christ—abiding in Christ (John 16:7). We can ask what we will, and it shall be done unto us only if we abide in Christ, and His words abide in us.

One of the principles of the kingdom is "draw nigh to God, and he will draw nigh to you" (James 4:8). God always hears Christ, and if we abide in Christ, He will always hear us. Conversely, we have the right to be heard if we abide continually in Him. We must admit that thousands of prayers go up to God that are not answered. Why? Either God does not fulfill His promises, or else those who pray are not fully abiding in Christ Jesus.

Matthews 7:7–8 says, "Ask, and it shall be given you; seek, and ye shall find; knock, and it shall be opened unto you: For every one that asketh receiveth; and he that seeketh findeth; and to him that knocketh it shall be opened." Asking, seeking, and knocking are all continual and progressive. Not one time, but repeatedly. We must keep the mind fixed, as much as possible, at the end of life and on that which follows it.

Prayer is Not Mindless Prayer

Christianity is not a mindless and reasonless faith that must be followed blindly. Christianity demands that the minds, understandings, reasons, and judgments of men and women play a part in their Christian faith, prayer life, and life. God has not made men and women some mindless machines, but rational beings with reasoning, understanding, and other faculties. When people become Christians, they do not lose their faculties and check their minds at the door.

Genuine prayer is not a mindless act, process, or state. It is united with the mind of God, and God forms in our mind the words of prayer to be spoken. God does not empty our minds of thoughts, nor does He demand that we use some sort of mental meditation. Instead, it is demons who want this. They seek to empty our minds to put their thoughts, directions, and desires into them.

In Matthew 6:7, Jesus said that we must not regard genuine prayer as a magical incantation where phrases or words are repeated like mantras. Mindless chants have no place in the Christian life.

Genuine prayer is speaking to God with His will in mind (1 John 5:14). One of the goals of genuine prayer is not a mindless prayer, but a prayer that reasonably conveys our needs and our concerns unto a merciful God. Paul points out that sincere prayer is not a mindless prayer. Paul pleads with his readers to "continue in prayer and watch in the same with thanksgiving" (Colossians 4:2). In the Greek language, the idea of Colossians 4:2 is a mental state of continual alertness or watchfulness when we vocally pray (see also Matthew 26:41; Mark 14:38; 1 Corinthians 16:13; Ephesians 6:18; 1 Thessalonians 5:6; 1 Peter 5:8). The watching is "to give strict attention to, to be active, to take heed lest through remissness and indolence some destructive calamity suddenly overtake one."[22] Alertness or watchfulness is part of genuine prayer. If not, prayer has no value. No method of prayer that supports the techniques of the New Age has any value for Christian life. On the other hand, passive receptivity does not mean a mindless state, but a state that is passive unto the movements of the Holy Spirit. For example, the prophets were not robbed of their self-consciousness, or their self-control, but were in a state of passive receptivity (Numbers 11:25, 12:6–8; 1 Samuel 10:5–6, 19:20–21; 1 Kings 18:28–29; 2 Kings 9:11; 1 Corinthians 14:32).

I asked my son, "What would be the best way to translate Colossians 4:2?" He said, "Continue steadfastly in the occupation of prayer, and be mentally alert in it with an attitude of thanksgiving." He concludes that a mental state of alertness (watchfulness) is required for a prayer to be a genuine prayer. Further, the Greek word Paul uses for prayer here in Colossians 4:2 is rarely without the article. The emphasis means that the term prayer is not a general term, but a separative term that separates words, requests, intercessions, and petitions of the saints from the prayers of the pagans. Just by this alone, the prayers of the saints must be separate from the prayers of the heathens. Therefore, the prayers of the saints must not follow the practices or techniques of the pagans.

However, a considerable portion of prayer today is nothing more or less than mysticism. Mysticism, a pagan practice, focuses on extended mental meditation, abstracts from the phenomenal world, and generally rejects vocal prayer. In these methods, mental prayer is used to make the minds of men and women lose their consciousness. In such a state, the minds become ready to be controlled and manipulated by demons.

Practices like these, being a part of the realm of the demonic, also incorporate into themselves hypnotism and the power of suggestion. Neither of these is part of genuine prayer.

Further, these practices open people up to instability, fanaticism, heresies, and above all, demon possession. Since these practices make the mind thoughtless (or mindless) in nature, this explains the rampant phenomenon today of Christians who are mentally unstable after trying these techniques. Only deliverance can help undo the damage done by such practices.

In such cases, people lose their minds, become irrational and lifeless in their faces, and accept the demonic spirits of the ancient world. These evil spirits take over the minds of men and women; in essence, they are mind snatchers.

A Few More Facts on Faith

Faith is a gift, a fruit, an act, a process, and a state. The Bible speaks of the importance of faith when it says that without faith, it is impossible to please God (Hebrews 11:6).

Faith is always tied to what God has already promised. Faith will never work with something that God has not promised.

Faith is something that a person has already: "God hath dealt to every man the measure of faith" (Romans 12:3).

Faith can be increased from glory unto glory. The Bible says that saints must "grow in grace, and in the knowledge of our Lord and Saviour Jesus Christ" (2 Peter 3:18).

Faith can only be increased by the Word of God, fasting, praying, and answered prayer (Matthew 17:20–21; Romans 10:17; Jude 20).

When we exercise our faith, if we have a proper motive, attitude, and behavior, God is obligated to answer our prayer as long as it is in God's will.

CHAPTER 10
PRAYER AND TRIALS

Prayer without some type of trials following it or at least being associated with it is foreign to the ancient church and the ancient Jews. Daniel prayed amid tribulation (Daniel 2–12). This is true for all the apostles and early Christians.

When facing a wall of opposition, men and women have found prayer to be the key to their survival and success. Jeremiah prayed regardless of the opposition; he had no real success from his prayers. He had no actual results, yet he prayed. Jeremiah's success came after his death—by the miracles God performed through Daniel (see Daniel 9).

We must pray, regardless of any visible success. Noah faced great odds alone. The Bible says that "Noah walked with God" (Genesis 6:9), which implies that he was a man of prayer. Noah sought prayer as a relief from the evil and sins of the world, and as a means of comfort and power. Noah heard the voice of God; God spoke to him as a friend (Genesis 6:13–7:1).

Abraham talked with God and had a visitation from God (Genesis 17–19). Abraham genuinely enforced the practice of praying in the history of the Hebrew patriarchs. The significance of the altar is that prayers must accompany it (Genesis 12:7–8, 13:3–4).

The three Hebrew children mentioned in Daniel 3 were men who did not bow, give in, or compromise their faith, despite tribulation. Their strength came from their lives of prayer, their relationship with God, and their knowledge that God was able. We must remember where our strength in God originates.

Jesus, the apostles, and the saints sought help through prayer against the opposition (Matthew 4:4–10; Acts 16:25).

My son translated 2 Corinthians 11:23–30 in the following manner:

Ministers of Christ, are they? I am speaking as if I was quite irrational–I am also more than them, in labors even more abundantly, in stripes much greater degree, in imprisonments much greater, in the dangers of deaths repeatedly. From the hands of the Jews, I received five times forty stripes, except one. Three times I was beaten with rods, once I received a stoning, three times I was shipwrecked, both a night and a day I have spent time in the deep sea; by journeyings frequently, by dangers within rivers, by dangers with robbers, by dangers with my own race, by dangers from the Gentiles, by dangers within the city, by dangers within the wilderness, by dangers in the sea, by dangers among false brethren; by toil and hardship, by sleepless nights frequently, by hunger and thirst, by fastings frequently, by cold and poorly clothed. Apart from those external things that are the regular routine of my office and my labors, there is the pressure that is on me daily, the anxiety about all the churches. Who is weak, and I am not weak? Who is led to commit sin, and I do not burn with indignation?

My Prayer Life and Trials

During the worst trials of my life, prayer was the only thing that kept me going. It put me on my knees and strengthened my faith. For prayer is an action of our faith. Prayer cannot be a force by itself; prayer focuses on the object of that power: God Himself.

It seems that I could not get through one trial before two or more began. It seemed like Satan had no one else to test. I felt his focus was on me and my life.

It was so hard to keep up with my son and his needs. And if that were not enough, my mother, my mother-in-law, and others were all in need.

I had to get to the place where I hated Satan and his evil spirits immensely. That is a shame. Saints must hate evil in all its forms. But many of us are oblivious that light and darkness cannot coexist (1 John 1:5–9). And many of us do not understand that we cannot be children of God and children of Satan at the same time. We either hate God or hate Satan. We cannot love both. Therefore, saints must, with a godly hatred, hate all evil (Matthew 6:24).

I had to hate Satan and all his evil spirits because I was not going to let my family go to hell. Desperation pushed me to begin to study everything I could find out about Satan and his kingdom. I had a hunger to understand my enemy and his wiles. But first, I had to learn about God and His angels. It is always better to study about good first and then about evil. It is very dangerous to research demonology first. Few saints are mature enough to study such a topic.

I went from one bookstore to another, purchasing almost everything that I could find about Satan and his evil spirits. I wanted to know how they worked and how I could fight them. The more I researched, the closer I came to the fight that I was ready to begin.

Demons Grabbing Me

One night, I woke up with something grabbing ahold of me. My arms were tied up. If I could get one free, I thought that I would be okay. Other times, in my sleep, I felt hands around my throat, trying to choke me. If I could whisper the name of Jesus, the hold would loosen. Night after night, I fought. My fight was daily and nightly.

It was common for my cover to be on the floor the next morning as I was waking up.

Car Wrecks

It was common for me to have one car wreck after another. I learned that highways are places where demons congregate. And I learned that demons love particular areas by highways, and time and again they struck my car, whether by a car wreck or by disabling my vehicle.

Once, I was driving on the highway, and I went through a blackness. This blackness, though spiritual, became a visible blackness to the point I had trouble seeing.

I read about this blackness in a book written by one of the most exceptional believers England has produced in modern times: Smith Wigglesworth. His message was filled with faith, prayer, healing, miracles, obedience, and confidence in the Lord God.

He preached a critical message in August 1914, just seven years after he had been baptized with the Holy Spirit. He preached the following words concerning Christ at Lazarus's tomb:

> I tell you what makes us lose the confidence is disobedience to God and His laws. Jesus said it was because of them that stood around that He prayed; but He knew that He heard Him always. And because He knew that His father heard Him always, He knew that the dead could come forth. There are times when there seems to be a stone wall in front of us, as black as midnight, and there is nothing left but confidence in God. There is no feeling. What you must do is to have fidelity and confidence to believe that He will not fail and cannot fail. We shall never get anywhere if we depend upon our feelings. There is something a thousand times better than feelings, and it is the naked word of God. There is a

divine revelation within you, that came in when you were born from above, and this is real faith.[1]

I have met that stone wall many times in my life, and during these times, I have seen the darkness of evil present before me.

I found that in some of these spots along highways, there are many car wrecks. One night, while I was praying, the Lord showed me the kind of demons that stay at Nassau River Bridge. A particular demon looked like a bear from the waist down, and like a man in the upper parts of his form.

About three weeks later, one night after working the four-to-twelve shift, I had to pass over that bridge. It was about 12:30 a.m. on a very foggy night. I could hardly see anything in front of me. When I approached that bridge, my car lights went out. I did not stop. Cars coming in the opposite direction were flicking their lights for me to turn on my car lights. I could not imagine how many people were calling the police about a car traveling down the highway without any lights.

I drove on until I came to a gas station. Thank God, a man was able to put a new fuse in my car. It is interesting that demons can affect even the fuses of our vehicles.

Another night, I made a left turn into a gas station to purchase gas. The light had turned red. The traffic should have stopped, but not all stopped.

As I was turning about to go into the gas station, a motorcycle came around the corner at a very high speed. The motorcycle hit my car on the right side of the passenger back door. The crash threw him from his bike, over my car, into the median, and onto the grass. The police were called, and an ambulance came. The medics put him into the ambulance and drove him to the hospital.

According to the motorcycle rider, when the crash happened, he felt a big arm wrap around him and protect him from being killed.

Through much prayer, the man did not die, nor was he hurt. The devil picked the wrong car for this to happen. My vehicle belonged to the Lord. I prayed over that car. I learned many years ago to pray over everything that I had and give it over to the Lord.

Even though the wreck was not my fault, my insurance stepped in and paid for everything.

The next day at work, my bosses sent me back home. I was told the wife of the motorcycle rider had called that morning, but the secretaries did not give her my phone number. I told the guards that if she called back, they were to give her my number.

His wife was finally able to call me and told me a fascinating story. Her husband had recently been released from prison. He had purchased that motorcycle for traveling. He was greatly discouraged about not being able to find a job. He had gone to church, received the Lord, and sought the Lord's help in finding a job. He prayed and prayed, but there was no answer to his prayers. On the day of the wreck, he was planning to rob a bank.

The policeman told the man of what I said about praying over my car. Those words made a true believer out of the motorcycle rider.

I took the car to see how much it would cost to be fixed. The adjuster said, "That man is dead." I said, "No! He did not even get hurt. This car belongs to God. I had anointed it with olive oil." The adjustor said back to me, "I used to believe like that." I said back to him, "So you are the reason I had this accident." I told the adjuster much about God and led him back to Christ.

Sometimes, bad things happen in our lives for just one person. If the bad thing had never happened, I might never have met that adjuster and led him back to the Lord Jesus Christ.

In my life, Isaiah 59:19 was proven time and time again: "So shall they fear the name of the LORD from the west, and his glory from the rising of the sun. When the enemy shall come in like a flood, the Spirit of the LORD shall lift up a standard against him." In my life, the enemy repeatedly came in like a flood, and God repeatedly built up a standard. In the end, God got all the glory out of that wreck.

In his poem "Crossing the Bar" (1869), Lord Tennyson wrote, "I hope to see my pilot face to face / When I have crossed the bar."[2]

Psalms 91:1 reads, "He that dwelleth in the secret place of the most High shall abide under the shadow of the Almighty."

Charles Henry Mackintosh, a nineteenth century minister, said,

> The Lord be praised for such words! They assure us that all Scripture is given of God; and that all Scripture is given to us. Precious link between the soul and God! What tongue can tell the value of such a link? God has spoken — spoken to us. His word is a rock against which all the waves of infidel thought dash themselves in contemptible impotency, leaving it in its own divine strength and eternal stability. Nothing can touch the word of God. Not all the powers of earth and hell, men and devils combined can ever move the word of God. There it stands, in its own moral glory, in spite of all the assaults of the enemy, from age to age. "Forever, O Lord, Thy word is settled in heaven."[3]

When a person studies prayer, intercession, and demons, he or she must know how to fight spiritual warfare. Cyprian, a father of the ancient church during the third century A. D., said quite well and with mind-blowing words, "We are still in the world; we are still situated in the front line of the battle; we fight every day for our lives."[4]

Jesus and the Wilderness

When Jesus was led out in the wilderness to be tempted by Satan, He used the written word as His main weapon.

One of the key phrases that I repeatedly used in my fights and battles against evil was, "It is written." Jesus used that critical phrase, "It is written," when He was tempted by Satan (Matthew 4:4–10). I told the devil and his evil spirits, "It is written, devil, if I stand against you, you must flee in the name of Jesus Christ." I have also used "it is written" in many other ways like, "It is written, devil, that God is the God of healing, and I stand upon that word. Therefore, I stand to be healed in the name of Jesus Christ."

When my husband and I studied spiritual warfare, we learned that Satan and his evil spirits are bullies, and they try to intimidate the saints. I learned that if saints resist the devil, he will flee from them (James 4:7). And I learned that I must be sober and vigilant as a saint because the devil walks about, seeking whom he may devour (1 Peter 5:8).

I also remember Galatians 6:9: "And let us not be weary in well doing: for in due season we shall reap, if we faint not." First John 4:4 reads, "Ye are of God, little children, and have overcome them: because greater is he that is in you, than he that is in the world."

I learned to continue to plead the blood of Jesus Christ over me and whatever I needed. I learned that Satan and his evil spirits flee from the mention of the blood of Jesus Christ. It did not take very long for me to understand that we, as saints of God, are soldiers and we are in a full-blown war against Satan and his evil spirits. We are warring against spiritual darkness (1 Corinthians 10:4).

Furthermore, the battle starts with the Word of God and ends with the Word of God. We must get God's Word into our spirits, souls, and minds if we ever want to be able to stand in faith and hold on to His promises when the adversary rises against us.

As we learn to battle in spiritual warfare, we must always remember who we are in Jesus Christ. We are nothing outside of Jesus Christ, but we are kings and priests in training with the Lord Jesus Christ.

Satan Came to Kill Me

One of the times Satan came to me to kill me, I used Romans 8:37–39 against him. This biblical passage reads,

> Nay, in all these things we are more than conquerors through him that loved us. For I am persuaded, that neither death, nor life, nor angels, nor principalities, nor powers, nor things present, nor things to come, Nor height, nor depth, nor any other creature, shall be able to separate us from the love of God, which is in Christ Jesus our Lord.

I primarily used "we are more than conquerors through him that loved us" repeatedly throughout my life in my fights and battles against Satan and his evil spirits.

There were seven key phrases that I used in battle, which never failed to assist me:

1. "It is written. . . in the name of Jesus Christ."
2. "If I resist you, devil, you must flee in the name of Jesus Christ."
3. "Greater is He that is in me, than He that is in the world."
4. "We are more than conquerors in the name of Jesus Christ."
5. "I plead the blood of the Lamb in the name of Jesus Christ."
6. "I plead the bloodline in the name of Jesus Christ."
7. "I plead the blood over my mind, subconscious mind, spirit, body, soul, and brain in the name of Jesus Christ."

I continue to use these seven critical phrases in my spiritual battles. These have become my seven blows against Satan and his evil spirits, first and foremost. I repeatedly use these. If these do not entirely work, I use other prayers that also are successful. I have learned that if prayer does not work the first time, I must repeatedly pray until the battle ceases, the oppression leaves or an answer has come.

In warfare, there are always both offense and defense. Too many Christians always take the defensive when it comes to the devil and his demons. They never take the offensive against them. As I have heard many times that the best defense is a good offense. So we, as Christians, must learn how to attack the forces of evil, and after that, how to live.

For example, offensive warfare may be tearing down the stronghold, which Satan has whispered into our minds. Ephesians 6:12–13 reads,

For we wrestle not against flesh and blood, but against principalities, against powers, against the rulers of the darkness of this world, against spiritual wickedness in high places. Wherefore take unto you the whole armour of God, that ye may be able to withstand in the evil day, and having done all, to stand.

Within the kingdom of evil, there is a preoccupation with offense. Witches, warlocks, and other occultists seek to take the high ground, strike first, and keep all others from ever striking back. They care little about defense. And that is their weakness. We, as Christians, should fight fire with fire and become proactive. Offense should be first in our strategy. But unlike the occultists, we must have a good defense before we become proactive in our warfare.

Pleading the Blood of the Lamb

Few people truly know the significance or the power of pleading the blood of Jesus. The word "pleading" is not found in the Bible in this connection. Its meaning deals with legal rights associated with the blood of the Lamb.

The practice of pleading the blood of the Lamb is traced back to the revivalists, men like John Wesley, and C. H. Spurgeon, the reformers—including the Puritans, and the liturgies of the ancient church. So it is not something foreign to Christianity.

Additionally, every time Christians practice the Lord's Supper (the Eucharist), they are practicing the pleading of the blood, regardless of what they may think (1 Corinthians 11:22–24). Each time we practice the Lord's Supper, we are to remember the body and blood of Christ, and what both have done, including conquering Satan, his forces, sin, and evil.

By pleading the blood, the saints of God are pleading their cause and their case before God according to the power of the blood (Revelation 12:11). And the blood of Christ is pleading our blood-brought rights before God.

In the Old Testament, it was common to plead someone's case before the Lord (1 Samuel 24:15; Job 16:21).

Here are three main benefits of pleading the blood of the Lamb:
1. Forgiveness (Matthew 26:28; Ephesians 1:7, 2:13)
2. Deliverance (Colossians 1:13, 2:15; Hebrews 2:14; 1 John 3:8)
3. Protection (Exodus 12:22–23)

Requirements for Pleading the Blood

1. Salvation
2. Full surrender
3. Faith
4. Purity
5. Simplicity
6. Obedience

The Basics of Pleading the Blood

1. Plead the blood over the object that needs to be protected.
2. Plead the blood against whatever type of evil could come against that object.
3. End the prayer in the name of Jesus Christ.

Offensive Prayers Used

Over the years of public ministry, my son and I have found many prayers that repeatedly work. They may not work the first time, but they will work progressively. Sometimes, it is not the first time we say a prayer that it will work; sometimes, we must say a prayer numerous times before we receive results. We must keep on knocking. Here are some examples of offensive prayers:

1. Father, I repent of all my sins of thought, word, and deed. I repent of my sins of omission and commission. Father, I ask for your forgiveness in the mighty name of Jesus and receive it by the precious blood of Jesus Christ.
2. I bind my calling, my election, my healing, my wealth, my ministry, my gifts, and my promises of God to me. I will not allow anyone to take them from me—they are mine!
3. I loose all ungodly prayers against me, and I send them back to the one who sent them, for their instruction and correction. Now, I apply the blood of Jesus over my mind, my subconscious mind, my spirit, my soul, my body, and my brain.
4. I break all curses, hexes, spells, and all prayers over me that are contrary to the will of God for my life.
5. In the name of Jesus Christ, by the power of His cross, His blood, and His Word, I bind the evil spirits, the evil powers, the evil forces of the earth, the underground, the air, the water, the fire, the

netherworld, and all other satanic forces of nature. I rebuke any curses, spells, or hexes sent against me, and send them directly to Jesus for Him to deal with as He will. Lord, I ask you to bless our enemies by sending your Holy Spirit to lead them to repentance. I bind all interplay, interaction, and communication of evil spirits. I claim the protection of the shed blood of Jesus Christ over any evil forces.

6. O Satan, O Satan, I openly and publicly announce that I have won the victory over you in the name of Jesus Christ. In the name of Jesus Christ, I have put my foot upon your neck, O Satan. I proclaim victory over my finances, over my wealth, over my health, over my job, over my children, over my mother, over my father, over my sister, over my brother, over my wife or husband, and everything in my life. I have put my foot upon your neck, O Satan, and I proclaim victory in the name of Jesus Christ. You shall not take from me any longer. I have put my foot upon your neck, and I say that enough is enough, devil, in the name of Jesus Christ. Now, I take authority over my life, over my ministry, and everything in the mighty name of Jesus Christ.

Praying the Psalms

Modern Christians, time and again, overlook or forget the power released by praying the Psalms. One of the reasons for the success of the ancient Christians' prayers rests in the fact that they repeatedly prayed the Psalms. Psalms cover every circumstance possible:

1. Psalm 1 emphasizes the flourishing of the righteous, while the wicked are destroyed. It is also the most important way to see blessings and prosperity.
2. Psalm 4 is a prayer of faith.
3. Psalm 9 is praise to God for deliverance so far, and a plea that the deliverance may continue: "When my enemies are turned back, they shall fall and perish at thy presence. ... Thou hast rebuked the heathen, thou hast destroyed the wicked ... O thou enemy, destructions are come to a perpetual end: and thou hast destroyed cities; their memorial is perished with them" (vv. 3, 5–6).
4. Psalm 12 is a prayer to God to rescue the godly from the wicked. Important: this Psalm is good to remember when the whole world

seems to be against you or seems to be out of control.
5. Psalm 15 is a prayer for a life pleasing to God.
6. Psalm 22 is a prayer of deliverance from enemies.
7. Psalm 23 is a prayer of deliverance from evil and from enemies.
8. Psalm 29 is a prayer of the power of the voice of God to shake.
9. Psalm 34 is a prayer of deliverance from evil and evildoers.
10. Psalm 54 is a prayer of deliverance from trouble, evil, and evildoers.
11. Psalm 70 is a prayer of deliverance from trouble, evil, and evildoers. David emphasizes that he is poor and needy.
12. Psalm 73 is a prayer about the rich and wealthy being destroyed in a moment, but the righteous have the happiness that lasts forever.
13. Psalm 78 shows that when Israel was obedient, God sent prosperity. When Israel was disobedient, God sent judgment.
14. Psalm 82 is a prayer of deliverance.
15. Psalm 85 is a prayer of mercy.
16. Psalm 94 is a prayer of judgment against evil and the wicked and a prayer of deliverance against evil and the wicked.
17. Psalm 102 is a prayer of mercy and help from distress.
18. Psalm 118 is a prayer over distress.
19. Psalm 121 is a prayer of protection.
20. Psalm 141 is a prayer of deliverance from evil and enemies.

A Psalter for Prayer

1. If you need deliverance, pray Psalms 77, 104, and 113.
2. If you need prosperity, pray Psalm 1 and 106.
3. If you need protection, pray Psalm 19.
4. Psalms 10 and 11 are used by the saints to express faith and prayer.
5. If you are in distress, pray Psalms 53, 55, 56, and 141.
6. If you need to be blessed, pray Psalms 1, 31, 40, 111, 118, and 127.
7. If you are persecuted by your own family and opposed by many, pray Psalm 3.
8. At your affliction's end, pray Psalms 4, 74, 114, and 115.
9. In great times of trouble, pray Psalm 5, especially when the wicked are ready to ensnare you.
10. If you feel yourself under the Lord's displeasure, pray Psalm 6 and 37.
11. If someone is plotting against you, pray Psalm 7.

12. For victory over your enemy, pray Psalm 9.
13. Under great distress, especially when the wicked and the backslidden are surrounding you, pray Psalm 11.
14. If someone blasphemes the Lord, pray Psalms 13 and 52.
15. If you are in warfare against the enemies of God, pray Psalms 16, 85, 87, and 139.
16. If you want to know how Moses prayed, pray Psalm 89.
17. When you have been delivered from these enemies and oppressors, pray Psalm 17.
18. If enemies are surrounding you, pray Psalm 24.
19. If the enemies of God persist, pray Psalms 25, 34, and 42.
20. If your foes press yet harder, pray Psalms 26 and 30.
21. If your safety is in question, pray Psalm 38.
22. If you wish to learn the value of endurance, pray Psalm 39.
23. Trust God and how He will deal with your enemies by praying Psalm 41.
24. If you have been slandered, pray Psalms 51, 53, 55, and 54.
25. If still, the persecution follows hard on you, and he who seeks your life enters, pray Psalms 56 and 141.
26. If you need deliverance from God's enemies, pray Psalms 63, 64, 69, and 70.

The Tools of Satan

While there are several tools of Satan, the main three tools are deception, temptation, and accusation. When we learn these three main tools and how to rebuke them by using Scripture, and my seven keys of warfare, we can win almost every time. Of course, not every battle is ours. We will win the battles that God has called us to fight, but not necessarily every struggle before us.

The deceptions used against the believers are based upon carnal reason, the guilt of conscience, jealousies, and fears (2 Corinthians 2:11, 11:3; Ephesians 4:14, 6:11 Revelation 12:9). Satan uses deception, accusation, temptation, false reasoning, and arguments in an effort to overthrow our faith.

Because of this, evil spirits study an individual and contrive the best plan of deception, temptation, and accusation to destroy that person. The whole business of evil spirits is to examine men, women, and children to terminate them. It is this reason that the demons go up and down upon the earth. Though they are not omniscient, demons know all the ranks and classes of men, women, and children in the state of grace and holiness. By studying us, they understand what deceptions, temptations, or accusations need to be used against each one of us (1 Peter 1:6).

Evil spirits are diverse and are capable of a diversity of suggestions and reasonings. But God's workings and with His saints are also various, and He desires to move upon His believers and teach them how to defend themselves.

The ignorance of the meaning of the Scriptures has become the downfall of many saints. And it is wise to remember that demons manipulate legalities, through which people cede illegitimate rights to them.

Satan and his evil spirits first put their false suggestions and solicitations of sexual and worldly objects into our hearts (John 13:2; 1 Corinthians 7:5; Ephesians 6:12; Hebrews 8:5). These false suggestions and solicitations do not come from sinners or saints. Rather, they come from outside the sinners and the saints. As long as people do not commit or fulfill these false suggestions and solicitations, no sin is committed.

Satan and his evil spirits have six main advantages over us when it comes to deception, temptation, and accusation:

1. They frequently convey false reasonings and suggestions unto us.
2. They can send us a multitude of false reasonings and considerations together at once.
3. They can hold the attention of our minds.
4. They add weight to their false reasonings and accusations by a powerful affirmation that it is so.
5. They back their false conclusions with warnings and terrors.
6. They try to make us think that their false reasonings and suggestions are from us.

No sinner or saint can avoid the false reasonings and suggestions of Satan and his spirits. They come to all of us. And no person can take the false reasonings and suggestions of Satan and his spirits off any other person; only God can do this. We can pray, but it is only God who can remove these darts of Satan (1 Corinthians 12; Ephesians 6:16).

Luther, in his sermon on the Gospel of John, adds another kind of advantage that Satan has over us. He says, "For the devil goes to work with might and main to impede and obstruct the Gospel, he uses every obstacle at his disposal. Besides, he enjoys the advantage of having as an ally within our own hearts that great piece of Adam, who is too lazy by nature, too sluggish, and too tired to engage in a battle like this and always draws us back, thus making it especially hard and unpleasant to keep on contending with opposition and obstacles of so many kinds and to fight to the finish."[5]

Lord's Prayer and Satan

In the Large Catechism, Luther, speaking about the Lord's Prayer, says, "The entire substance of all our prayer is directed against our chief enemy."[6] Why? Satan is proactively and offensively working against everything Jesus teaches us to pray for in His prayer. By the Lord's Prayer, we see the areas of conflict in the cosmic-earthly rebellion presented before us. No one describes this better than Luther in the Large Catechism.

> For no one believes how the devil opposes and resists them, and cannot suffer that any one teach or believe aright. And it hurts him beyond measure to suffer his lies and abominations, that have been honored under the most specious pretexts of the divine name, to be exposed, and to be disgraced himself, and, besides, be driven out of the heart, and suffer such a breach to be made in his kingdom. Therefore he chafes and rages as a fierce enemy with all his power and might, and marshals all his subjects, and, in addition, enlists the world and our own flesh as his allies. For our flesh is in itself indolent and inclined to evil, even though we have accepted and believe the Word of God. The world, however, is perverse and wicked; this he incites against us, fans and stirs the fire, that he may hinder and drive us back, cause us to fall, and again bring us under his power. Such is all his will, mind, and thought, for which he strives day and night, and never rests a moment, employing all arts, wiles, ways, and means whichever he can invent.
>
> If we would be Christians, therefore, we must surely expect and reckon upon having the devil with all his angels and the world as our enemies who will bring every possible misfortune and grief upon us. For where the Word of God is preached, accepted, or believed, and produces fruit, there the holy cross cannot be wanting. And let no one think that he shall have peace; but he must risk whatever he has upon earth-possessions, honor, house and estate, wife and children, body and life.[7]

The Main Strategies of Satan

Like a physical enemy, Satan has strategies that he continues to use against mankind, and especially the saints of God. Every sinner who goes to hell and every saint who fails God are proof that the strategies of Satan are quite successful. These strategies are older than humanity, and it is impossible for any man, woman, or child to defeat these strategies on their own terms and in their own strength.

A strategy is a plan of action devised, by Satan and his evil spirits, to attain a certain objective. The main strategies are as follows:
1. Deception (2 Samuel 24:1–8; 2 Corinthians 2:11, 11:3, 11:14; Ephesians 4:27)
2. Blinding the minds of men (Colossians 1:9; 1 John 5:20)
3. Working in men without the men knowing it (Ephesians 2:2)
4. Working to snatch away the truth from men (Matthew 13:19)
5. Giving men a false peace (Luke 11:21)
6. Inciting opposition to the truth (2 Timothy 2:25–26)
7. Counterfeiting the real work of God (Matthew 13:25–39)
8. Targeting the leaders of the church for disgrace and destruction (2 Corinthians 12:7)
9. Dishonoring the purpose of God with a person, nation, or church (2 Samuel 24:1–8)
10. Stealing, killing, and destroying (John 10:10)
11. Resisting the removal of the filthy garments spotted by sin (Zechariah 3:1)
12. Using others to tempt a saint to sin (Matthew 16:22–23)
13. Inflaming the life of nature into chaos, confusion, and strife (James 3:14–15)
14. Weakening the authority of the Scriptures (Galatians 1:8; 1 John 5:5–10)
15. Distorting the teaching of the Scriptures (Galatians 1:8; 1 John 5:5–10)
16. Adding to the Scriptures (Galatians 1:8; Revelation 22:18)
17. Putting the Scriptures entirely aside (Galatians 1:8; Revelation 22:18)

This is noteworthy here: While many have crazy dreams, visions, and other experiences that pull people away from Scripture, my experiences with the Lord, especially those where I was carried up into heaven in the spirit, have always pulled or pushed me more toward the Word of God. Any experience that pulls a person away from the Word of God cannot be of God. Both the Word of God and these experiences must line up together. If the experiences are of God, they will always agree with the Word of God and draw a person closer to God.

And always remember that the Word of God is superior to experiences. Spiritual experiences coming from the Holy Spirit are always subservient to the Word of God.

I dealt with a woman who held that her experiences superseded the Word of God. With no authorized anchor, she went from one extreme to another and finally ended up in occultism. Nothing could be done to help her.

Generally, after a saint receives revelation from studying the Word of God, the fight will be on, and the saint will be engaged in spiritual warfare. For the sake of the saint, God is a deliverer and not a destroyer.

Immediately after the fight is on, the saint will be tempted by the devil, mainly to stop the fight and turn back to the old ways. This is the reason James said, "My brethren, count it all joy when ye fall into divers temptations; Knowing this, that the trying of your faith worketh patience" (James 1:2–3).

When God promised me that, if I served Him, He would save my family, I had no idea the amount of warfare I would have to endure. Years went by, years of crying tears with much prayer. Each stage of my life became a stage of trials rather than peace or joy. One trial after another was common. During these trials, I had to remember the promises of God while going home and seeing my father drunk with alcohol. The promises were one aspect of my life, while the reality was another. I had to pray in the promises so that the promises would be a reality.

When trial after trial submerged almost my whole life, I had to remember the promises, like when one of my closest friends was using witchcraft against me. I know that witchcraft can hit, hurt, and make gains against Christians. Ignorance of how witchcraft works does not protect a saint from it. And ignorance of Satan does not protect a saint from him either.

Not knowing much about witchcraft, I was almost destroyed. Spells were sent against my family and me. Here is a list of the consequences of the spells being thrown against me:

1. House was caught on fire.
2. I had to run my son to the hospital repeatedly.
3. Wreck after wreck occurred.
4. I was unable to sleep and felt like I was in a bed of ants.

It seems that I was always being attacked. I had no idea that witchcraft had so much power. Nor did I know that I was in the midst of a war between the power of witchcraft and the power of God.

My Friend, the Witch

People distinguish between white magic and black magic, but all forms of magic, regardless of their names, have as their source of power Satan and his evil spirits. In that regard, they're all black.

My friend had become a medium and communicated with evil spirits. She performed séances and other rituals. Evil spirits spoke through her, and she was able to send out evil spirits against others. The witch was entirely into witchcraft, especially black magic. Her power was extreme with Satan.

Years went by, and the witch's children grew up. Then one night, her children, two women, were both killed in a car wreck. That is the cost of serving Satan. There is such a thing as satanic compensation. Whatever Satan gives, he demands more back many times over.

The witch did not know or believe that Satan had a part in this, but she blamed the driver of the car. A man ran a stop sign, hit them broadside, and killed both of her daughters.

One day, when I got off from working the midnight to 8 a.m. shift, I met with some women to eat breakfast, and one told me about the witch: "Don't leave us today. Her girls got killed last night."

If I had ever seen anyone who was in shock, it was the witch. Still, she went on all day doing her work. The Bible says, "For the wages of sin is death; but the gift of God is eternal life through Jesus Christ our Lord" (Romans 6:23). This witch proved that verse, and the lives of her daughters proved it as well.

My husband, my son, and I went to the funeral home and saw the corpses of the witch's grown children in two coffins. If anyone ever looked evil, it was the bodies of these two grown-up children. The bodies of these two adult children had the very appearance of evil and the very appearance of evil spirits. I will never forget this. If there was no other proof of such a thing as evil, this was enough. My husband, my son, and I were all in the presence of evil. There is no doubt about that.

A few weeks went by, and I sought to see how the witch was doing at her shop. As I walked in, every one of her employees said, "We are glad to see you."

I said, "Why?"

They said, "We don't like what is going on in the back office. Dot, go into her office and see what is going on."

I have never been fearful of a fight or a battle. I told the women, "I will do it." When I walked into the office, I saw the witch performing a séance. By the power of the Holy Spirit, I knew what she was doing—casting a death spell.

Immediately the power of God hit me, and I jumped on that witch, screaming. My screaming scared her. I jerked her by the collar and said, "Yes! The devil will take that life, but he will take someone else from your family too. Who else do you want to give up?"

The man whom the witch threw a death spell against did die. On the Gulf Coast of Florida, the man was catching lobsters with a full tank of oxygen and died of a lack of oxygen.

Let us understand this: The man had a full tank of oxygen, and still, he died of a lack of oxygen. Yet, many Christians do not believe that witchcraft, especially death magic, can touch their lives to destroy, kill, and to steal. Witchcraft touches both the wicked and the godly; along with other forms of occultism, it binds people into darkness. And if a Christian is their target, it oppresses him or her. The only protection we have is in Christ. Paul went through many things, and the power of Satan continued to strike him through the angel of Satan (2 Corinthians 12:7). To "buffet" means that the angel of Satan continually attacked Paul. The striking was like being struck with a fist day in and day out. The striking was painful attacks, from illness to adverse circumstances. The apostle Paul knew that Satan could strike against Christians, even those who are powerful in Christ. He knew that while there is nothing to fear, if we are in Christ Jesus, still we must understand the wiles of our enemy and how to fight back against our enemy.

Too many Christians believe that it is the fault of Satan when they sin rather than their own fault. But the notion that "the devil makes us do it" will not stand the ground of divine justice. The devil may suggest, tempt, or push, but we are responsible for our actions.

One year after the death of the witch's daughters, she was burying her husband. Yes, Satan killed the man who killed her children but at a cost. And still, the cost continued. The witch had to quit her job because of her eyes becoming worse and worse. Her sight was being taken away from her.

The witch was not a reprobate yet. I know that because God was still dealing with her. One day, I came into her shop, and she said to me, "I have a problem with your God."

I said back, "Why?"

She replied, "Because He took my two children."

I responded immediately, "My God did not take your two children. Your god, Satan, did that. My God came to give life."

Sometime after that, she said, "Last night, I saw my two children sitting on my chest of drawers."

"Oh no, you did not!" I said, "You saw demons appearing as them." She was not communicating with her daughters. She was communicating with demons, who are called "familiar spirits."

After much time had passed, I got a call from one of our friends. She asked me, "Dot, do you want to go with me to a funeral?"

I said, "Yes." I was glad that I went to that funeral. The preacher performing the funeral said that the witch had renounced the occult and renounced Satan and his evil spirits. She had received the Lord by a minister on TV. But he also led her into a repentance prayer afterward. He wanted to make sure that she was saved. My friend at the funeral said, "Dot, that is for you." The words of the preacher about the now-former witch were for me. He confirmed to me that the witch had received the Lord before her death.

Another Case of Witchcraft

In another case, I was working at the lab and could not make up the chemicals right. I told my husband just what was happening. He said, "Dot, I do not want to tell you, but a person whose name is JoAnn is throwing witchcraft on you." I knew that this JoAnn was not part of my family.

I told my husband, "I know who it is." My husband and I bound the prayers of that person and returned them to her, according to the biblical principle of sending out prayers as arms and missiles. That day, lightning struck her car. It brought the fear of the Lord unto her. She was using witchcraft to try and take my job.

In dealing with this kind of spiritual warfare, the saints must know that God is with them. We must also remember in these cases that we are "heirs of God, and joint-heirs with Christ; if so be that we suffer with him" (Romans 8:17). And we must remember to have confidence in Christ Jesus. Our faith must not be shaken by suffering or by attacks of Satan and his evil spirits.

B. C. Forbes once said,

> Pity the human being who is not able to connect faith within himself with the infinite … He who has faith has … an inward reservoir of courage, hope, confidence, calmness and assuring trust that all will come out well—even though to the world it may appear to come out most badly.[8]

Regardless of what Satan does, a saint has a deep reservoir of trust, confidence, hope, and courage that sustains him or her.

Heart Attack and Death

In 1985, I was always under so much pressure in various manners that I was not resting. Rest was impossible. It seemed that wave after wave of depression, oppression, and troubles did their best to overtake my family and me. Satan schemed over all of us.

The Book of James says, "Is any sick among you? Let him call for the elders of the church; and let them pray over him, anointing him with oil in the name of the Lord" (James 5:14). My son points out that "Is any sick among you?" is a rhetorical question. And the question needs to be answered with a positive answer (yes). Further, Paul said about Epaphroditus,

> But I trust in the Lord that I also myself shall come shortly. Yet I supposed it necessary to send to you Epaphroditus, my brother, and companion in labour, and fellowsoldier, but your messenger, and he that ministered to my wants. For he longed after you all, and was full of heaviness, because that ye had heard that he had been sick. For indeed he was sick nigh unto death: but God had mercy on him; and not on him only, but on me also, lest I should have sorrow upon sorrow. (Philippians 2:24–27)

All the pressure upon my life led to a heart attack. If I could go back in time, I think I would have known more about how Satan was attacking and how to try to prevent my heart attack.

My heart attack began at work in the lab. I started having chest pains. I fell on my knees, and asked the Lord, "God, what is going on here?"

He spoke back and said, "You are having a heart attack."

I said, "Father, heal me, if not for me, for my mother. Who will take care of her?"

At that moment, one of my bosses walked into the lab and said that I needed some vitamins. I thought to myself, "If you knew what I knew, you would be calling a helicopter to land in front of this lab."

Rather than going to a hospital or calling 911, I continued to work. I tried to pray, but my breathing was hard, and my chest felt like something was sitting on it.

That night driving home from work, I began talking to God. I told him, "I can't pray." But finally, I got these words out, "Father, in the name of Jesus, if you are not going to heal my heart, I am going to be like your Son Jesus and say, 'Let this cup of suffering pass from me.'"

When I finally arrived at 12:30 am, my mother was having a terrible night. She was calling out. I entered her room and checked to see what was going on. I tried to pray for her, but I could not get out the words.

The next day, I did the usual. I made sure that my mother had her medicine, and then I went back to work, driving from Jacksonville to Fernandina. I did not know what I was going to do with my mother if I had a heart attack. It would not be right to let my husband be responsible for keeping my mother.

At work, I waited on God and tried to do my job. As I was doing my work, I was whispering, "Father, make a way where there is no way." In this very dark time of my life, I did not know any Scripture to use except Isaiah 53:4–5: "Surely, he hath borne our griefs, and carried our sorrows: yet we did esteem him stricken, smitten of God, and afflicted. But he was wounded for our transgressions, he was bruised for our iniquities: the chastisement of our peace was upon him; and with his stripes we are healed."

The next day, my condition was still the same. I got up, did everything that I could do at my house and went back to work. God did not turn a deaf ear to my cries at this critical time. I whispered this prayer repeatedly in the name of Jesus, "Hear me. Help me!"

The day after that was Friday, and I was off. That morning, I woke to a small voice in my ear. The voice said, "Call your doctor." He even named the doctor. I called and told the doctor's secretary that I needed to see the doctor right away, then I drove to the doctor's office.

I explained to the doctor what was going on. He ordered an EKG, which showed that I did have a heart attack.

The nurses and the doctor became upset, even scared. They slowly moved me into a wheelchair and wheeled me down to the bottom floor of the building, and then wheeled me to the hospital.

A Glimpse of Heaven

I was admitted to the hospital on a Friday. By Monday, I had another heart attack, and I died only temporarily, just a few moments, which was long enough to go to heaven.

My spirit left my body, and I went to heaven. I landed on a beautiful lawn. The first person I saw was my sister, Ruby. She was standing under a gazebo, praising God. Beside her I saw my father, another sister, and one of my ancestors.

The grass and trees in heaven were a green that I could not explain or describe. The atmosphere and the air were so pure that neither could be explained or described. Every leaf and every blade of grass was cut the same length.

When Ruby saw me coming up a hill, she said, "Dot has made it. Now we can rejoice." They were so happy and had a wonderful time. The party had around thirty-three persons. I think all of them were relatives who had died and made it to heaven.

The experience was genuine and real—not necromancy since my spirit had left my body. Remembering I had died, and looking back to the earth, I saw the hand of Jesus Christ come down to where my body was. His hand hit my chest and said, "Not now, daughter." He brought my spirit back into my body.

Aftermath

The doctor said, "Ease her off the table."

I said, "Doctor, keep nothing from me. What did you find out?"

"You died."

"Yes! How did you know?" I said.

He replied, "Because I see where the artery had been closed and then opened."

I told the doctor, "I died Monday morning."

He asked, "You are not afraid?"

I told him about my trip to heaven and asked him if he was Jewish. He said, "Yes."

I told him, "My heart attack may have happened to let you know Jesus."

The doctor was concerned about trying to get me off that table. He told the aide to call my doctor. He thought that I could easily have another heart attack.

My doctor was not just my doctor, but also a friend. Our family doctor told my husband, "She is really in trouble because she is so run down."

I had to have open-heart surgery because the main heart valve was completely clogged. The surgery went very well.

After the surgery, I woke up to a nurse humming, "I will meet you in the morning." Having tubes down my throat made it impossible to speak. The song was blessing me, so I made a gesture to keep on humming that song. One nurse in the room was laughing and thought that I was telling the other nurse off. But I shook my head and moved my hand as if I were leading a choir.

In my room, the spirit of death hit me again after surgery. It happened when my doctor was in the recovery room with me. I knew I was in trouble when the doctor said, "Set her up." The nurses put me in a chair. I woke up enough to know that they had not tied me in that chair.

When they carried me to another room, a patient was speaking, and her voice became an annoyance and upset me to the degree that it made me sick. I balled up my fist and said, "I will shut her mouth once and for all."

My husband and a nurse held me in the bed. The patient made a beeline for the door and told the nurse to move from the door. There must have been something evil about that person. Even her words were upsetting and had the sound of evil.

After the surgery, I had lots of company on the weekend. When I looked around and focused on one of the walls of the room, it seemed as if it were moving toward the river near the hospital. I called for the nurse and told her that I knew this wall of the room was not moving, but it appeared as if it were.

It was not long before my doctor walked into the room and asked, "How much company did you have yesterday?" When I told him, he put a sign on my door, "No visitors." He told my husband, "She is going to need a lot of rest. She has gone through more than most women should, and she can no longer take care of her mother."

Thankfully, my brother came down to Jacksonville to take our mother back home with him. Our mother lived almost six months after that, and she did not die until her prayers were answered—that she would die on her property.

For her prayers to be answered, God had to move me out of the way. Many times, we ourselves can stand in the way of God, preventing Him from doing what He knows is best. I had to learn this the hard way. Going through a heart bypass was not easy, and I lost a year of work.

Being a Christian, I was bothered by how I had acted while in the hospital. I told my doctor about the lady standing at my door and that I balled up my fist to get to her. His opinion was worded as, "The medicine that you were on had affected your hearing." According to the doctor, the lady had a very high-pitch voice. The lady's voice sounded as if she were screaming in my ear. Also, when I told the doctor that I had not been tied in the chair, he looked up and said, "Are you sure?" Later, one of the nurses told me that a patient had fallen out of the chair and busted open her chest.

Because of the seriousness of my heart attack, I had to have another heart catheterization in another hospital several years later. Two friends were present with my son. At this time, the doctor said, "It is not her heart that is the problem. The bypass artery was working perfectly, and the blocked artery had opened up and was also working perfectly."

What brought on my heart attack? Anxiety. This has been called the age of anxiety.

Time at a Doctor's House

There was a time when my husband, my son, and I were called to pray over a house owned by a doctor. This was in the 90s. We did not want to go. When someone wants a minister to go to their home to pray, the minister does not know precisely what he is walking into, or what he will be facing. A minister is allowing Satan and his evil spirits to pick the battleground rather than God. Only if God has ordained that place to be the battleground can the minister know that the ground has been chosen by God for that battle and be assured that the battle will be won.

The doctor called our house and said, "If you do not come over, we all will die." I made an appointment with her to go over and meet her and her husband the following Saturday.

Rather than facing the demonic head-on, or even thinking about the demonic problem, she had my son, Ricky, check her computer.

The doctor and her husband said that God had spoken to them and said that we were the Lord's children and gave us the run of the house.

After arriving at their house, we went from working on the doctor's computer to eating and then to the demonic activity. What confusion! If a minister goes to a house to fight against evil spirits, there is no time to work on a computer or even eat. My husband, my son, and I learned much in this incident.

Working on the computer was a ploy to keep my son and the rest of us from prayer. By this alone, our focus on the Holy Spirit, prayer, and evil spirits was greatly misplaced.

This ploy kept us from seeing in the Spirit that an evil spirit occupied the doctor's recliner. The doctor failed to mention that no one would sit in the chair. Unaware, I sat down in the recliner and immediately started having chest pains. The evil spirit dwelling in that recliner knew quite well that I had had a heart attack in 1985, and it was trying to give me another.

I screamed out at my son and said, "Ricky, I feel like I am having a heart attack. You need to stop working on that computer, come over here, and pray for me."

He replied, "Mom, if you could just see what is sitting on your chest, you would know the reason you are having chest pains." He came over and took hold of the situation. He commanded in the name of Jesus Christ that the evil spirit stop what it was doing. He commanded the spirit to leave the recliner and get out of that house. That was the first evil spirit to go out of the house, but that was not the last one.

There were many other evil spirits in that house. I do not think that I have ever seen a more demon-infested house than theirs. While objects like houses cannot be possessed, they can well be heavily oppressed or infested with evil spirits. Evil spirits infest, oppress, haunt, and occupy objects. The objects become theirs. They own them. They have generally obtained the objects or places by illegitimate rights over those places. Once a place or object becomes theirs, it is still possible to take that place or object back. Some places or objects can quickly be taken back from them. Other places or objects are hard to take back. And in other cases, some places or objects, because of their inherent use or nature, may never be taken back from them. It is common to believe that every place or object can be taken back from them, but that is not the case.

It is noteworthy in the Bible that altars, shrines, temples, and other ungodly places were destroyed rather than used (Numbers 33:52; Deuteronomy 13:9, 33:29; 1 Kings 15:14, 18:18–40, 19:1–21, 22:43; 2 Kings 8:4–13, 9:1–10, 10:17–28, 12:3, 14:4, 15:4, 35, 23:8–20; 2 Chronicles 31:12).

And notice that almost all things in Jericho were cursed of God (Joshua 6:17–21, 8:26–27, 10:28). They had the anathema of God upon them and could not be used or even blessed. Blessing and prayers could not remove the curse, in this instance.

In the master bedroom closet, there was a spot of a red substance. Both the doctor and her husband said it was blood. Drops of that substance dripped from the top of the closet to the floor. I saw it. Both of them worked tirelessly to clean the spot away. But every time they cleaned the spot to where it was all gone, it later reappeared. Time and again they cleaned the red substance, and it soon after reappeared.

My son went to work over the house. He took authority over the red substance and the evil spirits, and he commanded all demonic activity in that house to cease. He went throughout the house, pleading the blood of the Lamb over it and pleading the bloodline over it as well. He went room by room, taking charge over the demonic activity. Evil spirit by evil spirit left. Finally, he arrived at the last room, but he merely pleaded the blood and the bloodline over the room without commanding the evil spirit out. That was a mistake, but it became an amazing example of the power of God and the power of the blood of the Lamb.

My son left that last room. The doctor and her husband were at peace; the atmosphere of the house was entirely changed. We all finally sat down to rejoice over what the Lord had done. Then my son went to finish working on the computer.

Suddenly a scream sounded from within the house. The doctor heard it and almost fainted. Fear came upon her face, and her body shook. Her husband almost fainted as well. Yes, they were Christians, but very weak.

We called my son to see what was happening. He asked, "What did the scream sound like?"

The doctor said, "Like a scream of pain and suffering. It was of another world. And it did not sound like a human scream."

Immediately my son knew what had happened. The evil spirit tried to go out of that room, but my son had pleaded the blood over that room. When the evil spirit tried to escape from that room, the blood of the Lamb caused pain upon that evil spirit, and the blood became a boundary that an evil spirit could not pass. Only once did that evil spirit try to go through the blood of the Lamb boundary, and that was enough.

My son ran back into the last room. The evil spirit my son had forgotten to command out was still present. In the spirit, my son saw an evil spirit in the corner of the room. It was shaking and fearful, afraid of being forced to pass through the bloodline. The room had been sealed off from evil spirits going and coming. That is the power of the blood.

Regardless, my son commanded the evil spirit to go out of the house. Since it was impossible for that evil spirit to go through the blood, it became known to all of us that God had lifted the blood of the Lamb as a boundary so that the evil spirit could be let out. Then God replaced the boundary. This is the power of the blood.

A Missionary, a Car, and a Mountain

I will never forget the following story, which was told to me by a missionary. God called a precious woman to be a missionary in Haiti. Her name was Mrs. Street. She went there with her husband, unafraid and uncompromised. The protection of God was great upon her. Many spells of Voodoo were pronounced against her, but none ever penetrated the protection of the Lord. While she was completely protected, the spells did hit her husband. Besides witchcraft being sent her way, there were several attempts on their lives. Still, everything that Satan tried did not work.

One day, Mrs. Street went on a mission outreach and drove all day. She had been warned not to drive at night on a mountain road leading up to a sacred mountain dedicated to Voodoo. But that road was the only way she could reach her home. If she drove on that road during the day, all was well. But at night, it was extremely dangerous. Her life could well be forfeited.

On this particular trip, Mrs. Street tried to drive through that mountain road before nightfall, but it was impossible. She had no choice but to pray and pray. Suddenly she saw coming her way on that road at least one hundred devotees of Voodoo. She knew she was dead if they got their hands on her. She closed her eyes and prayed and then felt a strange movement. When she opened her eyes, her car had been lifted and moved to the other side of the mountain. She saw the devotees of Voodoo behind her in the rearview mirror.

It was impossible for the car to go around the mob of people. There was no room for that. The road was too small. The only means was for the Lord to lift the car from where it was and place it on the other side of the mountain. And that is what He did. She went on her way and finally made it home. Only God.

No Solid Gold Buddha

Another time a five-million-dollar solid gold Buddha was given to a ministry. The minister wanted to sell the idol and use it for the ministry, but the Lord would not allow it. The Lord informed the minister that the idol could not be blessed, nor could the idol have the curse broken from it. Once God cursed the idol, turned it over to demons, and set his anathema upon it, it could not be uncursed, nor the demons leave it. Even the money was considered cursed if the minister had used it.

The Lord ordered the minister to destroy the golden idol and bury it. And the minister did just that.

CHAPTER 11
WARFARE AND INTERCESSION

The call of Jesus Christ is a call to warfare. And accepting Christ is being enlisted into His army.

In 1845, Christian authors Gurnall and Campbell wrote about the power of Christian prayers, especially imprecatory prayers.

> A word to the wicked. Take heed, that by your unmerciful hatred to the truth and church of God, you do not engage her prayers against you. The imprecatory prayers of the saints, when shot at the right mark, are murdering pieces, and strike dead where they light. "Shall not God avenge his own elect, which cry day and night unto him, though he bears long with them? I tell you he will avenge them speedily," Luke 18:7, 8. They are not empty words, as the imprecations of the wicked poured into the air, and vanish with their breath, but are received into heaven, and shall be sent back with thunder and lightning upon the wicked. David's prayer unravelled Ahithophel's fine-spun policy and twisted his halter for him. The prayers of the saints are more to be feared than an army of twenty thousand men in the field. Esther's fast hastened Haman's ruin, and Hezekiah's prayer against Sennacherib, brought his huge host to the slaughter.[1]

If we, as saints, could understand the power of prayer, nations could be changed for the good, and the powers of darkness could be pushed back. If only we understood the power of prayer, we could have a different life—a life where the powers of darkness are dethroned, and where we do not submit to anyone but God.

Moses and Possessing the Promised Land

God informed Moses at the burning bush,

> I am come down to deliver them out of the hand of the Egyptians, and to bring them up out of that land unto a good land and a large, unto a land flowing with milk and honey; unto the place of the Canaanites, and the Hittites, and the Amorites, and the Perizzites, and the Hivites, and the Jebusites. (Exodus 3:8)

In other words, God told Moses that the Promised Land was occupied with strange and demonic powers that had to be dispossessed.

When the Israelites came out of Egypt, the words of the Lord were again noteworthy.

> And it came to pass, when Pharaoh had let the people go, that God led them not through the way of the land of the Philistines, although that was near; for God said, Lest peradventure the people repent when they see war, and they return to Egypt: But God led the people about, through the way of the wilderness of the Red sea: and the children of Israel went up harnessed out of the land of Egypt. (Exodus 13:17–18)

The Israelites needed absolute discipline and faith in God to prepare themselves for the coming conflict with the nations of Canaan. Therefore, God demanded unconditional obedience and no compromise among His people. The demands of God were extreme, but the reasons were severe.

At Kadesh Barnea, Moses sent spies into the Promised Land. Out of the twelve spies, only two spies believed that the Promised Land could be taken. The remaining spies brought fear and doubt into the midst of the Israelites (Numbers 13:1–33). The two spies who took a strong stand against the unbelief and negative report of the other ten spies were Joshua and Caleb (Numbers 14:1–45). Despite their efforts, the Israelites became fearful and alarmed. Numbers 14:3–9 expresses their fear:

> And wherefore hath the LORD brought us unto this land, to fall by the sword, that our wives and our children should be a prey? were it not better for us to return into Egypt? And they said one to another, Let us make a captain, and let us return into Egypt. Then Moses and Aaron fell on their faces before all the assembly of the congregation of the children of Israel. And Joshua the son of Nun, and Caleb the son of Jephunneh, which were of them that searched the land, rent their clothes: And they spake unto all the company of the children of Israel, saying, The land, which we passed through to search it, is an exceeding good land. If the LORD delight in us, then he will bring us into this land, and give it us; a

land which floweth with milk and honey. Only rebel not ye against the LORD, neither fear ye the people of the land; for they are bread for us: their defence is departed from them, and the LORD is with us: fear them not.

Once again, the Israelites retreated in fear at the very thought of war against the nations of Canaan, which were steeped in demonism. Because of this sign of doubt, God led the Israelites around until almost all the old generation died off. The wilderness became their graves. And a new generation arose, with Joshua and Caleb still living, and was able to enter the Promised Land.

The Israelites had repeatedly witnessed the supernatural intervention of God in their deliverance from Egypt, and throughout their years in the desert. Israelites were shown a supernatural lifestyle, which many may hope for within their lives and never receive.

Paul speaks to the Corinthians about the Israelites who left Egypt.

All our fathers were under the cloud, and all passed through the sea; And were all baptized unto Moses in the cloud and in the sea, And did all eat the same spiritual meat; And did all drink the same spiritual drink: for they drank of that spiritual Rock that followed them: and that Rock was Christ. (1 Corinthians 10:1–4)

Experiencing the good pleasure of God, the Israelites saw bread come down from heaven, and their clothes never wore out in all those years of wandering in the wilderness (Deuteronomy 29:5). The pillar of the cloud over the tabernacle led them from one oasis to another.

Aaron repeatedly prayed this prayer over the Israelites in the wilderness:

The LORD bless thee, and keep thee: The LORD make his face shine upon thee, and be gracious unto thee: The LORD lift up his countenance upon thee, and give thee peace. And they shall put my name upon the children of Israel; and I will bless them. (Numbers 6:24–27)

The Israelites never took possession of their whole inheritance. While they went far and experienced so much, they never wholly experienced the heritage of God. Nor did they ever completely remove the nations of Canaan from the Promised Land.

The failure of the complete conquest of the land of Canaan is well documented in Judges 1:27–36:

Neither did Manasseh drive out the inhabitants of Beth-shean and her towns, nor Taanach and her towns, nor the inhabitants of Dor and her towns, nor the inhabitants of Ibleam and her towns, nor the inhabitants of Megiddo and her towns: but the Canaanites would dwell in that land. And it came to pass, when Israel was strong, that they put the Canaanites to tribute, and did not utterly drive them out. Neither did Ephraim drive out the Canaanites that dwelt in Gezer; but the Canaanites dwelt in Gezer among them. Neither did Zebulun drive out the inhabitants of Kitron, nor the inhabitants of Nahalol; but the Canaanites dwelt among them and became tributaries. Neither did Asher drive out the inhabitants of Accho, nor the inhabitants of Zidon, nor of Ahlab, nor of Achzib, nor of Helbah, nor of Aphik, nor of Rehob: But the Asherites dwelt among the Canaanites, the inhabitants of the land: for they did not drive them out. Neither did Naphtali drive out the inhabitants of Beth-shemesh, nor the inhabitants of Beth-anath; but he dwelt among the Canaanites, the inhabitants of the land: nevertheless the inhabitants of Beth-shemesh and of Beth-anath became tributaries unto them. And the Amorites forced the children of Dan into the mountain: for they would not suffer them to come down to the valley: But the Amorites would dwell in mount Heres in Aijalon, and in Shaalbim: yet the hand of the house of Joseph prevailed, so that they became tributaries. And the coast of the Amorites was from the going up to Akrabbim, from the rock, and upward.

Judges 1 says quite well that the tribe of Asher did not drive out the Canaanites but dwelled among them. What does that mean? They merged their customs, habits, behavior, and religion with that of the Canaanites. The Asherites who did not destroy or capture Tyre or Sidon but cultivated friendly relations with the Phoenician inhabitants utterly disobeyed the mandate of God. The Asherites may have, at first, made some hostile demonstrations against their pagan neighbors, but they were so thoroughly checked by the superior power and skill of their opponents that they soon settled down side by side with them, and made no further attempts at conquest or taking hold of their inheritance. Deborah, the judge of Israel, said it the best. "Asher continued on the sea shore, and abode in his breaches" (Judges 5:17).

The general estimate of the conquest here in Joshua 10:38–43 is the same time period of the conquest of Southern Palestine. With the exemption of the Gibeonites, the sons of Anak continued to live until the times of David, along with the Philistines and several groups of Canaanites. This shows that the

Israelites never carried the mandate from God, through Moses, to its completion in both Southern and Northern Palestine. Not until the reign of David was the Philistine power entirely broken.

God's Battle or Our Battle

As soon as the Israelites left Egypt, they were attacked by the Amalekites. The battle lasted one day. The Israelites ebbed and flowed but finally ended in victory (Exodus 17). The victory, however, was not due to the talent of the Jewish warriors. It occurred as a result of the deeds of Moses, Aaron, and Hur on the hilltop.

As Moses, supported by Aaron and Hur, held the rod of God in the air, the battle finally turned in favor of the Israelites. The lesson here is that the victory is first won in the spiritual world and that the real enemy of the Israelites was not the Amalekites, but Satan and his evil spirits who were using the Amalekites.

The conflict with the Amalekites was a dress rehearsal for what was to take place in the Promised Land. And it was a warning of what else would come upon the Israelites when they entered the Promised Land.

As the Israelites stood in their faith, they could and would experience nothing but victory. In this conflict with the Amalekites, the Israelites were taught the principle of faith. It was to be by this principle alone that they could defeat all their enemies.

If the Israelites unreservedly believed in God, they would experience maximum success. But if they only partly believed in God, they would only obtain some success in their endeavors. As they believed in God, so God would move for them. God Himself was to drive their enemies out before them, not they themselves. It came down to this fact: if they wanted complete success, they had to attain it by unconditional obedience and faith.

After the trouble with the Amalekites, the Israelites did not encounter any other enemy nation throughout their wilderness experience, until they reached the land of Canaan.

In all the superseding years, there were plenty of conflicts, but the main conflicts that faced the Israelites were of an internal nature. The Israelites had to fight themselves to gain success. And many times, they lost that fight because of sin.

What is Spiritual Warfare?

To Israel, spiritual warfare came in the outward form of physical, brutal, bloody battle. And victory or loss resulted from obedience or disobedience, rather than strength, skill, or numbers—as Moses declares in Deuteronomy 11:22–25:

> For if ye shall diligently keep all these commandments which I command you, to do them, to love the Lord your God, to walk in all his ways, and to cleave unto him; Then will the Lord drive out all these nations from before you, and ye shall possess greater nations and mightier than yourselves. Every place whereon the soles of your feet shall tread shall be yours: from the wilderness and Lebanon, from the river, the river Euphrates, even unto the uttermost sea shall your coast be. There shall no man be able to stand before you: for the Lord your God shall lay the fear of you and the dread of you upon all the land that ye shall tread upon, as he hath said unto you.

To the apostles, spiritual warfare is based on the sacrificial love of Christ that exemplified by His earthly ministry. It is empowered by Christ's work of the cross and the power of the resurrection. The physical war transitions into a spiritual war of invading the darkness and setting people free from demonic bondage and oppression. The purposes of the spiritual holy war are as follows:

1. To spread the gospel of the cross throughout the world
2. To defeat Satan in his own area and arena
3. To set the captives free
4. To heal the brokenhearted
5. To restore life as God intended it to be
6. To preach deliverance to the captives
7. To recover sight for the blind
8. To set at liberty them that are bruised
9. To expose and overthrow the kingdom of darkness
10. To significantly advance the kingdom of light
11. To move out under the authority of the Word of God, the name of Jesus, the power of the blood, and the power of the cross

To Jesus, spiritual warfare is an armed struggle between the forces of good and the forces of evil (Matthew 4:4–10, 8:1–3, 8:28–31, 9:1–7, 9:18–35, 14:21, 14:34–36, 15:29–31, 17:14–18, 21:19–20).

Spiritual warfare denotes spiritual resistance against all the evil works and operations of Satan through spiritual weapons of war.

To Paul, this part of the call of Christ is a call to arms. At the new birth, the person is (often unbeknown to him or her) enlisted in the army of God. Christian life means warfare.

According to Paul, our warfare is controlled and restricted under the domain of faith, the domain of a good conscience, and the domain of the Spirit (Romans 4:12; 1 Corinthians 8:7; 2 Corinthians 5:7; Galatians 5:16–17). It is impossible for a saint to be victorious in spiritual warfare without being in the domain of faith, the domain of a good conscience, and the domain of the Holy Spirit. The word domain is a term that originates in Greek grammar, as understood in the New Testament. For example, our faith has a domain, an influence, or an area of dominance. We must remain in that domain.

Furthermore, spiritual warfare is using our godly weapons and attacking spiritual strongholds of Satan and his evil spirits, which are against the gospel of Christ (Matthew 18:18–20). Spiritual warfare is possessing the authority of the believer in the name of Jesus Christ, and the power of the Holy Spirit by the baptism of the Holy Spirit (Luke 10:17; Acts 1:8).

The Modern Church

Today, most of us are like scared children hiding in the bedroom or lost in a dark forest with no light. Most of the church has become useless and pathetic, especially in the realm of prayer and spiritual warfare. Few are fighting, while the rest are on the sidelines. On the other hand, Paul told Timothy and the rest of the Christians at Ephesus to fight the good fight of faith (1 Timothy 6:12). And Paul asked the Corinthians a question in 1 Corinthians 14:8, "For if the trumpet give an uncertain sound, who shall prepare himself to the battle?" Paul understood the life of a Christian is war. Walter Martin, a minister and an expert on cults and occult, once said, "The methodology and the philosophy governing the Christians today, in many areas, is that there is no battle."[2] Walter Martin did not believe that there is no battle. He said, "The moment you enlist in the army of God, you personally become a target. You need to remember that if you're living for and walking with Jesus Christ, the powers of darkness are aligned against you."[3] And lastly, he said, "Christ imparts the capacity of conquest to our lives every single day that we are willing to believe Him."[4]

Some say that it is easy to pray against the forces of evil. Really?

We are in many ways defenseless, hopeless, and helpless against an evil that we cannot defeat on our own. We have refused to understand our enemy. We have denounced the weapons of warfare and laid down our sword and shield, hoping that the devil will not see us or come near our home or our families.

Denying the devil's existence will not save us. Lowering our weapons and refusing to take up our armor will not save us. Paul, the apostles, and the ancient church knew how to overcome Satan: through prayer and the Word of God (Ephesians 6:17–18). Paul longed to see the saints united in Christ, enjoying the riches of blessing in Him.

We all need to pick up our weapons and fight.

Weapons of our Warfare

Within the Bible, we can draw up a list of weapons to be used by the saints in our never-ending battle against Satan and his evil spirits.

I have never used extra-biblical weapons. These have no reference in Scripture and should never be used. They are not weapons authorized by God or by His Word. These supposed weapons are tied to the occult, and I have never seen them be successful. For example, some Christians use salt or holy water as a weapon. I have never seen salt or holy water work, nor have I ever used them to fight a spiritual battle. There is a biblical limit on weapons that should be used by Christians.

"Holy water" was officially used in 850 A.D. as a weapon by the Roman Catholic Church. Before that date, holy water was never used as a weapon; it was purely for Catholic rituals. As a weapon, it should not be used. Other conventional modern methods of spiritual weapons were never used by the ancient church. Such modern armaments hinder or destroy our attempt to stop Satan and his evil spirits. We should go back to the earliest times of the church.

Luther taught that we should not depend on holy water, sacred salt, and other sacraments as weapons, but we must now fight by the Word of God and the prayer of faith.[5]

Here is a general list of these weapons:
1. Word of God (Matthew 4:4–10; Luke 4:4–10).
2. Blood of Christ (Exodus 12:7; Acts 20:28; Romans 3:25, 5:9; 1 Corinthians 10:16, 11:27; 1 Peter 1:2, 1:19; 1 John 1:7, 5:6).
3. Name of Jesus (Matthew 18:19–20, 28:18; John 14:12–15; Acts 2:21–38, 3:6, 4:18, 5:40, 9:27, 16:18).
4. Power of praise (Luke 19:28–43; Revelation 5:11–12).
5. Power of the cross (John 19:30; Hebrews 2:2, 9:9).
6. Power of prayer (Mark 11:24; Acts 4:24–32; Roman 8:26).

7. Word of wisdom (1 Corinthians 12–13).
8. Word of knowledge (1 Corinthians 12–13).
9. Gifts of healing (1 Corinthians 12–13).
10. Working of miracles (1 Corinthians 12–13).
11. Gift of discerning of spirits (1 Corinthians 12–13).
12. Gift of faith (1 Corinthians 12–13).
13. Gift of tongues (1 Corinthians 12–13).
14. Gift of prophecy (1 Corinthians 12–13).
15. Gift of interpretation of tongues (1 Corinthians 12–13).
16. Power of love (1 Corinthians 12:31).
17. Power of hope (1 Corinthians 12:31).
18. Fruits of the Holy Spirit (Galatians 5:22–23).
19. Power of fasting (Psalms 35:13, 69:10; Daniel 10:1–21; Matthew 4:11; 1 Corinthians 7:5).
20. Gospel music (1 Samuel 16:15–23).
21. Repentance (Matthew 18:22, 3:11, 9:13; Luke 17:4; Acts 17:30; 2 Corinthians 7:8; Revelation 3:19, 3:3, 2:16).
22. Communion (Matthew 26:26; Mark 14:22–26; Luke 22:19; John 13:1–14:31; 1 Corinthians 11:23–34).
23. Walking in holiness (Luke 1:75; Romans 6:19–22, 8:4, 12:2, 13:8–10; 1 Corinthians 7:19; 2 Corinthians 7:1; Ephesians 4:24; Hebrews 12:10–14; 1 Timothy 2:15; 1 Peter 14:16).
24. Anointing with oil (Exodus 28:41, 29:7, 29:36, 30:22–27, 40:9–13; Mark 6:13; James 5:14).
25. Faith (Matthew 17:20; Hebrews 11:1–39, 12:2).
26. Suffering for Christ (Matthew 5:11; 1 Corinthians 4:9, 10:13; 2 Corinthians 4:8, 6:3; Hebrews 2:10, 11:25; 2 Peter 2:9).
27. Gift of truth (Ephesians 6:11–19).
28. Breastplate of righteousness (Ephesians 6:11–19).
29. Feet shod with the preparation of the gospel of peace (Ephesians 6:11–19).
30. Shield of faith (Ephesians 6:11–19).
31. The helmet of salvation (Ephesians 6:11–19).
32. Shield of protection (Job 1:10, 3:23).
33. Exorcism and prayers of exorcism (Matthew 8:16, 12:28; Acts 16:16).
34. Baptism in water (Matthew 3:6–16, 28:14–18; Mark 1:4; Acts 2:38).

How to Begin to Fight

The Bible teaches us how to fight Satan and his evil spirits. A general list of how to fight in spiritual warfare is as follows:

1. We must submit to God (James 4:7).
2. We must resist the devil (James 4:7).
3. We must draw near to God (James 4:8).
4. He will draw near to you (James 4:8).
5. We must keep our eyes on Christ.
6. We must take a public stand for Christ.
7. We must keep a balanced status in our faith.
8. We must not become fanatical in our faith.
9. We should join a balanced church.
10. We must begin a regular prayer life (Matthew 7:7–8).
11. We must read the Bible daily.
12. We must be faithful in giving to God (Genesis 28:20–22).
13. We must know the Bible.
14. We must know Christ, not know about Him.
15. We must know the authority of the Bible.
16. We must know that Christ is the victor over Satan.
17. We must remain in the presence of God.
18. We must be ready to receive divine authority for a battle.
19. We must step out of our safety zones.
20. We must know how to pray.
21. We must know our enemy.
22. We must focus on what we are spiritually attacking.
23. We must know our place and position in Christ.
24. We must know who we are in Jesus Christ.
25. We must know who is backing us up.
26. We must know our spiritual authority.
27. We must be righteous and holy.
28. We must be obedient.
29. We must keep our relationship with Christ in good standing.
30. We must not go into spiritual warfare over a situation unless we are ready to pay the cost and are ready to be attacked by Satan.
31. We must know our limits.
32. We must know the ploys and strategies of Satan.
33. We must know that Satan will use anyone to try to detour us from

our goal of victory.
34. We must know the limits of the weapons used.
35. We must be certain that God is leading us into spiritual warfare for a situation.
36. We must make sure that we have repented.
37. We must have on the armor of God.
38. In spiritual warfare, we must fight by the name of Jesus, the power of the blood, and the power of the cross through prayer.
39. In prayer, we must tell Satan and all his forces that they are rebuked and rejected by these weapons.
40. We must denounce the works of Satan.
41. We must loose and bind the forces of Satan.
42. We must use other weapons and other means, as God so directs.
43. We must focus on what Satan is doing and attack or counterattack that and all his strongholds.
44. In spiritual warfare, the saints of God must have determination, direction, specific prayer, and faith.

Seven Prayers of a Spiritual Warrior

These prayers are beyond what many know. Every spiritual warrior (intercessor) should recognize these prayers:

1. O Lord, open my eyes, like Elijah's servant, so that I may see the spiritual battles that are going on in my life in the name of Jesus Christ (2 Kings 6:17).
2. Teach, O Lord, my prayerful hands to war, and my prayerful fingers to fight in the name of Jesus Christ (Psalm 144:1).
3. O Lord, give unto me one heart and one way so that I may fear You always in the name of Jesus Christ (Jeremiah 32:29).
4. Uphold me, O Lord, with Your directing Spirit, in the name of Jesus Christ (Psalms 51:12).
5. O Lord, grant me Your divine authority and power so that I may fight against the forces of evil in the name of Jesus Christ (Colossians 1:29).
6. O Lord, give me heroic friends whose hearts You have touched in the name of Jesus Christ (1 Samuel 10:26).
7. O Lord, teach me to guard my words so that my words can be used as weapons against the forces of evil in the name of Jesus Christ (Psalms 141:3).

Battles in Biblical History

The apostle Paul explained one critical purpose for Old Testament battles. He said, "Now all these things happened unto them for ensamples: and they are written for our admonition, upon whom the ends of the world are come. Wherefore let him that thinketh he standeth take heed lest he fall" (1 Corinthians 10:11–12).

In Origen's commentary on the Book of Joshua, he speaks of the reason for the historical mentioning of all the Old Testament battles.

> Unless those physical wars can bear the likeness of spiritual wars, I do not ever suppose that the Books of Jewish History would have been delivered from the apostles to the disciples of Christ, who came to teach peace, so that they could be read in the churches. For instance, what can the description of these physical wars achieve unto those followers to whom it is said by Jesus, "My peace I bestow unto you; My peace I leave behind unto you," and unto whom it is being commanded and being spoken by the apostle, "Not avenging your own selves," and, "Rather, you receive injustice," and, "Rather, You suffer wrongdoing"? From that, in summary, knowing that now we do not have to conduct wars physically, but the struggles of the soul have to be performed with exertion against spiritual adversaries, the apostle, just as if a military commander, gives a command unto the soldiers of Christ, saying, "You put on the armor of God, in order that you may be able to stand stable against the cunning strategies of the devil." And so that we may have examples of these spiritual wars from the militaristic exploits of old, he wished such narratives of these militaristic exploits to be recounted aloud unto us in church, in order that, if we are spiritual, hearing that the Law is spiritual, we may compare spiritual things with spiritual in those things that we may hear. And we may consider very carefully, by the aid of those nations that battled against physical Israel, how mighty can the groups of opposing armies be from among the spiritual races that are being called "spiritual wickedness in the heavenlies," and how they can wage wars against even the church of the Lord, which is the true Israel. Both the Moabites and the Ammonites come, and all those kings and invisible races that we have already mentioned. They come against us, planning to give us battle, so that they may make us sin.[6]

When we read the Old Testament, we will find many records of battles fought in the physical world. The significance of these battles goes beyond their physical and immediate outcomes. These battles give us spiritual principles and strategies in the spiritual world to defeat our enemies, both Satan and his evil spirits.

From studying the physical battles recorded in the Old Testament, we can develop abilities, principles, and strategies to use in our battles against Satan and his evil spirits. Paul and the rest of the early church saints followed suit and developed their means of conflict based upon the natural battles of the Old Testament.

The physical battles of the Old Testament were fought for seven spiritual reasons:

1. So that the people of God could defeat their enemies.
2. So that the people of God would not be enslaved by their enemies.
3. So that the people of God would fulfill the promises of God in occupying the Promised Land and in other promises.
4. So that the people of God could take the territory of their enemies.
5. So that the people of God could chastise their enemies, which are also the enemies of God.
6. So that the people of God would be punished by their enemies when they are in a state of disobedience.
7. So that the people of God would inherit their inheritance and defend that inheritance once obtained.

General Principles of Old Testament Warfare

1. A battle must be ordered and endorsed by God (Deuteronomy 20:1–4).
2. We cannot be afraid of our enemies (Deuteronomy 20:1–4).
3. The Lord God will be with His people and will go before His people (Deuteronomy 20:1–4).
4. The battle is the Lord's (Deuteronomy 20:1–4).
5. We must prepare ourselves for the battle (Deuteronomy 20:1–4).
6. Our enemies must be utterly destroyed (Deuteronomy 20:1–4).
7. We must not run after the abominations of the Gentiles (Deuteronomy 20:1–4).
8. God promises protection to His soldiers (Deuteronomy 20:1–4).
9. The enemies of God's people are the enemies of God (Exodus 17:16; Judges 5:31).

10. We are to trust in God for victory (Exodus 17:16; Judges 5:31).
11. We are never to trust in our strength (Exodus 17:16; Judges 5:31).
12. The Lord makes war with the enemies of God's people (Exodus 17:16; Judges 5:31).
13. The presence of God must go before us in battle (Exodus 25:21–22, 30:6).
14. Without the presence of God, there can be no victory (Exodus 25:21–22, 30:6).
15. The presence of God must be in our camp; the Ark of the Covenant symbolized the presence of God with the Israelites during a battle (Exodus 25:21–22, 30:6).
16. We have to be a holy people for God to fight for us against our enemies. No holiness = no victory, but inevitable defeat (Deuteronomy 23:9–14).
17. Holiness is key for the saints of God in battle (Deuteronomy 23:9–14).
18. We must be and remain a holy people so that the battle can be won (Deuteronomy 23:9–14).
19. We must separate ourselves from anything sinful (Deuteronomy 23:9–14).
20. Repentance must go before a battle (Deuteronomy 23:9–14).
21. Those who live in fear cannot fight or win any battle (Deuteronomy 20:8; Judges 7:1–6). No cross, no crown.
22. Those who focus more on the affairs of life than the issues of the Lord are not permitted to fight for God or the people of God (Deuteronomy 20:5–8).
23. We are supposed to fight against our enemies until they are destroyed. So we cannot give up or retire until we attain total victory (Numbers 31:10–11).
24. Both offensive and defensive warfare are found in the lives of the saints.
25. We must become submissive to the command of God either to fight or to cease fighting (Judges 7:18; 2 Samuel 2:28, 18:16).
26. We must have spiritual walls around our lives by the pleading of the blood of the Lamb.

Strategies of Warfare

The Old Testament battles provide clear warfare strategies for the modern saint. These strategies can be brought beyond the natural world into the spiritual world. These strategies should be used daily by all the saints of God. Such a strategy can only be used in each battle if the strategy can be used in that case. Using all the strategies in each battle is impossible. Some battles may only need a few strategies. Other battles may require almost all strategies.

As pertaining to different strategies and their uses, Ignatius, an apostolic father, said it best in medical terms unto Polycarp, another apostolic father, "Not every wound is healed with the same salve."[7] The Greek noun may be translated *treatment* or *remedy*, but it is better translated as *salve*, which follows the full thought of the Greek.

Edward Longstreth summarized the strategies of warfare in the Old Testament times.

> Yahweh stated His relationship with men very positively and very explicitly to Moses, saying: I am the Lord your God, you shall have no other gods before me. You shall not make for yourself any graven image of anything that is in the heavens, on the earth, or in the water. For I am a jealous God and you shall worship Me only, and with all your heart and soul and mind.
>
> That was it! There was to be no compromise, no extenuation, no equivocation. There had never before been such a concept of a God. The impact of this unique idea shook the world. It could not be exterminated. It took root in the empty places in man, possessed him, fulfilled his unfulfillment. Death and disaster only made it grow. The point all the major prophets made was that any repudiation of, or lapse from, these two basic commandments would be punished. Any backsliding generation would wish it had never been born.
>
> In the decisive battles of ancient Israel, more was involved than the clash of arms. It was not his body the Israelite feared to have pierced, it was not his life he feared to lose; the loss he dreaded most was the loss of the favor of His God because he had broken his covenant with Him.[8]

The following three phrases describe the strategies extracted from the battles of the Old Testament better than any other: "No compromise, no extenuation, no equivocation."[9]

Here is a list of the overall strategies extracted from the battles of the Old Testament and from several books about the battles in the Old Testament:[10]

1. When a saint goes into the territory of the enemy, he or she must expect a battle (Genesis 14).
2. Victory in a battle rests upon implementation of the plan of God, and the involvement of God in the battle (Genesis 14).
3. The battle plan is not ours, but it is our Lord's (Genesis 14).
4. Without God, everything can stand against the saint of God (Genesis 14).
5. With God, everything, sooner or later, will crumble before His power (Genesis 14).
6. With God, sooner or later, we will be able to conquer what stands against us (Genesis 14).
7. In battle, we should fight only the portion that we can handle (Genesis 14).
8. We must refuse to give any help to the enemy (Genesis 14).
9. We must enter a battle with the right motive, behavior, and attitude (Genesis 14).
10. The credit of victory rests upon God (Genesis 14).
11. We must not look at the enemies or the evil circumstances with fear (Exodus 14:10–11).
12. We must not go back into captivity (Exodus 14:12).
13. Sometimes we must stand still or become unmovable (Exodus 14:13).
14. We must allow the Lord to fight since it is His battle (Exodus 14:14).
15. Despite our circumstances, we must keep our peace (Exodus 14:14).
16. We must go forward and rarely retreat (Exodus 14:15–16).
17. God moves for His saints in supernatural means (Exodus 14:19–31).
18. God will orchestrate events for our benefit in our conflicts (Exodus 14:19–31).
19. In prayer, we must call upon the Lord and learn to wait and minister unto the Lord (Exodus 14).
20. We must wait in faith and patience (Exodus 14).
21. We can only overcome or conquer the enemies of God through prayer (Exodus 17:9–11).
22. We must hold to the authority and power of God, regardless of our circumstances (Exodus 17:9).
23. We must follow spiritual leadership, as long as that leadership follows

the leading of God (Exodus 17:9–10).
24. We must go out from our safety zone and fight in plain sight (Exodus 17:9).
25. We need to seek help from the Lord (Exodus 17).
26. We must remember the victories and conquests that took place in the past (Exodus 17).
27. We should not grumble (Number 14:2–3).
28. We must never rebel against God in or outside a battle (Numbers 14:9).
29. We must not accept evil or slanderous reports (Numbers 14:36–28).
30. We must never do the reverse of what God has spoken (Numbers 14:25).
31. We must never go up when the Lord is not with the people of God (Numbers 14:25–28).
32. We must not be overoptimistic or arrogant, regardless of the circumstances (Numbers 14:42–44).
33. We must not make any decision in fear, but always make decisions according to the principles of faith (Numbers 14).
34. We must not be forced into a battle (Numbers 21:1–3).
35. Any failure experienced by the people of God is temporary and never permanent (Numbers 21:1–3).
36. We do suffer failures, but any failure of God's people is beneficial (Numbers 21:1–3).
37. Conflict in life, especially if a person is a saint of God, is inescapable (Numbers 21:21–32).
38. If we are to have the promises of God, spiritual warfare is unavoidable (Numbers 21:21–32).
39. Enemies will never allow the people of God safe passage through their territory (Numbers 21:21–32).
40. We must repent and purify ourselves before the battles (Numbers 31).
41. In battle, the interests of God's people are foremost (Numbers 31).
42. We must claim the promises of God (Deuteronomy 2:24–37).
43. We must allow God to fight for us (Deuteronomy 2:24–37).
44. We must possess the promises of God (Deuteronomy 2:24–37).
45. We must contend with the enemies in battle (Deuteronomy 2:24–27).
46. We must see that nothing is hard for the Lord (Deuteronomy 2:24–

37).

47. The enemies of God's people will be delivered into our hands by the Lord (Deuteronomy 3:1–11).
48. We must overcome all obstacles by the power of God (Deuteronomy 3:1–11).
49. We must claim victory and its consequences (Deuteronomy 3:1–11).
50. We must follow the ways of God and not our ways (Joshua 6).
51. Sometimes we must divide and conquer the forces of evil (Joshua 6). In such cases, we should fight one evil spirit, or one group of evil spirits at a time rather than take on many evil spirits.
52. We must trust God, regardless of our circumstances (Joshua 6).
53. We must fight the battle God's way (Joshua 6).
54. We should seek assurance from God (Joshua 6).
55. We should practice silence on occasion (Joshua 6).
56. We should never go against the directions of God (Joshua 7).
57. We must never underestimate our enemies (Joshua 7).
58. We should understand the reasons for defeat or failure (Joshua 7).
59. We must not compromise with the world (Joshua 7).
60. We must not accept any accursed thing nor violate the warnings of God (Joshua 7).
61. We must always be prepared and ready to do battle (Joshua 8).
62. We must use the sword of the Lord, which is the Word of God (Joshua 8).
63. We must turn toward the enemies and face them (Joshua 8).
64. We should not run from our enemies unless God demands us to retreat for some reason (Joshua 8).
65. We must face our enemies in the strength of God (Joshua 8).
66. We must focus on the Lord God, nothing else (Joshua 8).
67. We must put our enemies under our feet (Joshua 10:1–27).
68. We must be stable and of good courage (Joshua 10:1–27).
69. We must learn to attack key strongholds (Joshua 10:28–43).
70. We must persevere and remain faithful in battle (Joshua 11).
71. We must never fear the type or the size of any enemy (Joshua 11).
72. We should always heed the warnings from the Lord God (Judges 6:1–8:35).
73. We must be restored from God (Judges 6:1–8:35).
74. We must learn to be alone with the Lord God (Judges 6:1–8:35).

75. We must destroy all our altars of idolatry (Judges 6:1–8:35).
76. We must persevere by the Spirit of God (Judges 6:1–8:35).
77. We must seek greater and more powerful levels of faith (Judges 6:1–8:35).
78. We must learn to depend upon the Lord (Judges 6:1–8:35).
79. We must learn to move and not hesitate when God commands us to move (Judges 6:1–8:35).
80. We must not fear our enemies (Judges 6:1–8:35).
81. We must call down and invoke the authority and power of God (Judges 6:1–8:35).
82. We must learn that God can turn a defeat into a victory (Judges 15).
83. We should acknowledge God as our provision and support (Judges 15).
84. We must be refreshed by the Lord (Judges 15).
85. We must ask the counsel of God (Judges 20).
86. We must accept corporate discipline (Judges 20).
87. We must not stop fighting (Judges 20).
88. We must be patient in the day and hour of crisis (1 Samuel 13–14).
89. We must stress commitment, but never highlight numbers (1 Samuel 13–14).
90. We must draw strength from past victories (1 Samuel 17).
91. We must have faith that is strengthened in the difficulties of the past, which always yields faith for new challenges (1 Samuel 17).
92. We must see obstacles and other trials as opportunities of God (1 Samuel 17).
93. We must use a proven armor and not a new armor (1 Samuel 17).
94. We must face the enemies in the name of the Lord (1 Samuel 17).
95. We must not be limited by our capabilities (1 Samuel 17).
96. We must confess our victories (1 Samuel 17).
97. We must recognize the purposes and reasons for spiritual warfare (1 Samuel 17).
98. We must not give in to despair (1 Samuel 30).
99. We must claim restoration of all things that have been taken by our enemies (1 Samuel 30).
100. We must realize that victories, whether personal or corporate, are for all (1 Samuel 30).
101. We must not be intimidated by the mockeries of our enemies (2

Samuel 5:1–16).
102. We must fight offensively (2 Samuel 5:17–25).
103. We must attack our enemies in the Lord's timing (2 Samuel 5:17–25).
104. We must overcome the giants in the land (2 Samuel 21:15–22).
105. We must know that God uses different methods in battles (2 Samuel 21:15–22).
106. We must remember that our enemies will return (1 Kings 20).
107. We must not be deceived by flattery (1 Kings 20).
108. We must set appropriate priorities (1 Kings 20).
109. We must praise God for revelation (2 Kings 3).
110. We must repeatedly pray, especially in battles (2 Kings 6:8–23).
111. We must develop spiritual perception (2 Kings 6:8–23).
112. We must allow the power of God to be manifested (2 Kings 6:8–23).
113. We must move toward the realm of the impossible (2 Kings 6:24–7:20).
114. We must not be critical or untrusting of God's power (2 Kings 6:24–7:20).
115. We must worship God (2 Kings 17).
116. We must understand the consequences of sins in our lives (2 Kings 24:1–25:30).
117. We must hold on for victories (1 Chronicles 14:8–17).
118. We must humble ourselves before the battle (2 Chronicles 12).
119. We must learn to submit to the service and tasks of God (2 Chronicles 12).
120. We must not make any unholy alliances (2 Chronicles 18).
121. In a battle, we must use discernment (2 Chronicles 18).
122. In a battle, we must use fasting as a means of defeating our enemies (2 Chronicles 20).
123. We must always keep our eyes upon the Lord God (2 Chronicles 20).
124. We must believe and trust in God rather than ourselves (2 Chronicles 20).
125. We should rejoice during the occurrence of a battle (2 Chronicles 20).
126. We should follow good and godly advice if it agrees with the will of

God (2 Chronicles 25:5–16).
127. We must rebuke pride in our lives (2 Chronicles 25:17–24).
128. We must not allow corruption to come into our lives because it will bring destruction (2 Chronicles 28).
129. We must cut the supply line of our enemies (2 Chronicles 32:1–23).
130. We must reject all types and forms of deceptions (2 Chronicles 35:20–24).
131. We must always listen when God speaks (2 Chronicles 35:20–24).

My Continued Experience with Spiritual Warfare

Becoming a prayer warrior and a soldier for the Lord was something that I had no idea the Lord God had ever wanted from me. From the pulpit, I had never been taught that God required His people to pray and become a soldier for Him. I never knew that when I accepted the Lord, I was enlisted into an army. For years, I had been a soldier on the sidelines. I was a soldier doing nothing for the kingdom of God and doing nothing against the kingdom of Satan.

When W. V. Grant Sr. called me up before the whole congregation and said, "The Lord wants you to lay your family on the altar and leave them there. You are called to be an intercessor," I thought to myself, *What is intercession?* Further, the minister said, "You have been called a warrior for Christ."

From that moment, I knew that I must get into the Bible. I had previously believed that the minister was responsible only for studying and reading the Bible. I did not know I must study and read the Bible for myself. I trusted only the minister to tell me what the Bible said.

When I began studying and reading the Word of God, I did not know what I was reading at first. I went from subject to subject.

Studying prayer, I found that it must be the lifestyle of true Christians. It is the responsibility of every Christian to pray because praying is entering a deeper relationship with God.

I got so excited about knowing that God would teach me to pray. From that moment, God knew my spirit. He knew that my battle cry was, "Lord, teach me to pray."

I knew one passage of Scripture to help me. First Timothy 2:1–2 reads, "I exhort therefore, that, first of all, supplications, prayers, intercessions, and giving of thanks, be made for all men; For kings, and for all that are in authority; that we may lead a quiet and peaceable life in all godliness and honesty."

I thought, *my Lord, if I did not know that I had to pray for all of this. I will just pray.*

Another passage of Scripture I used was, "Praying always with all prayer and supplication in the Spirit, and watching thereunto with all perseverance and supplication for all saints" (Ephesians 6:18). I learned here that I must pray for the saints.

One other passage of Scripture that touched my heart was James 5:15, "And the prayer of faith shall save the sick, and the Lord shall raise him up; and if he have committed sins, they shall be forgiven him."

Reading this passage made me believe that I must base my prayers upon Scripture. When I was healed of an ulcer, I used these three passages of Scripture only.

I learned that the prayer of petition is asking God for something, whereas the prayer of intercession is praying for others. An intercessor prays primarily for others.

Ezekiel 22:30–31 reads as follows:

And I sought for a man among them, that should make up the hedge, and stand in the gap before me for the land, that I should not destroy it: but I found none. Therefore, have I poured out mine indignation upon them; I have consumed them with the fire of my wrath: their own way have I recompensed upon their heads, saith the Lord GOD.

Most of my prayer life has been to pray for others rather than myself. In many respects, I have been forgotten in my prayer life for the sake of others.

But Luke 18:1–8 helped me through by teaching me to not give up praying for what I needed:

And he spake a parable unto them to this end, that men ought always to pray, and not to faint; Saying, There was in a city a judge, which feared not God, neither regarded man: And there was a widow in that city; and she came unto him, saying, Avenge me of mine adversary. And he would not go for a while: but afterward he said within himself, Though I fear not God, nor regard man; Yet because this widow troubleth me, I will avenge her, lest by her continual coming she weary me. And the Lord said, Hear what the unjust judge saith. And shall not God avenge his own elect, which cry day and night unto him, though he bear long with them? I tell you that he will avenge them speedily. Nevertheless when the Son of man cometh, shall he find faith on the earth?"

My Mother with Bird Fever

For days and nights, I stayed alone at the hospital with my mother. Somehow, she was infected with bird fever. When I could not go any further because of exhaustion, I began crying and asking the Lord, "Why is my life so hard?" For three days and nights, I had stood over my mother as she was sick. She was repeatedly coughing. Her coughing was like whooping cough. Every time she coughed, her bowels moved. The nurses brought me a bedsheet.

When I had gone as far as I could go, I looked upon the Father and cried out, "Help!" The Lord informed me what type of virus she had.

Only a few minutes later, the phone rang. It was a friend, and she came up to sit with my mother for the rest of the night. She had the nurse get me a bed and food.

Jesus and His Prayer Life

Studying the life of Jesus, I found that prayer was the priority in his life. To Jesus Christ, prayer was communication with His Father. He teaches us that we must talk to our heavenly Father.[11]

Prayer and Intercession

While intercession is a form of prayer, there is a difference between general prayer and intercession.

When I was first saved, there were very few books on prayer, especially on intercession. Since I had few resources beyond the Bible, I followed the simple path of prayer as found in the Bible. I experienced many types of prayer.

I had been doing intercessory prayer ever since I was saved. At night, I would sneak out of my house and crawl over our fence. Alone in the field, I would cry and cry over my family. I went from one state of mourning and groaning to another: deeper and deeper into prayer. My heart was crying over my family. I knew that all of them were going to hell. The burden was so intense, I thought that my heart was going to burst open.

As time went on, some books were written about prayer that I was able to purchase. I could not understand the differences between general prayer and intercession from these books. Intercession is a prayer for others, while general prayer does not necessarily follow that pattern.

After much study, my prayer life and my style of prayer made sense. So many times, God moved me to pray for various people. Sometimes, I knew the person whom I was to pray over for their benefit. Other times I did not know the person or even the name of the person.

Definitions and Nature of Intercession

Intercession means "to intercede for," "stand in the gap for," "to stand in proxy for," "to mediate," "to intervene," and "to desire to be part of what God is doing." Intercessory prayer is standing in for a person.

The foundation of intercession is to have the mind of Christ. By having the mind of Christ, we join with Christ to fulfill the will of God and to intercede for the fulfillment of His will.

Intercessory prayer is for all the saints. All the saints are priests (Revelation 1:6). All saints of God have been given the ministry of reconciliation (2 Corinthians 5:17–18).

At its heart, intercession is standing in the gap or proxy for another person. When a person stands in the gap, he is so concerned about a person, that he will intercede for him or her and stand in his or her place for a point of contact or so all other people can have a visible representation before their eyes for which to pray (Isaiah 53:12, 59:16; Jeremiah 7:16, 27:18, 36:25; Romans 7:25, 8:26–27, 8:34, 11:2; 1 Timothy 2:1).

In intercession, the ultimate criterion remains not the worthiness of the pleader, but God's will and those for whom the person is pleading (Ezekiel 14:14–20).

Intercession originates in a revelation from God. Such prayer is praying God's will into the world. Intercession is making a demand upon the abilities of God. If we pray right, intercession begets wealth, power, and rewards.

Intercession takes upon itself two aspects: warfare and travail (taking on a burden). The warfare aspect is facing Satan on behalf of a person, while the travail aspect is beseeching God for an answer to a situation for a person.

One powerful intercessor that the church has forgotten was Pandita Ramabai, a Pentecostal revivalist, missionary, and pioneer. Speaking of the burden of young intercessors, she said, "The burden of their prayer is intercession, that all the mission and all India may be converted, may experience a great revival and receive the Pentecostal baptism."[12]

Lastly, intercessors repeatedly pester God with prayer until He does something. Whether He punishes them or moves and brings forth a manifestation of His power, they continue to pray. The idea of pestering God through prayer has its origin in Old Testament times. Abraham and the other intercessors of the Old Testament pestered God repeatedly.

Intercessors and Fanaticism

Most Christians do not understand intercession. They do not understand the ministry of reconciliation, which is a form of intercession. And intercession is a closet ministry—away from the public eye.

Intercessors receive no recognition. If the spirit of intercession should come to a person, that person should find someplace to pray.

One time, an intercessor asked me, "If an intercessor knew that she or he had to pray, what would you do if she or he ran up on the platform while praise, worship, or preaching was going on?"

I replied, "God does not move in confusion; go find yourself a place in the back where the service is not hindered. And if you laugh or groan, put a cloth over your mouth." The intercessor will do nothing that brings confusion into the church.

An intercessor is in a ministry of love. We cannot do spiritual warfare over someone if we do not have love in our hearts. It is impossible for a person to be an intercessor without the love of the Lord God. As an intercessor, one can and does stand between an individual or nation and the wrath of God. That is the essence of love.

To be an intercessor requires a lot of self-discipline and a continual crucifying of the flesh. This has been hard for me.

We, as intercessors, become the cutting edge of the Lord's sword. We pull down strongholds of darkness and prepare the way for others. We are birthing the will of God upon the earth. We are posted as watchmen on the walls. Isaiah 62:6–7 reads, "I have set watchmen upon thy walls, O Jerusalem, which shall never hold their peace day nor night: ye that make mention of the LORD, keep not silence, And give him no rest, till he establish, and till he make Jerusalem a praise in the earth."

During the Great Awakenings of the past, the ministers spoke of the "sword of the Lord." This was a manifestation of the power of the Lord. When it was used, hundreds and more would experience a great conviction of sin. The meeting place would resemble a battlefield full of people slain in the Spirit. Some of the ministers of these revivals spoke of the spirit of revival and the spirit of prayer. The spirit of prayer was a supernatural ability to pray for revival and to pray for God's moving. The spirit of revival was groaning for revival, a groaning for change in the church, and groaning over the sinners. No wonder the Lord wanted someone to stand in the gap (Ezekiel 22:30–31).

Today, we need intercessors like Moses and Daniel. Daniel prayed three times a day and received remarkable revelations of present and future events. His example inspired me to make an appointment with the Lord God three times a day in prayer.

Job was the man who gave me courage when I thought that God hated me. Indeed, I went to the Book of Job almost all the time. The hand of Satan killed Job's servants, sons, and daughters. Job longed so many times to die. I could relate to that feeling many times.

The Prayer of Agreement

Matthew 18:19–20 reads, "Again I say unto you, That if two of you shall agree on earth as touching anything that they shall ask, it shall be done for them of my Father which is in heaven. For where two or three are gathered together in my name, there am I in the midst of them."

As a baby Christian, I read this and said, "Wow! God the Father or the Lord Jesus Christ will come down and will be with us on earth when two or more agree." This was so exciting.

To look at this, it would seem easy. It is easy to bind and loose, but agreeing is not so easy.

I have learned that when someone else is praying for me, I must repeat what they are saying very quietly. It keeps my mind on the subject.

One night, my son was ministering to a lady. She asked him to agree with her. My son was about to say something like, "I will agree with you." But the Lord said, "Be careful here. She wants you to agree with her that you and she will marry. She is not to be your wife."

In my life, it has been so important to have a person to pray with during my trials and troubles. Once in our prayer group, I asked the others to agree with me in prayer over a situation.

One in the prayer group said, "I cannot agree with you to pray that way."

I said, "Okay." Then I asked, "Whoever will agree with me, please go over on the other side of the church. And all others continue to pray what you were already praying."

After much studying on agreement, I discovered that we must be in one accord. If one does not agree with our prayers, it can hinder or block those prayers from being answered. We must agree in prayer and leave our feelings at the door.

Prayer of Binding and Loosing

Matthew 16:19 reads, "And I will give unto thee the keys of the kingdom of heaven: and whatsoever thou shalt bind on earth shall be bound in heaven: and whatsoever thou shalt loose on earth shall be loosed in heaven." When I read this, I knew that I must learn how to get these keys.

At first, I thought it meant that God in heaven had these keys. I found out that first I had better pray for the baptism of the Holy Spirit. With this I would receive the anointing, and it is the anointing that breaks the yoke (Isaiah 10:27).

A Prayer Partner and Me

My prayer partner and I were going downstate to check on her house. As I was driving, I knew I had to pray. Tears began filling my eyes so much that it became hard to see. I was crying, groaning, and screaming in pain. In the Spirit, I saw a lady sitting in a beautiful bed. The bedroom suite was beautiful. But the woman was crying and saying, "I am so sick. I have no one to pray for me, and I am dying."

God had given me revelation knowledge of what this sister was going through in her life. I did not know how long this went on. After a while, I began laughing, and the burden left me.

The next day when I got to work and told my co-workers what had happened to me, they said that they knew the woman. She was healed.

Another Healing

One night, while praying in my bed, I began to travail and groan in the Spirit, crying and praying. I opened my eyes and saw a lady standing at the foot of my bed, looking at me. I knew from the Holy Spirit that she was a living missionary who was in great need. In the name of Jesus, I came against the danger in her life and commanded the evil spirit to leave her alone.

This was one time I was happy that God had taught me spiritual warfare. I repeatedly learned that Christian life is a battle.

Violent Intercession

Intercession can become violent. I learned this in a butterbean patch as I prayed for my sister Sue. I fell on my face and felt as if I were having a baby. This reminds me of Psalms 48:6, "Fear took hold upon them there, and pain, as of a woman in travail."

Soon after, I became angry and told Satan, "Satan, you are not going to kill my sister." I used Matthew 16:19 in my prayer against him.

I began binding up that murdering spirit and loosing life to her. That day, I stood between the power of darkness and the power of light. In the name of Jesus Christ, Satan was not going to kill my sister. I would not stand for this. Sue was not saved, and Jesus had promised me that my family would be saved.

Tertullian viewed the prayers of the saints as violence going up to the Lord God. Tertullian wrote,

> Now I will proceed and display at once the duties of the Christian society, that, as I may refute the evil things charged against it, I might also draw attention to its good things. We are a body united together as such by a common conscience of religion, by unity of discipline, and by the bond of a common hope. We assemble in a meeting-place and congregation, that, approaching God in prayer, as if massing into a united force, we might struggle with Him in our prayers. This violence is pleasing unto God. Further, we pray for emperors, for their ministers, and their magistrates, for the state of the world, for peace on the earth and the delay of the final consummation.[13]

William T. Ellis, a writer for the Heritage Magazine, described his experience with Pandita Ramabai, and other intercessors in Kedgaon, India, on July 24, 1907. His description of the intercessors and how they were praying is utterly remarkable. The intercessors were practicing violent intercession. Ellis describes what was before his eyes, and then Pandita Ramabai speaks about testing the spirits.

> For half an hour I had been hearing strange sounds, now of one person shouting in a high voice, then of the mingled utterance of a crowd, and later of song. At last, it settled down into a steady roar. "What is that?" I asked. "It is the girls' prayer meeting," was the answer. "Could I visit it?" I pointedly asked my guide, after hints had proved unavailing. "Why—I—suppose—so, I'll see." In a few minutes I found myself witnessing a scene utterly without parallel in all my wide experience of religious gatherings.
>
> In a large, bare room with cement floor, were gathered between 30 and 40 girls, ranging in age from 12 to 20. By a table sat a sweet-faced, refined native young woman, watching soberly and without disapproval the

scene before her. After a few minutes she too knelt on the floor in silent prayer.

The other occupants of the room were all praying aloud. Some were crying at the top of their lungs. The tumult was so great that it was with difficulty that any one voice could be distinguished. Some of the girls were bent over with heads touching on the floor. Others were sitting on their feet, with shoulders and bodies twitching and jerking in convulsions. A few were swaying to and fro, from side to side or back and forth. Two or three were kneeling upright, with arms and bodies moving.

One young woman, the loudest, moved on her knees, all unconsciously, two or three yards during the time I watched. She had a motion of her body that must have been exhausting. She also swung her arms violently. And often the gestures of the praying figures showed one or both hands outstretched, in dramatic supplication. Several girls would clap hands at the same time, though each seemed unconscious of the others. The contortions of the faces bespoke extreme agony, and perspiration streamed over them. One girl fell over sideways, asleep, or fainting from sheer exhaustion.

All had their eyes tightly closed, oblivious to surroundings. Such intense, such concentrated devotion I had never witnessed before. It was a full of 15 minutes before one of the girls, who had quieted somewhat, saw me. And thereafter she sat silent praying or reading her Bible in comparative tranquility …

"We do not make a special point of the gift of tongues," Ramabai insisted gently; "our emphasis is always put-upon love and life. And undoubtedly the lives of the girls have been changed. About 700 of them have come into this blessing. We do not exhibit the girls that have been gifted with other tongues, nor do we in any wise call special attention to them."

"We try to weed out the false from the true; for there are other spirits than the Holy Spirit and when a girl begins to try to speak in another tongue, apparently imitating her sisters without mentioning the name or blood of Jesus, I go up to her and speak to her or touch her on the shoulder, and she stops at once. On the other hand, if a girl is praying in the Spirit I cannot stop her, no matter how sharply I speak to her or shake her. My own hearing is peculiar," continued Ramabia, "in that I can understand most clearly when there is a loud noise (a well-known characteristic of the partially deaf) and I move among the girls, listening to them in awed wonder. I have heard girls who know no English at all utter beautiful prayers in your tongue. I have heard others pray in Greek and Hebrew and Sanskrit, and others again in languages that none of us understood. One of my girls was praying in this very room a few nights ago and although in her studies she has not gone beyond the second book she prayed so clearly and beautifully in English that the other teachers marveled who could be praying, since they did not distinguish the voice."[14]

The Holy Spirit and My Sister Ruby

My sister, Ruby, saw what was going on in the butterbean patch. She thought I was going crazy, or at least having a nervous breakdown. It scared her. She had never seen the Holy Spirit work like this, and she had never seen the power of intercession.

What Ruby saw so scared her that after I left to go home, she fell on her face before God and cried out to God that if this experience was real, she wanted it. She prayed in her home and on her knees for the baptism of the Holy Spirit. The baptism fell upon her with evidence of speaking in tongues.

The next day at work was hard. The devil was busy doing all he could do to make me think my sister, Sue, would be murdered that day. About 11:30 a.m., a phone call came in for me. As I walked to the phone, my mind was battling. I repeatedly quoted Ephesians 6:12, "For we wrestle not against flesh and blood, but against principalities, against powers, against the rulers of the darkness of this world, against spiritual wickedness in high places." I knew that it was war. There was no time to let doubt come into my mind.

From the phone call, I learned that someone fired a gun at Sue seven times, but the shots had missed her.

The Bible tells us to stand during the battle. According to Ephesians 6:12, we must be on the front line in the fight. And the Bible speaks of the wiles of the devil.

Thank God, I learned to put on the whole armor of God and keep it on. God does not put the armor upon us. We put it on, and we must keep it on (see Ephesians 6:11).

Times like this with Sue taught me that our faith must not fail us. We must know and make sure that our faith is strong and ready for battle. After all, faith that has never been tested is no faith. How do we know that we have faith if that faith has never been tested?

Though I did not know that when I became a Christian, I became a soldier, that is exactly what happened.

Most of my fighting was over my family, my husband, my son, and myself. I thank God that I knew about, and then experienced, the gifts of the Holy Spirit.

The gifts of knowledge and wisdom became very important to me. These two gifts helped me so many times while my mother was in the hospital. God repeatedly told me what was wrong with her. And God would let me know if my mother-in-law was in trouble with her sugar levels.

My mother went from healthy to extremely sick time and again. Many times, the doctors gave up on her, but I could not. She was unsaved, and I still held on to the promises of God about my family. The practice of intercession was my lifeline for my mother and me.

Danger

One of my prayer partners became a very good friend. She and I could pray together for hours.

I will never forget one incident of our praying together. The Lord spoke to me, "Go on a fast." I began to fast. The Lord led me back to her house after fasting for fifteen days. Then I walked across her daughter's property, and the Lord said, "Danger, danger." That was all I could receive from the Lord.

After fasting twenty-one days, the Lord gave me peace over the problems.

Later that week, my prayer partner called me and said, "I know why you had to go on that fast." Her daughter had some politicians over for a cookout. But before that, someone had put a shotgun shell in her barbecue pit.

When her daughter lit the charcoal pit, the shotgun shell blew up. Miraculously the shotgun shell pellets hit the bricks and did not go outside the charcoal pit. The pellets chipped out some of the blocks, but no one was hurt. My prayer partner called, just crying, knowing why I went on that fast.

My Husband and I

My husband and I had to learn that spiritual warfare is a battle. The Bible says, "For in death there is no remembrance of thee: in the grave who shall give thee thanks? I am weary with my groaning; all the night make I my bed to swim; I water my couch with my tears. Mine eye is consumed because of grief; it waxeth old because of all mine enemies" (Psalms 6:5–7).

My husband and I studied the Book of Ephesians and realized it is all about spiritual warfare. I asked my husband, "What does all this mean?" He looked at me kind of funny. I asked, "What is the sword of the Spirit?" Again, we had to go back to the Word of God and study it. That made me realize I had to change some things in my life. I knew that I had to give up my softball team. We had to get into the Word of God.

Further, my husband and I learned to wrestle all night against evil spirits. During these times, evil spirits tried to choke us or tie up our arms. They even tried to throw us out of bed. We had to whisper the name Jesus repeatedly. Every time, the enemy or his evil spirits fled. We must remember that Satan does not have the last moment or the final say. Our God has the final say: "Weeping may endure for a night, but joy cometh in the morning" (Psalms 30:5).

If we can get through the night of storms and trials, joy will come in the morning.

Though I was a baby Christian, people were telling me to do spiritual warfare. But how can a saint fight something that he or she cannot see?

Baby Christians should go easy on spiritual warfare. It is very dangerous for baby Christians or unstable Christians to cast out demons. They need to grow and mature in faith and their identity in Christ. If not, they may be able to have success for a time, but a time will come when they will face a principality, and they will be destroyed.

Spiritual warfare has levels, and baby Christians cannot go to the highest level of spiritual warfare first.

My son preached about John Cassian and his views on spiritual warfare. Cassian was an apologist and theologian during the fourth century. He wrote a considerable portion of work on spiritual warfare based upon the lives of the monks. He showed that every aspect of their life had been patterned to spiritually combat Satan and his forces.

With words, John Cassian painted the life of the saint as a spiritual contest with victors and losers. He said that in this spiritual contest, for one to obtain the greatest rewards, he or she must enter the highest contest where there is no quarter given. In this type of contest, Satan pushes forth extremely hard against the saint, but the saint attacks and counterattacks extremely hard against the forces of evil.

Cassian discussed four levels of spiritual warfare between the saints and the forces of evil.

1. The level of babies in Christ. Baby Christians receive the least attacks by Satan and the least rewards.
2. The level of immature youth. More attacks, and more rewards; power to combat; few crowns and prizes seen by Satan upon these Christians in the spiritual world.
3. The level of maturity. For the saints to reach this level, they must have carefully been tested and have passed all tests; more attacks, and more rewards; power to combat; more crowns and prizes seen by Satan upon these Christians in the spiritual world.
4. The level of victors (overcomers). These are saints who have already become victors many times against Satan and are decked out with many crowns and prizes already seen by Satan in the spiritual world. Those saints who reach the level of victors can do the most damage against Satan, the power of Satan, and all the forces of evil.[15]

A Baby Christian and a Principality

A woman once came to our services and saw how my son cast out demons. She wanted that power, but she would not wait, pray, study, and prepare herself. A person must be founded upon the Word, fasted up, prayed up, and be mature in Christ Jesus.

The woman traveled and set up a ministry in India. For a time, she had great success. People were healed, and several were set free from evil spirits. She only used the Word of God, the name of Jesus Christ, the power of the cross, and the power of the blood.

All these wonderful things were occurring through a baby Christian who was unstable. God honors His Word, the name of Jesus Christ, the cross, and the blood.

Finally, Satan threw down the gauntlet before her and sent a principality her way. Because of her immaturity, instability, and ignorance, the principality tore into her. By the time the battle was over, there was nothing left of that baby Christian. She did not die, but she was stricken with disease and various curses. By disobedience, she had lost everything. Her faith was gone, and she became the property of evil.

Her ministry was over. Only then did she remember the words of my son.

He had warned her not to speed into ministry. He told her to study the Word of God and allow the Lord to mature her.

She flew from India to New York, and from New York to Jacksonville, where she called the office. I received the phone call and told her, "Rarely does my son see people and pray for them separately from the services." I went to my son and asked him, "What do we do?"

He said, "She needs to come to the services. Tell her to come to the service."

She came to the services, and we could see that the principality had taken possession of her, cursed her, and afflicted her.

What a night. Whether an exorcism is done in private or publicly, God will honor it. However, according to the ancient church, removing an exorcism from the public removes its primary purpose. According to the ancient church, the main use of exorcism is to show the power of God over the power of Satan.

Not only had the principality possessed, cursed, and afflicted this woman, her whole family had been cursed and afflicted as well. My son has repeatedly warned baby Christians and unstable Christians not to go into spiritual warfare unprepared and unstudied. He warns them that a time will come when principalities will show up. A saint must be mature and stable to face them. We must remember that not every battle is ours.

This woman stood before my son. Almost everyone in the service was praying. The principality wrestled, screamed, and snarled. As far as I can remember, the principality did not speak. I think that my son came against its speaking.

It took some time, but by the end of the service, the principality was rebuked and cast out, never to bother her again. The curses and afflictions were broken over her and her family. She repented and renounced Satan and regained what she had lost.

My son is continually concerned about baby Christians fighting battles that they are not ready for and suffering the way this woman did. It takes time to be able to face the most evil and powerful of Satan's forces and win the victory.

Bill Bean, a well-known deliverance minister, taught an associate about exorcism. The associate took on a case, which he should have left alone. He faced an Egyptian Baal, a principality, that was possessing a young man. The evil spirit faced the associate with little fear. The spirit threw him back to a couch, and the man ran away from the house. He called Bill Bean, and Bean came to the house and did the exorcism. This time—with the mature, seasoned minister—the Egyptian Baal was cast out of the young man.

We should remember that the purpose of the coming of Jesus Christ was so that "he might destroy the works of the devil" (1 John 3:8).

Historian Ramsay MacMullen wrote in his book on the church's history,

> The manhandling of demons through exorcisms–humiliating them, making them howl, beg for mercy, tell their secrets, and depart in a hurry–served a purpose quite essential to the Christian definition of monotheism: it made physically (or dramatically) visible the superiority of the Christian's patron power over all others. One and only one was God.[16]

Formalism, Fanaticism, and Necromancy

An anonymous minister once said, "If you have the Bible only, you have formalism, but if you have the Holy Spirit only, you have fanaticism." If a church has formalism, it is dead and has no life. If a church has fanaticism, there is no balance, stability, nor consistency with the Lord. In fact, fanaticism will lead to movements and manifestations that are not of God. Commonly, it will lead to necromancy and blending occultism with Christianity.

There was disagreement among both reformers and revivalists. They sought not to be in formalism, fanaticism, or necromancy. They warred to stay balanced in the Word of God and in experiences. They did not want to be pulled into extremes.

Princeton theologian and scholar Dr. Charles Hodge rightly warned,

> No amount of learning, no superiority of talent, nor even the pretension to inspiration, can justify a departure from the . . . truths taught by men to whose inspiration God has borne witness. All teachers must be brought to this standard; and even if an angel from heaven should teach anything contrary to the Scriptures, he should be regarded as anathema, Gal. 1:8. It is a matter of constant gratitude that we have such a standard whereby to try the spirits whether they be of God.[17]

A balanced Christian will want the ministry of the Bible and the ministry of the Holy Spirit to have a place in their lives and church services. The movements and manifestations of the Holy Spirit never supersede the Word of God. Instead, they confirm the Word of God.

Many of the revivalists throughout history have followed this view about the ministry of the Bible and the ministry of the Holy Spirit. Almost all ancient Christians also accepted this concept.

Peter Cartwright, a Methodist revivalist in the Second Great Awakening, held the Word of God as the only infallible guide in trying the spirits. He judged all movements and experiences by the Word of God.

Cartwright faced many types of fanatics in the Second Great Awakening. Fanaticism unrestrained will lead to deception and finally to death. One fanatic believed that he became immortal in this life. Regardless of arguments to the contrary by his friends, he still believed that he had become immortal. He refused to eat and drink. Within sixteen days, he died. His death helped restrain much fanaticism.[18]

Peter Cartwright wrote about one class of fanatics that he faced and his view about the Word of God.

> First, there are many that are truly awakened and soundly converted to God, and are pious, but instead of taking the word of God for their only infallible guide, and trying the spirits, and their impressions, or feelings, by that as a standard, they take all their impressions and sudden impulses of mind as inspirations from God, and act accordingly. If you oppose them, they say and believe you are fighting against God. If you try to reason them out of their visionary flights, and settle them down on the sure foundation, the word of God, they construe it all into the want of religion and cry out persecution.[19]

In another part of his autobiography, Peter Cartwright mentions a woman who received a wrong Jesus Christ and a wrong doctrine over the Word of God. He stood against this woman with the Word of God and prayer. He was proven right in his views on Jesus Christ and his opinions on the Word of God. He wrote,

> There was a very confirmed Arian lady in the congregation who denied the supreme divinity of Jesus Christ. Late on Monday, she professed to get very happy, and shouted out aloud; but said, while shouting, among other things, she knew I was wrong in my views of Jesus Christ, but she desired someone to go and bring me to her, for she wanted to show me, that though I was in error, she could love her enemies and do good for evil. At first, I refused to go; but she sent again. I then thought of the unjust judge, and less by her continual coming she might weary me, I went. She told me she knew I was wrong, and that she was right, and that God had blessed her and made her happy. Said I, "Sister, while I was preaching, did you not get mad?"

She answered, "Yes, very mad; I could have cut your throat. But I am not mad now, and love you, and God has blessed me." Said I, "I fear you are not happy; you have only got in a little better humor and think this is happiness. But we will test the matter. Let us kneel down here and pray to God to make it manifest who is wrong." "But," said she, "I don't want to pray; I want to talk." "Well," said I, "I have no desire to talk; I always go to God in prayer; and I now believe God, in answer to prayer, will recover you out of the snare of the devil, for you certainly are not happy at all."

So, I called upon all around–and they were many–to kneel down and help me to pray God to dislodge the lingering Arian devil that still claimed a residence in this woman's heart. We knelt, and by the score united in wrestling, mighty prayer; and while we prayed it seemed that the bending heavens came near; and if the power of God was ever felt among mortals, it was felt then and there. The woman lost her assumed good feelings, and sunk down into sullen, dumb silence, and so she remained during the meeting; and for weeks afterward many of her friends feared she would totally lose her balance of mind.

She became incapable of her business till one night she had a dream or vision, in which she afterward declared she saw her Savior, apparently in all his supreme glory, and he told her she was wrong, but he frankly forgave her; and when she came to herself, or awoke, she was unspeakably happy, and never afterward, for one moment, doubted the supreme divinity of Jesus Christ. She joined the Methodists and lived and died a shining and shouting Christian.[20]

The counsel of John Wesley about manifestations is quite wise, even today,

Do not hastily ascribe things to God. Do not easily suppose dreams, voices, impressions, visions, or revelations to be from God. They may be from him. They may be from nature. They may be from the devil. Therefore, "believe not every spirit, but try the spirits whether they be of God." Try all things by the written word and let all bow down before it.[21]

Smith Wigglesworth, a Pentecostal revivalist, seeing all the movements and manifestations of the Holy Spirit most of his life, was a man of the Word. He had a "consuming love for the Word of God," and "he had an overwhelming confidence in the God of the Word,"[22] which settled any matter for Wigglesworth.

Having learned the secret of God's power, which is His Word, Wigglesworth said,

> I understand God by His Word. I cannot understand God by impressions or feelings. I cannot get to know God by sentiment. I can only know Him by His Word. . .. It is a dangerous practice to be governed by feelings. We are saved not by feelings, but by the Word of God. Salvation does not fluctuate as do feelings.[23]

Wigglesworth, with all his movements and experiences of the Holy Spirit, condemned any experience that excluded the Word of God.[24]

Lastly, Wigglesworth held the Word of God supreme and said, "Nothing substitutes for the Word of God."[25]

It is common to hear today about experiences that do not agree with the Word of God. And there has become a fascination with seeing the dead, or necromancy (Leviticus 19:11, 20:6; Deuteronomy 18:11; 1 Samuel 28:7, 25; 2 Kings 21:6, 23:24; 1 Chronicles 10:13; 2 Chronicles 33:6; Isaiah 8:19, 19:3, 29:4).

There is a popular minister who claims to have gone to heaven and communicated with the dead apostles. This is an abomination before God.

Another strange manifestation on the rise is the appearance of Jesus Christ as a woman. Run! If that Jesus Christ prophesies ten prophecies to a person and all are fulfilled, that person must still run away from that experience. Jesus Christ must be the same Jesus Christ who ascended. If not, rebuke that false Christ. Jesus Christ will not appear as a woman.

When my sister Frankie died, her husband cried out unto the Lord God, "If I can just hear her voice one more time." When he came home, the phone rang, and her husband heard the words, "Goodbye, Al," and the person hung up. When I heard about this, I told him to denounce that voice. The voice was not of God. It was a demon speaking in the voice of Frankie, and it would have tempted him into necromancy. I will never forget that.

I believe in the movements and manifestations of the Holy Spirit, but they will agree with the Word of God. And they will not be part of the abominations mentioned in Scripture.

Many forget that God is bound to His Word. He will never do anything contrary to His Word.

False Visitations of the Dead

One thing the modern church needs is a proper theology of the dead. Today, some Christians claim that they are having visitations of the dead saints. Apostle Paul, David, Abraham, Ezra, and a host of other dead saints are proclaimed to be seen and heard. It is said that these dead saints are speaking to people and giving them insight into biblical interpretation, their faith, and their lives. Those who are experiencing these visitations claim that all these visitations are within the bounds of Christian experience. But this experience is spiritualism and necromancy. As already stated, communication with the dead is forbidden. It is not the dead speaking, but it is demonic forces (Deuteronomy 18:11; Isaiah 8:19; 1 Samuel 28; 1 Chronicles 10:13).

We must never allow a vision or other experience to interpret Scripture. Such experiences are very dangerous, and they do not follow the rules of interpretation for Scripture. The more we enter the spiritual world, the closer we must be to the Word of God. We must judge an experience by the Word of God, not the Word of God by the experience.

Consequently, I only accept the experiences ordained by the Holy Spirit and authorized in the Bible, especially in the New Testament.

Moving our authority from Scripture to spiritual experience changes the end zone from that which is certain to that which may not be certain. Such changes allow us not only to be deceived but also to become fanatical. And if that is not enough, we will become devotees to mysticism and other forms of paganism.

Scripture has boundaries. And such boundaries give Christians security from false and demonic experiences. Second Peter 1:3 reads, "According as his divine power hath given unto us all things that pertain unto life and godliness, through the knowledge of him that hath called us to glory and virtue." Moving away from the authority of Scripture means the destruction of Christians.

Counterfeit Christians and True Believers

Paul warns that Satan will certainly disguise himself as an angel of light (2 Corinthians 11:14) and that demonic manifestations may behave like the manifestations of the Holy Spirit in order to deceive and destroy people.

Paul states that people may depart from sound doctrine and adhere to the doctrines of demons (1 Timothy 4:1). He warns us to never fall into the snare of the devil nor end up ruined by the devil's wiles (Ephesians 6:11; 1 Timothy 3:7; 2 Timothy 2:26).

It is interesting to note that Paul never worried about genuine Christians being influenced by counterfeit gifts. This fact is seen in the pagan city of Corinth (1 Corinthians 10:20, 14:2). To Paul, it was impossible for genuine Christians, who have the Holy Spirit working through them and abiding in their life, to receive anything counterfeit.

He utilizes 1 Corinthians 12:3 as reassurance that demonic and pagan worship, medieval (Oriental) mysticism, as well as other contrary (alien) or occultic practices, cannot influence, nor corrupt the genuine spiritual gifts of the Spirit. The verse reads, "No man speaking by the Spirit of God calleth Jesus accursed: and that no man can say that Jesus is the Lord, but by the Holy Ghost." This passage sets forth a clear understanding that the genuine gifts of the Holy Spirit are not used by mediums or other occultists. Their gifts come from Satan and his evil spirits.

It is quite clear that Satan can counterfeit the gifts of the Holy Spirit for unbelievers (Matthew 7:22–24; John 10:10; Ephesians 5:11). On the contrary, it is impossible for Satan to counterfeit the gifts of the Holy Spirit for genuine believers who do not fall into a state of lukewarmness and continue to manifest positive fruits in their lives from the Holy Spirit (Matthew 7:16–20; 1 Corinthians 12:3; 1 John 4:4).

Appropriately, genuine Christians do not manifest counterfeit gifts, regardless of what people may think. Those who do manifest counterfeit gifts are deceived, have become lukewarm or backslidden, and may even be demon-possessed unbelievers. When Christians accept counterfeit gifts and their demonic origin and do not heed the strong warnings from the Bible, they become deceived, lukewarm, or backslidden, and become the property of the devil again. If Christians manifest such counterfeit gifts, it is impossible for them to remain saved and still be in a state of holiness, grace, and faith. A principle should be noted here: "A good tree cannot bring forth evil fruit, neither can a corrupt tree bring forth good fruit" (Matthew 7:18). A person using counterfeit gifts, or producing evil fruit, points to the fact that the person has become an evil tree.

The Danger of Mediumistic Abilities and Powers

The Bible consistently links occultism and sorcery with mediumistic abilities and powers (Leviticus 20:6, 20:27; Deuteronomy 18:1–12). In Acts 16, Paul calls the mediumistic power of the damsel demonic. These abilities emerge in a person through generational inheritance, transference by the laying on of hands in occultic prayer, or through occultic experimentation. There are some ten to twenty types of mediumistic (occultic) gifts, which are all demonic in origin.

The effects of occultic practices are various and never good. Here is a short list of the negative effects upon the lives of people:

1. The faith of a Christian is greatly affected.
2. The person who is under occultic influence or infestation is unable to practice his or her faith.
3. The person is unable to keep a stable and living relationship with Christ.
4. The person often falls victim to damning sects and heresies.
5. The person is plagued with doubts.
6. The rational mind of a person is wounded, and rational thought is almost entirely gone in that person's life.
7. In such a state, the person is unable to concentrate on the Word of God or to pray with a rational mind.
8. In such a state, the person regularly becomes immune to the working and movements of the Holy Spirit and does not know the difference between genuine manifestations of the Holy Spirit and those that are counterfeit.
9. The character of the person is greatly changed.
10. Mental and emotional illnesses will regularly be present.
11. Involvement in magical practices and sorcery will affect the whole family, even to the third and fourth generations.

Beware of Voices

We should be cautious of several types of Christians. For example, beware of Christians who are quitting their fifth or sixth church because a voice or a feeling directed them somewhere else. Beware of Christians who keep hearing a voice telling them not to work. Beware of those who every time they change their husband, wife, underwear, or their business plan it is because they say God's voice told them so. Beware of a voice if,

1. It is always telling you to say "no" (especially to reading and studying the Bible).
2. The voice keeps telling you to say "yes" to every request for help.
3. The voice tells you to go where the money is.
4. The voice tells you what other people should do and never what you should do.

5. The voice tells you something different from the last instruction.
6. The voice assures you that you are always right.
7. The voice tells you that you are an exception to the rule.
8. The voice leads you away from the Bible, Jesus Christ as the only means of salvation, the power of the cross, and the power of the blood.

Tests of Jonathan Edwards

In response to the criticisms against the moving of the Holy Spirit in the First Great Awakening, Jonathan Edwards developed tests to determine the genuine movements of the Holy Spirit. Such movements or manifestations are of the Holy Spirit when:

1. an activity is such as to raise the very esteem of Jesus Christ who was born of the Virgin and was crucified (Matthew 10:32; Romans 15:9; 1 Corinthians 12:3; Philippians 2:11; 1 John 4:1–3, 4:15);
2. such operation is used to shine a light upon the gospel of Christ (Matthew 10:32; Romans 15:9; 1 Corinthians 12:3; Philippians 2:11; 1 John 4:1–3, 4:15);
3. such operation seems more than anything else to confirm and establish in the minds of people the truth of what the gospel declares to all that Christ is the Son of God and the Savior of men (Matthew 10:32; Romans 15:9; 1 Corinthians 12:3; Philippians 2:11; 1 John 4:1–3, 4:15);
4. a spirit operates against the interests of Satan's kingdom (1 John 3:8, 4:4–5);
5. a spirit operates in such a manner as to cause in men a greater reward for the Holy Scriptures and establishes these men more soundly in their truth and divinity (Ephesians 2:20; 1 John 4:6);
6. a spirit operates in such a manner as to lead people into the full truth of the fundamentals (1 John 4:1–6);
7. a spirit operates in such a manner as to promote a spirit of love for God and man (1 John 4:6–7);
8. a spirit operates in such a manner as to promote agreement with the Holy Scriptures (1 John 5:5–10);
9. a spirit operates in such a manner as to promote the holiness, greatness, and majesty of God (Luke 1:75; Romans 6:19–22, 8:4, 12:2, 13:8–10; 1 Corinthians 1:8, 7:19, 34; 2 Corinthians 7:1; Galatians 5:14,

6:2; Ephesians 4:24; Philippians 1:11; 1 Thessalonians 3:13, 4:3–7, 5:23; 1 Timothy 2:15; Titus 2:5; Hebrews 12:10–14; 1 Peter 14:16; 1 John 4:1–7,5:5–10);

10. a spirit causes unusual and extraordinary events and effects upon the lives, minds, and bodies of persons that emphasize the holiness of God, His greatness, and His majesty (Luke 1:75; Romans 6:19–22, 8:4, 12:2, 13:8–10; 1 Corinthians 1:8, 7:19, 34; 2 Corinthians 7:1; Galatians 5:14, 6:2; Ephesians 4:24; Philippians 1:11; 1 Thessalonians 3:13, 4:3–7, 5:23; 1 Timothy 2:15; Titus 2:5; Hebrews 12:10–14; 1 Peter 14:16; 1 John 4:1–7, 5:5–10). In such cases as these manifestations, people will have an extraordinary conviction of the dreadful nature of sin, a very uncommon sense of the Christian life, extraordinary views of the certainty, and glory of divine things, will be proportionally moved with extraordinary affections of fear, sorrow, desire, love, or joy, and will be changed suddenly with no infringing upon Scripture. Reactions include tears, trembling, groans, loud outcries, agonies of body, the failing of bodily strength, and what has been known as being "slain in the Spirit." All of this will always be in the realm of God's holiness, His greatness, and His majesty.[26]

My Husband and a Baby Boy

One night at church, the singing went on longer than usual. I thought to myself, *God is holding this service up for someone.*

A man came into the church with a baby boy in his arms. Tubes were hanging down from the child's head. The baby boy had leukemia.

The minister of the church told the boy's father to put his son on the altar. The man did not want to lay his son on that hard altar. The minister spoke back to the father, "Do as I say." At the right time, my husband and the minister went to the altar and prayed for the young child. Immediately, the young boy came up from the altar and ran around the church. The minister said, "We must keep our minds on Jesus. The baby deserves to play." That night, the Lord healed the young child entirely.

That night, the minister recognized the gifts of the Holy Spirit upon my husband's life and allowed my husband to work in the power of the Holy Spirit without any hindrance.

My Husband and the Wheelchair

My husband and I were told that a man was coming to church in a wheelchair, and we must be prayed up for his sake. My husband was told by the Lord, "I shall set him free from that wheelchair. That man is going to walk out of this church tonight."

As the church service was going on, a man in a wheelchair came rolling into the church. The minister looked at my husband with a smile. When the time came, my husband and the minister laid hands upon the man. Immediately, the man jumped out of his wheelchair. He ran across the front of the building and up and down the aisle, praising the Lord God.

The next morning, he had to go to the hospital to see his wife. When he walked into the room, she thought she was seeing his spirit. It scared her so badly that she almost had a heart attack. She thought he had died.

It took some time to calm her down. Of course, the hospital workers came running to see what was happening. They saw that her husband no longer needed the wheelchair, and they all worshipped the Lord.

My husband reminded me of what A. W. Tozer once said, "The man who has been taught by the Holy Spirit will be a seer rather than a scholar. The difference is that the scholar sees, and the seer sees through; and that is a mighty difference indeed."[27]

Church to be Built

One morning, my husband, Elias, said, "Dot, the Lord showed me a place for a church to be built. It is out from Yulee." He went on to explain all that he saw.

When I went to work and told several women about what my husband saw, they all knew about the property. One woman said, "My father had said that a church would be built there someday."

The building, which was just a beginning, was very small. It could only seat about forty people, but I can say God anointed that place. The Holy Spirit was drawing people from all over Florida and Georgia to the little church built in a cow pasture. My husband became known as the "Cow Pastor."

Elias worked all day or night and went out to the building to pray. The Lord showed him the first evangelist to teach there, besides him. My husband saw even what kind of suit the evangelist would wear.

Though the building was very small, the power of the Lord God was not small. During one service, the power of God overshadowed the building so much that the building shook for a considerable time. I have never experienced this since. The power of the Lord God manifested so strongly that the whole building shook.

My mother attended the service that night and it made her into a believer. From then on, when someone would mention the power of God, my mother would share this incredible experience with them.

One night, a lady ran into the little church. She said, "The Lord told me to come here. I ran in the ditch and finally in the woods. I asked for help and was able to find this church."

My husband had been expecting her, and when my husband expected a person, God always moved. The Lord met her needs.

However, God's entire purpose has never been accomplished at that place.

First Evangelist in the Little Church

Around 1975–1976, the first evangelist appeared at the little church. We were told about this man from another minister in Tennessee.

As a baby, the evangelist had been left in a trash can. A dear African-American woman was walking by and heard a baby crying. She stopped, looked in the trash can and saw a pitiful white baby. When she picked him up, she fell in love with him and said to herself, *I am going to raise him as my own*. It was very much like the beginnings of the life of Moses. The lady did not know that she would raise a prophet of the Lord God.

One key day in the revival held by this evangelist, Elias came out of his room in our house and said, "That little evangelist has sugar problems. God is going to heal him this very night." The music began in the church service, and there was no evangelist. He had not come into the church service. They continued singing until finally, the evangelist arrived. My husband stepped onto the platform and told him, "This is your night to be miraculously healed of diabetes."

When my husband and the evangelist touched hands, it was as if each had felt an electric wire. The evangelist flew under the organ, and my husband ended up under the piano!

When the evangelist got up from the floor, he was shaking all over. He said, "Brother Roberts, take over the service. All day I have been trying to use the bathroom." He ran to the bathroom.

Later, the evangelist remarked that he had been prayed for by some of the most prominent healing ministers in America, and nothing happened. He said, "It is just like God to bring me to a new, beginning pastor in a cow pasture to heal me."

That was the night the church was filled with angels, and the Lord shook the building.

We also called Granny and Grandpa Neal to come to that service. She said, "The angels are in this place."

Granny and Grandpa Neal were a godly couple. No one would even imagine just how God had blessed this couple. They were multi-millionaires, but it was impossible to prove that by how they lived.

This couple did much work of the Lord. They collected clothes and put them in a room until they could fill a whole airplane. Several times, they bought electrical generators and sent them overseas. Granny Neal owned several churches in Jacksonville.

The Neal's paid the Lord His tithes, offerings, and alms. Immediately, on the first day of January, she gave her tithes, offerings, and alms unto the Lord for that year. It was common for her to give five hundred thousand dollars at the beginning of the new year. She expected that God would give her at least five million dollars in financial blessings that year. Every year like clockwork, she gave, and God gave back much more. She lived Luke 6:38: "Give, and it shall be given unto you; good measure, pressed down, and shaken together, and running over, shall men give into your bosom. For with the same measure that ye mete withal it shall be measured to you again."

Jealousy and Steaks

During the revival at that little church, the young evangelist rarely had any good food to eat. The people he was staying with only gave him beans, rice, and potatoes, or potatoes, beans, and rice—for days. No meat. He was starving for something good to eat.

On Friday, I got off work so I could go to the revival. I was sitting there, and the Lord impressed upon me to invite the evangelist and several others who were serving in the church to dinner. I invited fourteen people to my home. Saturday, I went by the store and picked up seventeen T-Bone Steaks. I told all that we would eat at 6 p.m.

The steaks were ready to take off the grill, and yet my house was empty. No evangelist. No other people. None had made it to my home. I became more nervous about the meal. All I could think was, *The steaks will be ruined.*

Immediately, my husband went back to our bedroom and prayed. He knew what to do. He came out into the kitchen and said, "Let us eat. They have been deliberately detained. God will show them the way to our house." When we finished eating, the evangelist and his company came in the back door, and all of them said, "This is the place. Let us eat."

He was very weak and had been praying for many people. He needed protein.

It is a shame how the supposed people of God treated this minister. How can God bless such people who treat His servants so unkindly?

Granny Neal and the Volkswagen

One night, we were at a church service with Granny and Grandpa Neal. The preacher was teaching on prosperity. He said, "If you are driving a Volkswagen, that is the kind of faith you have." Immediately, Granny rose up and said to the preacher, somewhat out of order, "That is not so! I drive a Volkswagen because that is what I want to drive. Now I can buy ten cars right now, and I will pay cash for them, but we do not want ten cars. We want our old Volkswagen."

This couple did not think of purchasing anything for the service of the Lord. They bought a camper for this same evangelist. They saw his need. The camper could be used by the evangelist to carry his family along with him.

So many times, the Holy Spirit showed Granny Neal that her only son was in trouble. She prayed, and God always moved for her.

As she became older, she could not cook as she once did, so I cooked many meals for them.

One time, the Lord woke me up to go to the garden to pick vegetables for dinner. The Lord said, "Granny and Grandpa Neal are hungry. They will be coming over for dinner." Yes, they were multi-millionaires, but they became too old to take care of themselves. They did not believe the money that God gave them was also for them. They refused to take even a little of that money for themselves. That was a problem. God did want some of their money to be used for their necessities.

It was common for me to cook chicken and dumplings. I called them to come, and sometimes I picked them up. I tried to get them Lunch-On-Wheels, but they said they could not pay for it. One day at their home, I said, "Granny Neal, you have sixty thousand dollars right here, fifty thousand dollars over there, a hundred thousand dollars under that mattress, and fifty thousand dollars under another mattress. Now God is not pleased that you are going without food."

When she died, the undertaker was upset at how cheap the funeral was. I told him, "She could buy that funeral home and more. That is how she lived. She gave out to the poor and to churches." The undertaker was glad to hear that.

Out of all ministers, she liked to help tent preachers more than any other. I see now that I am reaping what I sowed by helping Granny and Grandpa Neal. Now in my old age, I have several people to help me the way I helped this old couple.

Granny Cherry and My Husband

During this same time, my husband had to take Granny Cherry, our friend and sister in Christ, to Georgia. He did not have any money with him. He looked down at the gas gauge and saw that it was almost on empty. He began to pray. The gas gauge never moved after driving nearly three hundred miles.

Transport Truck and a Wreck

As always, Satan will raise his head and send forth fiery darts against the saints. A transport truck hit my husband's vehicle during the revival at that little church. The driver of that transport truck said, "This is my job."

My husband asked, "What do you mean?"

He said, "My boss had told me that one more wreck, and I will be fired."

The policeman was writing down the information. My husband stopped the policeman and said to the man, "I tell you what. Tell your boss what has happened. And then tell him that I am going to have my truck fixed if you will promise me to go to the church of your choice for one year."

The policemen said, "That is all right with me."

Six months went by, and the phone rang. My husband picked it up and heard, "Brother Roberts, this is the man to whom you gave another chance. I am going to a Baptist church and playing on their softball team. You are the only person in my whole life who has ever given me a break."

A year later, the same man called back and said, "I am now teaching Sunday school." It cost us six hundred dollars to repair the truck. That was a small price for a soul to be added unto the kingdom of God.

My Husband's Arm

One day, my husband was at work and suddenly realized he could not lift one of his arms. His shoulder was frozen up. His co-workers were Christians. All of them said, "Brother Roberts, don't worry. We will help you." My husband and I kept on praying and fasting about this.

About eighteen months went by with no hint that God was going to heal my husband. Then one day, Elias went to work, and one of his co-workers said, "Brother Roberts, look at what you are doing!" He was using his arm and was able to move his shoulder. God had completely healed him. This proves one of my expressions, "You can't out give God. One way or the other, God will bless you back."

Not a Perfect Vessel, but a Willing Vessel

My life is not an example of a perfect vessel, far from it. Instead, my life is an example of a willing and forgiven vessel. Though weathered and battered with the storms of life, my life has been used by the Lord.

God has used my imperfections and removed them in His fiery furnace of trials and testing. In His fiery furnace, I thought that God mistreated me. Still, despite my storms, and unpleasant experiences, God was working out a plan for my life. And that plan was for my betterment. In so doing, He prepared me for better jobs and worse battles that I was to face. It was impossible for me to survive or even prosper throughout my life without the Lord toughening and developing me for what was to come.

God took nothing and made something out of it. He made me a chemist and a safety engineer. But more than that, my co-worker who acted like a big Jezebel repented, was changed, became our sister, and is now the anchor that keeps the retirees together.

My life was not only changed by the Lord, but my life also touched others. People saw the change in my life and wanted the same change. Knowing Christ will always result in a changed life. If there is no changed life, then there is no knowing Christ.

The storms of life did not destroy me. Instead, they made me a well-developed saint, ready to lift up the cross and fight against the forces of evil. I was never a powder puff, snowflake, or tumbleweed Christian (where there is no foundation), but I was made to be an EFC—Effective, Forceful Christian. If only most Christians were Effective, Forceful Christians, Satan and his forces would be pushed back, victory would come more often than defeat, and nations could be changed in another movement of the Lord.

ENDNOTES

Author's Note

1. Dr. Ricky Roberts, *A Walk Through Tears: One of the Greatest Miracles in Modern Times* (CreateSpace Independent Publishing Platform; Third Edition, April 10, 2017).

Introduction

1. P. L. Tan, *Encyclopedia of 7700 Illustrations: Signs of the Times* (Garland, Texas: Bible Communications, Inc., 1997), 995.
2. John Wesley, *The Journal of the Rev. John Wesley* (N. Curnock, Ed. London, England: Robert Culley; Charles H. Kelly, 1909–1916), 3.102.
3. E. Jones Lewis, *I've Anchored in Jesus* (Words & Music: Lewis E. Jones. Renewal, 1928, Brentwood Tennessee: Lillenas Publishing Co. Owner, 1901).

Chapter 1
Did Satan Know?

1. Ignatius, *Epistle to the Ephesians*, 19; my son's own translation of the Greek text.
2. Ignatius (spurious), *Epistle to the Philippians*, 8; my son's own translation of the Greek text.
3. Ibid.,4.

Chapter 2
Why?

1. Josephus, The Antiquities of the Jews, 2.9.3–6.
2. *Ibid.*, 2.9.2.
3. The Targum of Jonathan, Exodus 1:15.
4. Josephus, The Antiquities of the Jews, 2.9.4.
5. Josephus, *Against Apion*, 2.2.

6. John Glanvil, *Evidence Concerning Witches and Apparitions* (London, England: Printed for A. L., 1678), 1–60.
7. Origen, *Homilies on Joshua 14.1;* my son's own translation of the Latin text.
8. John Foxe, *Acts and Monuments* (New York, New York: AMS Press Inc.; Reprint, 1965), 4:653.

Chapter 3
Early Miracles

1. *The Cordelle Dispatch*, "Crisp County mob Disposes of Cobb" (Cordele: Georgia, May 23, 1918).
2. Mark Water, *The New Encyclopedia of Christian Quotations* (Alresford, Hampshire: John Hunt Publishers Ltd., 2000), 527.
3. I*bid.*, 527.
4. Roy B. Zuck, *The Speaker's Quote Book* (Grand Rapids, Michigan: Kregel Publications Inc., 1997), 142.

Chapter 4
Life Growing Up

1. Mark Water, *The New Encyclopedia of Christian Quotations* (Alresford, Hampshire: John Hunt Publishers Ltd., 2000), 335.
2. Dwight D. Eisenhower, *At Ease: Stories I Tell to Friends* (Conshohocken, Pennsylvania: Eastern Acorn Press, 1967), 95–96; Oursler, Grace Perkins, *A Question of Courage,* (Reprinted from a 1959 Readers Digest School Reader, condensed, and adapted from a Guideposts article).
3. Richard V. Pierard and Robert D. Linder, *Civil Religion, and the Presidency* (Grand Rapids, Michigan: Zondervan, 1988), 96–97; DeMar Gary, *America's Christian History: The Untold Story* (Powder Springs, Georgia: American Vision, 1993), 101–102.
4. *Freeport Weekly Journal,* "The Victory of Truth," a Discourse Preached on the Day of National Thanksgiving, November 24, 1864, in the First Presbyterian Church of Freeport, Illinois, by Isaac E. Carey, Quote appears in *Freeport Weekly Journal,* December 7, 1864, 1; *Lincoln Memorial Album*, 508.
5. Lincoln Memorial Album, 366; O. H. Oldroyd, *Words of Lincoln* (New

York, New York: Mershon Company, 1875), 154.
6. Ida Tarbell, *The Life of Abraham Lincoln* (New York, New York: The Doubleday & Mclure Co., 1900), 1.406.

Chapter 5
Introduction to Pentecost

1. John Wesley, *The Journal of the Rev. John Wesley* (N. Curnock, Ed. London, England: Robert Culley; Charles H. Kelly, 1909–1916), 3.490.
2. John Wesley, *The Sermons of John Wesley*, "The More Excellent Way" (London, England: Wesleyan Methodist Book Room, 1872), Sermon LXXXIX, 7.26.
3. David W. Dorries, Assemblies of God Heritage, Volume 12, No 3, Fall (Springfield, Missouri: Assemblies of God Archives, 1992), 22.
4. Olney Hymns (1779), 53, Book 1, Hymn 41, *Faith's Review and Expectation*, 1 Chronicles 17:16–17, vv. 2–3.

Chapter 6
My Husband's Family

1. H. D. M. Spence-Jones, *John 11–12* (London, England; New York, New York: Funk & Wagnalls Company, 1909), 2.11–12.

Chapter 7
Introduction to Pentecost

1. Roy B. Zuck, *The Speaker's Quote Book* (Grand Rapids, Michigan: Kregel Publications, 1997), 364.
2. Elizabeth Elliott, *A Chance to Die—The Life and Legacy of Amy Carmichael* (Grand Rapids, Michigan: Fleming H. Revell Company; Reprint, 2005), 85.
3. G. B. Kelley, "The Life and Death of a Modern Martyr," *Christian History Magazine, Issue 32, Dietrich Bonhoeffer: Theologian in Nazi Germany* (Worcester, Pennsylvania: Christian History Institute, 1991).
4. David W. Dorries, *Assemblies of God Heritage, Volume 12, No. 3, Fall* (Springfield, Missouri: Assemblies of God Archives, 1992), 7.
5. Ben H., Price, *Alone* (Chicago, Illinois: Homer A. Rodeheaver, 1914).
6. P. L. Tan, *Encyclopedia of 7700 Illustrations: Signs of the Times* (Garland,

Texas: Bible Communications, Inc., 1997), 1283.
7. Clement of Alexandria, *Christ the Educator 1.5.18;* my son's own translation of the Greek text.
8. Caesarius of Arles, *Sermons 160.2*; my son's own translation of the Latin text.
9. A. W. Tozer, *The Best of A.W. Tozer Book One* (Camp Hill, Pennsylvania: Wing Spread, 2007), 103.
10. Mark Water, *The New Encyclopedia of Christian Quotations* (Alresford, Hampshire: John Hunt Publishers Ltd., 2000), 769.

Chapter 8
Ministers who Helped Us

1. Russell P., Spittler, "Du Plessis, David Johannes," in *The New International Dictionary of Pentecostal and Charismatic Movements*, eds. Stanley M. Burgess and Eduard M. Van Der Maas (Grand Rapids, Michigan: Zondervan; Expanded, Revised Edition, 2002), 590.
2. Peter Cartwright, *The Autobiography of Peter Cartwright, The Backwoods Preacher* (Cincinnati, Ohio: Swormstedt & A. Foe., 1859), 75.
3. Ibid., 76–77.

Chapter 9
Teach Me to Pray

1. John Owen, *The Works of John Owen* (London, England: W. H. Goold, Ed. Edinburgh: T&T Clark, 1862), 6.446.
2. J. Calvin & J. Pringle, *Commentaries on the Epistles of Paul the Apostle to the Corinthians* (Wheaton, Illinois: Crossway Books, 1999), 1.210–211.
3. Charles Hodge, *Commentary on the Epistle to the First Corinthians* (Wheaton, Illinois: Crossway Books, 1995), 104.
4. Tertullian, *On Prayer 29;* my son's own translation of the Latin text.
5. L. Ginzberg, H, Szold, & P. Radin, *Legends of the Jews* (Philadelphia, Pennsylvania: Jewish Publication Society, 2003), 621; Sanhedrin 10:28b.
6. Roy B. Zuck, *The Speaker's Quote Book* (Grand Rapids, Michigan: Kregel Publications Inc., 1997), 298.
7. P. L. Tan, *Encyclopedia of 7700 Illustrations: Signs of the Times* (Garland, Texas: Bible Communications, Inc., 1997), 1052.

8. Leslie K. Tarr, *Christian History Magazine–Issue 1:* "A Prayer Meeting that lasted 100 Years" (Worcester, Pennsylvania: Christian History Institute, 1982).
9. Harry E. Bowley, Assemblies of God Heritage, Volume 2, No. 2, Summer (Springfield, Missouri: Assemblies of God Archives, 1982), 1 and 3.
10. Mark Water, *The New Encyclopedia of Christian Quotations* (Alresford, Hampshire: John Hunt Publishing Ltd., 2000), 766.
11. Leonard Ravenhill, "Have we no Tears for Revival?" Sermon.
12. Mark Water, *The New Encyclopedia of Christian Quotations* (Alresford, Hampshire: John Hunt Publishing Ltd., 2000), 519.
13. Leonard Ravenhill, *Why Revival Tarries* (Eastbourne, England: Kingsway Publications, 1959), 7.
14. Randy C Alcon, The Law of Rewards: Giving What You Can't Keep to Gain What You Can't Lose (Carol Stream, Illinois: Tyndale Momentum, 2003), 18.
15. Charles Finney, *Lectures to Professing Christians* (New York, New York: Fleming H. Revell Company, 1837), 75.
16. Mark Water, *The New Encyclopedia of Christian Quotations* (Alresford, Hampshire: John Hunt Publishing Ltd, 2000), 777.
17. *Ibid.,* 1032.
18. Charles Finney, *Memoirs of Rev. Charles G. Finney* (New York, New York: Fleming H. Revell Company, 1876), 122–123.
19. Kenneth E. Hagin, *Praying to Get Results* (Tulsa, Oklahoma: Kenneth Hagin Ministries, Inc., 1990), 14.
20. Mark Water, *The New Encyclopedia of Christian Quotations* (Alresford, Hampshire: John Hunt Publishing Ltd., 2000), 104.
21. Ibid., 107.
22. Kenneth S Wuest, *Word Studies in the Greek New Testament* (Grand Rapids, Michigan: Eerdmans, 1953), 6.233.

Chapter 10
Prayer and Trials

1. Smith Wigglesworth, "The Confidence that We Have in Him," Sermon, *The Complete Collection of His Life Teachings,* compiled by Roberts Liardon (Tulsa, Oklahoma: Albury Publishing, 2008), 13.
2. Lord Alfred Tennyson, 1889, in *Crossing the Bar, St. 3.* John Bartlett,

Bartlett's Familiar Quotations (Boston, Massachusetts: Little, Brown and Company, 1855, 1980), 535.
3. Charles Henry Mackintosh, *Notes on the Pentateuch* (New York, New York: Loizeaux Brothers, 1885-86), 1.13–14.
4. Cyprian, *Epistle 6.2;* my son's own translation of the Latin text.
5. Martin Luther, *Luther's Works* (Saint Louis, Missouri: Concordia Publishing House, 1972), 24.383.
6. Luther, *Large Catechism, The Lord's Prayer, Book of Concord* (Saint Louis, Missouri: Concordia Publishing House, 2005), 422–423.
7. *Ibid.*, 415–416.
8. B.C Forbes, *Forbes Book of Quotations: Thoughts on the Business of Life* (New York, New York: Black Dog & Leventhal, 1991), 250; Demakis Joseph, The Ultimate Book of Quotations (Scotts Valley, California: CreateSpace Independent Publishing Platform, 2012), 108.

Chapter 11
Warfare and Intercession

1. W. Gurnall, & J. Campbell, *The Christian in Complete Armour* (London, England: Thomas Tegg, 1845), 731.
2. Walter Martin, "Curtains for Walter Martin and Doug Clark at TBN," 1985, YouTube video, 24:50 https://youtu.be/wYviYC5f_6Q.
3. Walter Martin Quotes. BrainyQuote.com, Brainy Media Inc, 2020. https://www.brainyquote.com/quotes/walter_martin_306426 accessed June 3, 2020.
4. Walter Martin Quotes. BrainyQuote.com, Brainy Media Inc, 2020. https://www.brainyquote.com/quotes/walter_martin_306412 accessed June 3, 2020.
5. Marc R. Forster and Benjamin J. Kaplan, *Piety and Family in Early Modern Europe: Essays in Honour of Steven Ozment* (Milton Park, Abingdon-on-Thames, Oxfordshire, United Kingdom: Routledge, 2005), 90–91.
6. Origen, *Homilies on Joshua 15.1–2;* my son's own translation of the Latin text.
7. Ignatius, *Ignatius to Polycarp;* my son's own translation of the Greek text.
8. Edward Longstreth, *Decisive Battles of the Bible* (Philadelphia, Pennsylvania: J.P. Lippincott, 1962), 16–17.
9. Ibid., 7.

10. Edward Longstreth, *Decisive Battles of the Bible* (Philadelphia, Pennsylvania: J.P. Lippincott, 1962); Boyd Seevers, *Warfare in the Old Testament* (Grand Rapids, Michigan: Kregel Academic, 2013); Stephen Leston, *Illustrated Guide to Bible Battles* (Uhrichsville, Ohio: Barbour Publishing Inc., 2014); Brenda Lewis, *Battles of the Bible* (New York, New York: Chartwell Books, Inc., 2009).
11. Elizabeth Alves, *Becoming a Prayer Warrior* (Ventura, California: Regal Books, 1998), 23.
12. William T. Ellis, Assemblies of God Heritage, Volume 2, No 4, Winter (Springfield, Missouri: Assemblies of God Archives, 1982–1983), 1.
13. Tertullian, *Apology 39;* my son's own translation of the Latin text.
14. William T. Ellis, Assemblies of God Heritage, Volume 2, No 4, Winter (Springfield, Missouri: Assemblies of God Archives, 1982–1983), 1 and 5.
15. John Cassian, The Institutes of the Coenobia, 5:12–18.
16. Ramsay Macmullen, *Christianizing the Roman Empire* (New Haven, Connecticut: Yale University Press, 1984), 28.
17. Charles Hodge, *Commentary on the Epistle to the Romans* (Wheaton, Illinois: Crossway Books, 1995), 395.
18. Peter Cartwright, *The Autobiography of Peter Cartwright, The Backwoods Preacher* (Cincinnati, Ohio: Swormstedt & A. Foe, 1859), 102.
19. *Ibid.,* 275.
20. *Ibid.,* 221–223.
21. John Wesley, *The Works of John Wesley* (London, England: Wesleyan Methodist Book Room, 1872), 11:429.
22. Smith Wigglesworth, *The Secret of His Power* (Tulsa, Oklahoma: Harrison House Inc., 1982), 29–30.
23. *Ibid.,* 32.
24. *Ibid.,* 33
25. *Ibid.,* 33.
26. Jonathan Edwards, *The Works of Jonathan Edwards* (Carlisle, Pennsylvania: Banner of Truth Trust, 1834), 2:261.
27. A. W. Tozer, *Man: The Dwelling Place of God* (Harrisburg, Pennsylvania: Christian Publications, Inc., 1966), 167.

ABOUT THE AUTHOR

Dot Roberts has been called a modern-day Hannah for the intensity with which she prayed sixteen years over her disabled son.

Dr. Ricky Roberts is an authority on ancient languages. He has been honored by Who's Who in America, Who's Who in the World, 1,000 Great Americans, and other gracious rewards.

www.ingramcontent.com/pod-product-compliance
Lightning Source LLC
Chambersburg PA
CBHW030320100526
44592CB00010B/498